Praise for Eric Booth's
The Everyday Work of Art

"This book is important, taking us in a direction we've forgotten or ignored. I hope it will remind us of the necessity of the arts for the growth and health of the human spirit. Eric Booth has done a great service, and I thank him for it."
>—Madeline L'Engle, author of *A Wrinkle in Time*

"Eric Booth's *The Everyday Work of Art* shows us all in hundreds of ways that perhaps the greatest art is the art of living. This book provides an insightful look at the wonder with which we can approach our lives and reminds us of the importance of perceiving the extraordinary in the ordinary. It was a joy to read."
>—Yo-Yo Ma

"Eric Booth understands what art is about and communicates that knowledge with great clarity and verve. *The Everyday Work of Art* is a ringing and liberating answer to the killer question, 'What good are the arts, really.'"
>—Mihaly Csikszentmihalyi, author of *Flow*

"Booth shares his rich experiences as an artist and an educator and his love for experiment and innovation in this creative approach to daily life."
>—*NAPRA Review*

"What a thrilling book this is—passionate, provocative, and profoundly useful. One of the finest explorations of creativity ever written, it restores our sacred birthright as artists. Eric Booth shows us how creativity is as natural as breathing, how the things of ordinary life are there to be orchestrated by us into art and wonder."
>—Jean Houston, author of *A Mythic Life*,
>*Passion for the Possible*, and *The Possible Human*

"This book is a powerful tool for change educationally and personally. In theory and its practice, *The Everyday Work of Art* provides us a way of connecting back to the artist in all of us, no matter what we do in life. Once read, you will never look at the arts and the world quite the same."

—Scott Noppe-Brandon, Executive Director,
Lincoln Center Institute

"In this fascinating study, Eric Booth skillfully revises the limiting and conditional beliefs that surround art in our professionalized culture. He boldly cuts across institutional approaches in order to reframe the phenomenon of creativity as something that is used daily by ordinary people in concrete moments of living. *The Everyday Work of Art* will surprise, enlighten, irritate and beguile you into a new sense of what art is about."

—Suzi Gablik, author of *The Reenchantment of Art*
and *Conversations Before the End of Time*

"Eric Booth's book was a revelation to me. It gave me a vivid new definition of art and work as a vivid kind of serious play, a profoundly satisfying moment to moment awareness. I still think about this book every day."

—Robert Landy, Professor of Theater,
New York University, author of
Persona and Performance

"This book will help all readers to see, appreciate, and understand our world, and, will give them skills needed to improve it."

—*Library Journal*

"...an engaging look at a different aspect of art and aesthetics."

—*Publishers Weekly*

"*The Everyday Work of Art* is an effective and pleasant reminder of how arts fill our daily lives even if we are unaware of their presence."

—Schuyler G. Chapin, Commissioner,
City of New York Department
of Cultural Affairs

"Much more than the usual 'feel-good' book about yourself that nowadays passes for psychology, *The Everyday Work of Art* is full of wisdom and common good sense. You don't have to be an artist to want this book on your shelf—and on the shelves of all those whom you care about. Absorbing and uplifting...and highly recommended."
—*Art Times*

"Reading Eric Booth's book is a real 'Touched by an Angel' experience. Your eyes will be clearer and your ears keener to life's simplest rhythms, thus your enjoyment factor substantially enhanced."
—Thomas Leahy, President,
Theatre Development Fund

"I am moved and impressed by the charm, wisdom, and originality of *The Everyday Work of Art*. Eric Booth brilliantly highlights the significance of making things and attending to things for a more meaningful life."
—Maxine Greene, Former Professor Emeritus
at Columbia University, Teachers College,
author of *Releasing the Imagination* and
Landscapes of Learning

"This book is a wonderful companion for those 'in the arts,' because it provides reminders of how to tap the energizing artistic processes. For those not in the arts, the book offers the opportunity for more fully realized lives."
—Bennett Tarleton, Executive Director,
Tennessee Arts Commission

"Eric Booth has written an important book. Our times demand that we bring new levels of creativity and meaning to every aspect of our lives. This book can help us greatly in this critical task."
—Charles Johnston, M.D., Director,
The Institute for Creative Development,
author of *The Creative Imperative* and
Necessary Wisdom

"In this engaging, practical, amusing and provocative book, Eric Booth has created an effective, no-nonsense approach to an enriched life through the processes of art....Particularly wonderful is Booth's ability to make art understandable as a plain part of all life and learning—not just as a pleasant pastime for a few."
—Alexander Bernstein, President, Leonard Bernstein
Education Through the Arts Fund

"You can escape the ordinary groove of daily living with *The Everyday Work of Art*. It's a cookbook of brilliantly original recipes for making everyday use of the arts in our lives, delivering insights you can put to immediate practical use today—even in the kitchen."
—Roberta Ciuffo, President,
Nashville Institute for the Arts

"It grieves me constantly that in our society, creativity and imagination are undervalued, endangered treasures of our birthright. We should be cultivating them in our lives and playing with endless possibilities. Eric Booth's book is an insightful, stimulating exploration of how to do so: full of epiphanies, experience and invitations."
—Karen Elizabeth Gordon, author of
The Ravenous Muse and *Paris Out of Hand*

"*The Everyday Work of Art* brings together the divergent, elusive reasons that witness the need for the arts in everyone's life."
—Helen Marie Guditis, Executive Director,
The Broadway Theater Institute

"At times I think our task is to preserve and nurture spirit against all the encroachments of the organizations and institutions that we create, as if we sit and design our own prisons and cells. And then Eric Booth describes how to see the world differently, literally—how to shift perceptions, and the spirit is freed to see, and thereby to act. Action is the creation of the world—and that is what *The Everyday Work of Art* guides us to do."
—David O'Fallon, Executive Director,
Minnesota Center for Arts Education

"This wide ranging exploration of everyday creativity returns the notion of art to its useful origins as a verb that means to simply 'put things together,' a thrilling process that brings order to chaos and beauty to ugliness. Here is a demystifying approach to bringing the soul into every aspect of our lives, and the life of our communities."

—Phil Cousineau, author of *Soul Moments* and
Soul: An Archaeology

"Eric Booth reminds us in *The Everyday Work of Art* that living to the fullest is a work of art done on an expense budget of inquiry, questioning and curiosity....An exciting piece of work for those of us whose lives are given such meaning by living with art."

—Marianna Houston Weber, Education Director,
Theatre Development Fund

"Eric Booth presents a fresh philosophy for looking at and engaging in the world around us. His book illustrates the power of the arts and presents us with clear strategies for tapping more fully into the artists within each of us."

—Derek E. Gordon, Vice President, Education,
The Kennedy Center

"Filled with illuminating insights and warm anecdotes, *The Everyday Work of Art* is an inspiring work offering a stirring argument for the importance of art. *The Everyday Work of Art* is an impressive contribution to the national dialogue on the essentialness of art in American culture, schools, and communities."

— *The Midwest Book Review*

"Eric Booth's book explores how artists encounter daily life in a unique way, and how the habits and routines artists develop in order to create, can help all of us find new approaches to our problems and the solutions."

—Thomas Cahill, Executive Director, The Studio
in a School Association

"A useful reminder that in life, as in art, attitude is everything."
                                                    —*Independent Publisher*

"*The Everyday Work of Art* is alchemy. Let it in, and it will change your life, make it richer, sweeter, deeper, and a whole lot more fun. It's already having that effect on me, delightfully and unexpectedly."
                              —Carl Frankel, U.S. Editor of *Tomorrow Magazine*,
                                        author of *In Earth's Company*

"*The Everyday Work of Art* is a pleasant surprise. The vast majority of books written about art examine what individuals, whether artist or audience, bring to art, and almost always from a specialized or professional point of view. It is refreshing to read a book about art that opens the field to generalists and examines what art brings to us."
                                                    —*Artspeak*

Eric Booth

The Everyday Work of Art

Awakening the *Extraordinary* in Your Daily Life

Sourcebooks, Inc.
Naperville, IL

Published by Sourcebooks, Inc., P.O. Box 372, Naperville, Illinois 60566
(630) 961-3900 FAX: (630) 961-2168

Library of Congress Cataloging-in-Publication Data
Booth, Eric.
    The everyday work of art: awakening the extraordinary in your daily life / Eric Booth.
        p. cm.
    Includes index.
    ISBN 1-57071-438-X
    1. Art—Psychology. 2. Visual perception. I. Title.
N71.B66 1997
701' . 15—dc21   97-22796
                                                                        CIP

Printed and bound in the United States of America
10 9 8 7 6 5 4 3 2 1

This book is dedicated to my father, who created many
fine things in the medium of business—though he would have scoffed if
I had called him an artist. We felt the closest in the music at the symphony.

Contents

Part 1

Art
is a
Verb

Chapter One:

Trade Secrets

Art, like sex, is too important to leave to the professionals[1]—too important because of the delight and satisfaction it provides, and too important because of its role in creating each person's future. This book is dedicated to restoring our artistic birthright: an endless intercourse with attractive things.

Art is not apart. It is a continuum within which all participate; we all function in art, use the skills of art, and engage in the action of artists every day. Underneath the surface distinctions that make individual lives seem very different, art is a common ground we share; the work of art is a way we all do things when we are working well. Our unheralded everyday actions of art comprise one end of the human spectrum of artistry; the other end is the creation of masterpieces in the arts that we readily label as art: newlyweds setting the table for their first Thanksgiving dinner on one extreme, and da Vinci's painting *The Last Supper* on the other; a businesswoman shifting the sequence of the slides in her presentation on one extreme, Sam Shepard transposing the order of the scenes during rehearsals of *True West* on the other. The differences are obvious, easy to identify and laugh about; the similarities (which are the focus of this book) may be less evident, but they construct the way we experience being alive. If we can acknowledge and honor the art we perform, if we can stay aware of and develop the skills of art we use daily, if we can borrow appropriate and

*Art is not apart.
It is a continuum within
which all participate; we
all function in art, use
the skills of art, and
engage in the action
of artists every day.*

If we can acknowledge and honor the art we perform, ...we can dramatically enrich the quality of daily life.

When we assume that the work of art exists only in these isolated peaks, we shrug off our birthright.

useful trade secrets from artists, who are the experts and exemplars of this field, we can dramatically enrich the quality of daily life.

The main artistic media (music, theater, dance, visual and literary arts) have survived because we thrill to witness what humans can accomplish, what the body can express, what the human voice can do at its best—what subtle truths people can communicate. Masterworks in art invite and reward our best attention; they also enable us to extend the range of our own overlooked artistic competencies. Apprehending the magnificence of the soprano's aria increases our proficiency to hear the wide range of organized sound we encounter throughout our lives. Perceiving Cézanne's accomplishments in a painting of an ordinary house among trees can radically alter what you see on your daily drive to work. Responding to Shakespeare's King Henry the Fifth as he wanders all night, reflecting before the big battle, develops a wiser you to confront your next crisis.

But those occasional celebrated masterpieces are merely the tip of the artistic iceberg to which all of us, including many fine-but-not-famous artists, contribute less visibly and far more frequently. When we assume that the work of art exists only in these isolated peaks, we shrug off our birthright. Human bodies do wonderful things all the time, not just when the dance company Pilobolus performs, not just for a few days every two years at the Olympics. We all have human voices, and even though they are less developed than the diva's, they are rich in sonic subtlety that we ply in many ways. We live in an abundant playhouse of sound that rewards the best hearing we can apply. We need to attend to the artistic experiences throughout our lives, not just at ticketed events. In doing so, we reclaim many dwindling passions; we awake dormant skills with which to construct good answers to life's hardest questions.

We all have a natural knowledge of the processes and perspectives that artists use, even if we have not focused our efforts on developing these skills the way artists have. Yes, maybe you sing like a squawking crow, and you might think *contrapposto* is an Italian side dish; but you certainly have expertise about what sounds and tastes and feels good. You may not be trained for center stage leaping, but you have made many beautiful things with that body of yours, like dives into the deep end and waltzes on the dancefloor or charades clues and wedding choreography. You have entertained others by performing clever impersonations. You've played red light/green light. You've made love. You are also, I'm sure, intimately aware of choreography in the world: on the street, on the playing field. You get annoyed when someone bungles their role on the dancefloor of the sidewalk by crossing in front of you, or in the reception hall by stealing your spotlight, or on the gridiron by missing a block on a tailback sweep. You appreciate the balletic steps of the furniture movers as they maneuver your dining room set or of your spouse chopping vegetables in the kitchen. You said of the Japanese chef's preparation of teriyaki at your table, and of the carpenter's work on your cabinets: "It was a work of art."

Even those famous artists want you as a creative peer. Here is a secret truth they might not tell you—they really seek colleagues, but settle for admirers. Alvin Ailey and George Balanchine would rather have had the choreographically competent you than the venerating follower who paid to sit in row G.

You have all the necessary background. To engage fully in the work of art, all you really need are the skills you already have, the birthright you were given, and the perspectives and practices this book will remind you about.

The Meaning of "Art"

Contrary to conventional wisdom, art has not always been a noun, a valuable object relegated to a museum or a ticketed event in a performance hall. At the birth of the word "art," it was a verb that meant "to put things together." It was not a product but a process. If we can reclaim that view of art—as a way of looking at and doing things, as a series of experiences and experiments—all of us gain a fresh grasp on the proven, practical ways to construct the quality of our lives.

Yes, the verb "art" often produces nouns. When artists apply themselves to certain media, they create those magnificent things we hang on well-lit walls or pay forty bucks to hear at Carnegie Hall. But the prevailing view of art is built upon a simplistic equation: art equals

To engage fully in the work of art, all you really need are the skills you already have.

Art (ärt) v. to put things together

those "things." While not overtly wrong, this formula for art is stingy. It sadly overlooks the down-to-earth actions that result in art objects, the perceiving that brings such objects to life in us, and the impact of artworks on the way we think, understand, learn, and make changes in our lives. We get caught up in the games of that materialistic view, with buying, selling, judging, and discussing art (if we bother with it at all), and we leave art to a few supposed "experts," abandoning our own innate capacities, our own curiosities and artistic potential. We cash in our inheritance of conscious participation in the action of art for too little payoff in convenience and comfort.

This book seeks to put the verbs of art back in your hands for intentional, effective use in the rich media of your everyday life.

This book seeks to redress this imbalance by putting the verbs of art back in your hands for intentional, effective use in the rich media of your everyday life. The following pages focus not on "works of art," but rather on "the work of art." The phrase may sound awkward at first, perhaps too taxing with its emphasis on labor. But in practice, you will see that it is neither heavy nor laborious—the work of art you will find in these pages is familiar, engaging, and fun. In other words, the work of art is serious play.

For the message of this book to make a difference, you need to embrace two ideas:

1) You do the same kinds of work Beethoven did. You may not believe this until later in these pages, but it's true. The way you put things together—solve a problem at the office, tell a story, make sense out of a mess, let your spouse or child know your love—may not be as densely articulated as the Third Symphony or be performed by a medium as expressive as a seventy-piece orchestra, but they are successful accomplishments; they are filled with the work of art; and they are worthy of investigation.

2) You need to set things apart from the commonplace to attend to them in a special way. The special place need not be literalized as a museum or performance hall. It is a kind of experience—an attitude—created inside you; and the habit of setting aside such a place and making effective use of it is developed through the work of art.

This book builds upon those two ideas, and their implications will fill these pages. However, let me cement another critical truth in place at the beginning, though we will revisit it only occasionally. Just because we do some of the same work as Beethoven, it doesn't mean our results are the same. The accomplishments of master artists are stupendous, the result of fearsome diligence, vision, hard-earned skill, profound understanding of their discipline, and an extra dash of something we might call genius. They engage in many of the same actions, ply the same universal skills of art as the rest of us, but they put them together in superb, inspiring ways. The rest of us can do a little of what Rudolf Nureyev could do in abundance; the rest of us do not focus our talents with the understanding of a Matisse. In claiming our rightful partnership with such masters, we neither diminish their achievements, nor set unrealistic expectations for our own efforts. We can learn from what they know; we can refocus the way we see and work; we can transform the quality of our daily living.

How I Came to This World View

Let me recount the unexpected journey through which I found my way to the world view of this book. My reasonable plans for life met a Mack truck in college when I was cast in a play. It was Dylan Thomas's *Under Milkwood*, and the rehearsal and performance experience was so ecstatic and challenging, made me feel so alive in new ways, that I knew I had to have more. I pursued theater through graduate school and right into a successful twenty-year professional career.

Mine was not a rich-and-famous career (though I did fantasize about my Academy Award acceptance speech), but it was satisfying to play many of the great roles in Shakespeare, as well as many modern characters. I acted in a number of shows on Broadway and toured for a year in a one-man play. I enjoyed many brief appearances on television and even produced and directed plays. I also taught theater arts on the side, and, stealthily, my passion for teaching slowly wangled its way to my life's center stage.

By now, I have taught at every level, from pre-kindergarten, to graduate school, to professional actors' training, to continuing

In claiming our rightful partnership with such masters, we neither diminish their achievements, nor set unrealistic expectations for our own efforts.

education for senior citizens. I have taught everything in the theater from acting, to how to make hideously realistic scars, to how to stage a good broadsword fight, to how anyone can love a good play; and I have taught many subjects outside of the theater, too. In the late 1970s, I discovered a program called aesthetic education at Lincoln Center Institute (with which I am still affiliated).

Aesthetic education is a practice that uses teaching-artists to engage people of any age inside works of art. The teaching-artist designs challenges related to a particular artwork under study. The students' work on the problem pays off when they attend a culminating performance. The activities involve real artistic problems the artist solved in the piece under study (e.g., something Beethoven was working on in the Third Symphony). When those students attend the concert, they are peers, interested in seeing how Beethoven solved the problem they also solved. In this process, people develop their own perceiving skills, enabling them to step into works of art by themselves. They discover how their own creative work connects to that of the masters. (I know the process sounds a little vague—if we practitioners had a simpler way of describing why it works so well, it would be a household term by now.)

Aesthetic education is a practice that uses teaching-artists to engage people of any age inside works of art.

Much of the innovative work I have done in this powerful practice has been at the Nashville Institute for the Arts (NIA), where I was given carte semi-blanche to experiment and expand my workshop practice over many years of visiting Music City. Particularly valuable for me was a three-year think-tank at the NIA with a selected group of fine thinker-artists from New York and Nashville (we called the group Bob because we couldn't think up a proper name for it). Bob explored the implications of aesthetic education as it met big issues such as learning and understanding, the way the mind works, and the sources of art.

The insights I gained from working with Bob could have provided good fodder for theoretical writings about the arts for colleagues in the field of education, but something unexpected happened. Instead of conceptual and abstract ideas, I found that my curiosity carried me into constant experiments in the testing grounds of the real world. I carried the investigation of the processes of art beyond my work in theater and teaching and began studying the everyday aesthetics in my marriage, in my friendships, and in the way I did chores and constructed a daily life.

The biggest breakthroughs came in the least "artistic" realm: my business. I had started a small business in New York that gathered research on Americans' lifestyles and consumer behavior—we handled over one thousand studies done by various organizations each year, each with hundreds of pages of statistical data. We analyzed, synthesized, and humanized those tomes into quick-reading articles of highlights, which we then made available in newsletters for business people and anyone else who needed to know the latest objectively measured trends among Americans. The business became very successful. (I sold Research Alert and the other newsletters to New York's EPM Communications in 1992, and they still thrive.)

At the office, my imaginative theater background ran head-on into the practical walls of running a business. Lofty artistic concepts and the deluxe words that often go with them didn't count for much in the daily bustle of the bottom line. Try telling an angry customer that he is relying on hackneyed images in his dialogue; try suggesting that the overpriced supplier adjust her super-objective. The pragmatics of my business had no connection to the aesthetics of my previous artistic life—or so I thought at first.

Eventually, I began to notice that when I was working on my favorite tasks at the office—like devising a marketing plan, or analyzing the results of a study—the actual experiences felt a lot like my favorite work in the arts. *Hamlet* it wasn't, but to tell the truth, many parts of the process and payoff were indistinguishable from when I had acted the role of Hamlet and directed the play. My mind and energy were fully engaged; I was creatively challenged and absorbed; I was enjoying myself; I felt fully satisfied. I didn't know what to call these art-like experiences that had no "artistic" connection and began to question my previous definitions and beliefs about art.

I was hesitant to mention this heretical fascination to my artist-friends; had I "sold out"? Did I dare to liken my excitement in

I began to notice that when I was working on my favorite tasks at the office, the actual experiences felt a lot like my favorite work in the arts.

discovering the statistical patterns of future vacation travel in national forests with the joy my theater colleagues and I felt in staging a production of *A Midsummer Night's Dream*? I pursued my unorthodox interests anyway—experimenting, testing, and gingerly sharing my thoughts. My diffidence proved to be unwarranted, I'm relieved to report; artists have been enthusiastic colleagues in the observations and experiences that have formed the basis of this book.

The Inner-City Child

I currently teach about art and education at The Juilliard School in New York where many of the world's finest musicians are trained. My first lesson for a new group of students often consists of a simple request: Give me one good reason that an inner-city kid just a few blocks from Juilliard should give a damn about classical music. The students immediately offer a range of plausible reasons they have heard in their years of dedication to making music: it is beautiful, it is so well made, it is its own language. But even as they utter their instinctive responses, they quickly realize that none of their justifications would fly with a kid who grew up in the projects without their sophisticated background. They can't think of a single compelling reason why *every* person should care about fine musical art.

Juilliard students are not alone. I have met few people, even few arts professionals, who can convincingly make a case for the actual importance, for any real usefulness, of the arts. I struggle too. I've had many occasions to address different kinds of groups about the importance of the arts. Some groups already share a commitment to the arts (these choirs are delightful to preach to), and some are full of skeptics (they provide a litmus test for my verbal BS). Through my years oat Research Alert, I know the nail-gun power of a perfect statistic. How often I have wished to tell audiences that "one hour of arts experience raises your IQ 6.9 points," or "a good regional theater reduces a city's violent crime by 11 percent," or "ballet lessons in prison cuts criminal relapse in half." Won't someone please prove that watercolor painting cures arthritis?

The American choreographer Agnes De Mille said, "We are a pioneer country. If you can't mend a roof with it, if you can't patch a boot with it, if you can't manure your field with it or physic your child with it, it's no damn good." Does art mend a roof or physic a child?

Can the word "art" mean something important in America? My answer is that it *has* to; further, I have come to see that it does, although not in conventionally understood ways.

There are, in fact, bits and pieces of statistical evidence that shore up the case for the arts. According to scientific research, hearing complex music stimulates your spatial intelligence; making music increases synaptic development in the very young. A school curriculum that dedicates at least 25 percent of its time to the arts produces academically superior students, and using the arts in history classes increases students' retention of facts. It has been proven that good high school arts programs reduce dropout rates and absenteeism. But as encouraging as these slivers of certainty may be (and there are many more), we will never have a perfect "objective" pitch for the primacy of the arts, no slam-dunk case that will score over skeptics' objections. I believe we must look elsewhere to find the roof-mending, boot-fixing, child-healing relevance of art for that inner-city kid.

In my years of lecturing and leading educational workshops, I have come to believe that the answer lies in the doing of "the work of art." When I speak to a group about the importance of the arts, particularly a business group, I am almost always asked what I've come to think of as *the question*: "How are the arts really *useful?*" The inevitability of the question became disconcerting. The pattern: I would address the issue with my best stuff in the presentation; and then, there would be a raised hand next to a face that bore the unmistakable look from which the question blurts. The question is as blunt as Audrey II, the carnivorous plant in *Little Shop of Horrors*, who demands that we, "Cut out the crap and bring on the meat."

Never once have I been asked *the question* during or after a substantial workshop in which participants have had the chance to engage in the work of art. There is something about the *doing* of the

It has been proven that good high school arts programs reduce dropout rates and absenteeism.

arts that communicates their importance, that incontrovertibly answers *the question*. When people dig into the work of art, they no longer have to ask about its value because they know.

Art over the Telephone

Do you recall the children's game "Telephone"? One player starts with a secret statement and whispers it in a neighbor's ear. The neighbor in turn whispers it to the person next to her, and so on down a line of communicators. At the end of the line, the last person announces the statement as she heard it, and everyone compares it with the thought at the start. Low-tech as it is, children still play "Telephone" because it is amazing to see how well-intended communicators can insanely garble a simple thought.

The view of art we now hold in America is the sad result of a modern era telephone game. We began this century with inherited views about the purpose and practices of art, views already far from those that had prevailed for the previous thousands of years. And here at the end of the line of this century, the average citizen holds peculiar definitions and understandings of art that just don't make much sense. Perhaps the declaration from the end of the whispering line is Andy Warhol's definition of art as "anything you can get away with."

Well, the telephone game ends here.

Let's take a closer look at the currently accepted American view of the arts. We believe that serious art is attractive and marvelous. We say it is for everyone, but in practice, it is peripheral to most, irrelevant to many, and threatening to some. The average citizen thinks that art:

- Is about precious objects like Van Gogh paintings that sell for millions of dollars, or about expensive performances by masters in performance halls;
- Requires specialized skills, extensive training, and educated responses that usually include big words;
- Has a separate category called "modern" art, comprised largely of incomprehensible and unpleasant pieces;

- Is about government funding, sometimes for people to photograph sadomasochistic acts and to pour urine on crucifixes;
- Is a "treat" for the rich and sophisticated, but not meant for regular people, except in watered-down versions that elicit condescension from "those who know about art";
- Has glitz and romance attached to it, is nice, but not really important.

If you believe that misguided set of beliefs captures art, then you would believe that the human relationship to animals is completely described by the rules of polo.

I am not enough of a scholar to trace the bizarre generation-to-generation whispering route that our Western understandings of art have taken to bring us to our current muddle. In Paleolithic times, art was a life-essential, right up there with food, water, shelter, sleep, sex, and worship. Art activated and celebrated the important but invisible aspects of life that still hold people together. Art assumed full participation as a social norm and was so infused into daily living there was no special grunt or word to name it. The practices of art taught humans how to live in society and how society could function at its best. For thousands of years, even if she was not one who painted the cave wall, even if he was not a performer in the medieval pageant wagon play, he gave his heart to engage, she gave her mind to extend, through art.

I sense that our confusion about art began around the time of ancient Greek civilization when "philosopher" was becoming a shingle you could hang outside your house. Conflicting views about art's place in life began to appear: Plato banned poetry from his utopia because it was too dangerous, while Aristotle wrote in *Poetics*, "greater than all things is to be a master of metaphor." We have been arguing about art ever since and still never have set a good definition.

In daily life, however, the experience of art remained strong, active, and important for average people. Artists were not seen as existing

In Paleolithic times, art was a life-essential, right up there with food, water, shelter, sleep, sex, and worship.

apart from the rest of society. Art was connected to mysteries and spiritual impulses, as natural a part of social cohesion as the parental impulse.

This durable, active engagement in art in the West carried into the eighteenth and nineteenth centuries, and then things began to change. I will not propose a particular theory to explain this change; there was much going on, and I wasn't there. But by the time we tripped into the twentieth century, the average Western citizen no longer saw art as his or her birthright. Art was not viewed as a critical tool for connecting to the most important things in life, nor as a means to teach and develop understandings about how a society should be and how we should be in society. Art became institutionalized, museum-ized, and separated from daily life; it required experts. Art objects became commodified as a currency, and many art events became too expensive for all but the privileged. Art became what was done by a special talented few. Many romantic notions became attached to the arts: artists became special, hyper-emotional, heroic, not altogether reliable, and a little oversexed; self-expression emerged as an artistic end in itself. Art became fused with a particular, educated, abstracted way of looking at things.

It's true that artists are often very talented, and their accomplishments often magnificent. But artists are not apart. Brilliant soliloquies and sparkling trumpet riffs don't magically spring from some God-given talent or visitations by evanescent muses in billowing gowns. Artists create masterpieces the way we all accomplish things in life, by putting small component pieces together in complex, satisfying ways. In this book, we will explore the basic skills they use and the practices they develop. These are not things like the ability to recite iambic pentameter while you execute the choreographed moves of a fencing duel, or knowing how to load oil paint on a pig-bristle brush. They are skills like asking good questions, solving interesting problems in innovative ways, making stories, using intuition, not-knowing things for a while, paying attention, and making good choices.

Even though our views of art have changed and our equipment for art has diversified over the millennia, we still haven't improved on those

Artists create masterpieces the way we all accomplish things in life.

original tools (call them technologies) that ancient cave painters knew about: metaphor, improvisation, following impulses, making things that hold personal meaning, exploring the worthwhile things others have made, creating rituals in a special place. Once you scrape off the romance and irrelevant crud of common misconceptions about what artists actually do, you see the actual actions of art.

Think about it: Why do many of the smartest, most talented, most demanding people work like maniacs in fields that won't make them wealthy or secure? What is it about the arts that draws and satisfies so many of the best and brightest people who could be high-achievers in more lucrative professions? What is it about art that has kept it near the top of the human priority list for the last tewnty thousand years, until its slippage in recent generations?

Artists are not foolish; they are not old-fashioned; they're onto something.

Through practice, artists learn trade secrets. They pay attention to these basics as if their lives depended on them, because they do. These secrets are so powerful that they transform everyday, ordinary experience into a wealth more valuable than bankable currencies. Artists make masterful use of the perspectives and skills we all naturally apply in unnoticed moments throughout our lives. These secrets have been rediscovered and passed along, hand-to-hand not through whispering, for thousands of years; and they are responsible for much of the good humankind has managed, and most of the joy.

What Goes on in Works of Art

Let me give you a pop quiz about the work of art, using a frivolous example. I am going to suggest an ordinary situation we all encounter. Play it through in your imagination. Then see how many moments you can identify in the scene that you would classify as part of the work of art. Here's the insipid plot:

The scene is a restaurant. You are greeted, ushered to your table. You sit with your friend. You order your meal, and you eat it. It is delicious. You pay the bill. You get up and leave. That's it.

Artists are not foolish; they are not old-fashioned; they're onto something.

Play that scene through in your imagination, and see if you can pick moments that involve the work of art—that is, activity that engages the same kind of work that artists undertake when making their art. Try to stay realistic. In other words, don't jump up and grab the violin from the strolling musician and play "Flight of The Bumble Bee"; keep your hands from sculpting the mashed potatoes like Richard Dreyfus in *Close Encounters of the Third Kind*. Begin, and read on when you are done.

How many work-of-art moments did you find? None? A few? Too many to count?

If you found none, you hold a lofty definition of art and high standards for its label. If you found a few, you are flexible in your thinking and willing to credit small actions with larger meaning. If you found too many to count, you and I share a point of view.

Let me talk you through the way I imagine the restaurant visit. *Every action in it is one I would describe as pertinent to the work of art.*

a) You follow the hostess through the dining area, attending to whatever you happen to notice as you pass: an interesting painting of an ocean, the color of the carpet and walls, the lighting; you hear music, something classical with strings; you smell some curry-like dish and try to identify it; you note a particularly attractive young diner, see someone who looks like someone you know; you watch for possible problems like noisy groups, crowdedness; you pass a grumpy infant. You focus in on your table, evaluating it based on past history and this evening's expectations. To this point, you have noticed things that were attractive, surprising, or of concern. You probably made mental notes of things that were in some way beautiful or the opposite.

b) Cut to ordering from the menu. The printed words and numbers invite your sensory imagination to play. You scan the menu and your memory, consult how you feel, and check the prices. Your task may be complicated by the power of a live performance from the server with a "tonight's specials" recitation, enhanced with little embellishments of voice, face, detail, and professional recommendation. Now, with a sense of the pertinent landscape, you engage in the work of choice more strategically.

You may have a particular notion you brought with you that guides this evening's process of choice: you have always wanted to try the osso buco this restaurant is famous for; you planned to reprise an experience from last time; you only recognize one thing on the menu; you consider digestive or health repercussions. You take your time, as long as it takes for the decision to emerge. You may have organized the choosing process to the point where you need a few last bits of specific information from the server, the representative of the hidden experts in the kitchen. You state your selection, and the server makes a notation, offering a subtle acknowledgment of your accomplishment with a raised eyebrow.

Your mouth may water, your stomach may rumble, the anticipation of the pleasure may begin; you have begun the meal experience. In review, what you have done is take the information you have been given in many media (words, numbers, feelings, intuitions, past experience of many kinds, body awareness) and participated in an imaginative improvisation based on the data. The purpose of the work is to solve the problem of what to choose. You invented your own strategy, juggled the complex multi-media data with grace, pleasure and some sophistication, and arrived at a good solution. And finally, you established expectations of the outcome based on many variables, including the dollar gauge (you expect a better salad for $9 than for $2). You have transformed the menu into the meal. So does the chef.

c) Cut to the action in the kitchen. Each dish is constructed from a limited list of ingredients—some simple, some complex. This available palette of ingredients could provide an infinite number of different-tasting combinations. The possibilities need to be narrowed and shaped in brilliant specific ways to create a dish that connects to your imagined dish; the performance must deliver, and exceed, the promise of the playbill-menu.

The problems involved are multidimensional. While they center around issues of taste, with the hundreds of subtle challenges involved in that medium, the kitchen team's assignments spread far wider. They have to attend to your plate's presentation, smell, timing, and quantity.

They must calculate and plan on a moment-to-moment basis, as well as on a minute-to-minute, hour-to-hour, day-to-day, and every other kind of timetable. There are issues of supply and demand, personnel and personality and politics, health and safety, and many considerations about beauty. There is also the insoluble mystery of three unexpected parties of eight and an inexplicable reason why no one is ordering the chocolate soufflé.

Through its many processes, people, choices, and attitudes—whatever the action in the studio-world behind the closed door—your dish arrives. The server presents your selection. You begin to meet it as you follow its trajectory from the server's hand down toward the open center stage outlined by silverware in front of you. The curtain rises, and you take it in with multisensory attention and assessment. Again, you compare your expectations and past experience to this particular creation.

Without being aware of it, you begin a strategy for solving this next sequence of delightful problems—you reach for the fork to begin with the glazed garnet yams on the right side, as opposed to the lamb chop on the left. You enter a new kind of participation in the evening's improvisation.

d) Cut to standing up to leave the restaurant. It was a terrific meal; it encouraged great conversation; you feel satisfied. You navigate your way out of the now-familiar place, no longer needing a guide.

Again, you enjoy the framed seascape you noticed on the way in, connecting it with the many fish offerings you saw on the menu; the curry-like dish wasn't curry at all, it was the gumbo you saw served at a neighboring table; the cranky baby has gone to sleep; that beautiful young stranger is long gone. Each observation marks a change. Things now make a different kind of sense, enriched by this second, connected noticing.

You see the restaurant's wave-like logo painted on the entry window and note that it fits with the music (Handel's *Water Music*, you discovered from the waiter), the menu, the whole feel of the place. You look to the awning over the entry, and there's something you hadn't noticed before: the color is the same as the color of the border on the plates and the wainscoting on the wall. You think about the impact of that odd linkage—awning with walls and plates—you wonder if you have done something similar in your own home. You notice the color coordination between the scarf and purse of a lady who walks by you. You replay a joke from dinner, making a pun about the lady's silk purse. You turn to say good-bye to your dinner companion. You easily pull together a few words that sum up your experience of the evening. And just before you part, you say "Let's do this again soon, but let's try the new Thai place next time. I have heard the chef is very inventive and works marvels with vegetarian dishes."

That sequence sounds pretty reasonable, doesn't it? We focused in with exaggerated detail, but all the pieces of experience feel familiar and "real."

Every action, every moment, every step described above is filled with the work of art—the same tasks, skills, perspectives, energies, and actions that artists use when creating their work. You may have your doubts: "Eating at The Four Seasons is not art, and imagining that it is will not be something that changes my life." However, I'm convinced that the attending, responding, and choosing you do at The Four Seasons or Red Lobster is *very much* related to art. I know that gaining intentional command of the skills you use in these practices can greatly enhance the quality of your everyday life.

The Basic Actions of Art

The media in which we can engage in the work of art are infinite, as are the number of creations that might result. However, amid this plenitude of options and variations, I propose there are just three basic actions in the work of art.

1) Making Things with Meaning

Referring back to the original meaning of art ("to put things together"), this is the most obvious of the three parts of the work of art. I include the words "with meaning" to differentiate this kind of

Every action, every moment, every step is filled with the work of art.

construction from assembly-line manufacturing, or fretfully snapping together the "Barbie bus" late on Christmas Eve, or hooking fifty identical crocheted pot holders.

Making things is a peculiarly powerful act. Rather than the "things" you make, it is the making itself, the experience, that is the real payoff. Artistic disciplines provide particularly potent ways in which to make things, but they don't own the patent on these powerful experiences. We can, and do, make things with meaning in any medium. The difference between ordinary and extraordinary results does not reside entirely in the medium you work with, rather, it also lies in the qualities of the process.

2) Exploring the Things Others Have Made

Attending to things—perceiving them well—is a natural outgrowth of making them. We're used to paying attention to master artworks, but there are many more things in this world that merit and reward our fullest exploration. The same skills we use in perceiving master artworks can be directed toward decoding and making deeper connections with the many meaningful objects and opportunities that fill our lives. This kind of noticing is a skill to deepen for a lifetime.

In the humbling process of making things with meaning, we have insights that deepen our study of other people's work. We learn that: many choices, of many kinds, are made along the way; each part is placed where and how it is for a reason; one's first impressions might be second rate; that liking or disliking is one of the least useful responses we can have; the surface is only part of the story, and not the best part.

3) Encountering Daily Life with the Work-of-Art Attitude

The skills that result from a practice of making complex things and from perceiving those made by others fosters an attitude that artists know about. This attitude carries beyond the studio or the object itself; it makes connections among the various kinds of experiences we have in life. Artists make sense of their lives through the serious interplay of life and work, by asking, attending, and making connections. This

Making things is a peculiarly powerful act.

In the humbling process of making things with meaning, we have insights that deepen our study of other people's work.

work appears throughout our lives, too, as we find a moment comic, as we notice the natural choreography captured by prints in the day-old snow. This attitude weaves a fabric from the many chaotic threads of modern life. It might be called a curious way of seeing, or lifelong learning, perhaps full-tilt participation, or life jazz.

These three endeavors—making things with meaning, exploring things others have made well, and encountering daily life with the work-of-art attitude—comprise the triangle of actions that artists use to find their deepest satisfaction. These three angles of approach provided the unconventional artistic fulfillment I experienced in my business. I have found that doing the work of art, even just a little, reminds people of the following truths they somehow already know deep inside:

> We are shaped by what we extend ourselves into; our attending and our participation inform our lives. We must be very careful with the objects and actions we present to ourselves and to our children because we are changed by them. The work of art lends shape to passion and to yearning. Works of art are the best containers for yearning because they are so rich, so human, so satisfying on so many levels. Art-work gives serious outer shape to serious inner yearning. If our yearnings are informed by less rich objects, they will go to sleep, will die, or will eventually distort themselves in the harmful expressions that fill the pages of the daily newspaper.

All of us, even those who would derisively snort if you called them artists, engage in the actions of art. We do it naturally, we do it beautifully—without a hint that we have done anything that has to do with art. We commonly call it "doing our best" or "getting lost in our work." It might also be described as absorption in a process, as "flow," as being "in the zone." Call it what you like—it is made of the same work as the work of art. As the painter J.M. Whistler put it in *Ten*

All of us, even those who would derisively snort if you called them artists, engage in the actions of art.

O'Clock, "Art happens—no hovel is safe from it; no prince may depend upon it; the vastest intelligence cannot bring it about."

Your positive future lies in your "work of art": your skills, habits and practices, the way you choose to look at and engage with the objects and activities that fill your life.

What Lies Ahead

In Part Two, we will explore the basic skills of art. These are not the physical talents we think of as artistic skill; rather, these are the inner abilities that lead to the overt physical expressions of art. In Part Three, we will investigate those three actions of art just described, especially as they apply in non-"artistic" media. And in Part Four, we will get practical with some final suggestions about ways to bring the work of art into every part of living.

Part 2

The Infrastructure of Excellence

Chapter Two:

The Invisible Skills of Art

At the end of the last section, I introduced the three actions that comprise the work of art: 1) making things, 2) exploring things others have made, and 3) bringing the skills from 1 and 2 into active play in daily life. Before we delve into the skills used in all three, I would like to re-title these three art-actions, linking them to one of the key metaphors of art: worlds. The fluid cycle of "world-work," is comprised of: 1) making worlds, 2) exploring worlds, and 3) reading the world.

Like the word "art," "world" originally had a broader, more complex meaning. Two prehistoric German words—"weraz," meaning man (the root of werewolf and virile) and "ald," meaning age—married and gave birth to a new word that meant something like "the age of humankind." When early humans spoke this word "world," they referred to the mysterious aspects of human existence on earth. Over centuries, the meaning of the word evolved toward the tangible and mundane and away from the original etheric, spiritual meaning. Time has brought our sense of the world down to earth.

As we will use the term, a "world" is an organized, whole construction with a symbolic connection to something significant about being a human. A world is complete in some internally coherent way, although not fixed and final. A world has two concurrent lives: one as an actual real thing and another in the set of connections we make when we engage with it. A painting can be a world. A story we tell can be a world.

World (wûrld) derivative of *weraz* and *ald* (German) n. the age of humankind

A "world" is an organized, whole construction with a symbolic connection to something significant about being a human.

A solution to a problem, a garden, a poem, a session of lovemaking—whether small or large in scope, whether in the media of "the arts" or not—almost anything we make can be a world if it holds a complex truth that evokes a meaningful response. For example, a urinal in the Grand Central Station men's room could hardly be described as a world; however, when Marcel Duchamp presented one, titled *Fountain*, for display in a 1917 art exhibition, it immediately became a world that people still discuss.

1) World-Making

I call the practice of making things of significance "world-making," because those things we make in any work of art have more than mundane meaning. World-making draws out the raw material in us—past experience, unarticulated understandings, simmering passions, used and unused skills—whatever we've got. The process of world-making focuses our attention to capture and hold what we know—most excitingly, some things we didn't know that we knew. It organizes our current understandings to make new sense. World-making is a series of absorbing improvisatory processes with some sort of shape, most simply viewed as a beginning, a middle, and a closure, with an inherent, spontaneous bounce that sparks further world-work.

The process of world-making is most visible and most familiar in the arts. For example, anyone who encounters my friends Andrew Krichels and Donna Rizzo of the Tennessee Dance Theater can't miss the world-making when they are choreographing a new dance; they become the process for months. The things they talk about, what they notice about passers-by, the books lying open on their tables, the images that linger from their dreams, the opinions they solicit, even the music they play in the car, all become grist for their creative mill. They collect bits that somehow fit with the patterns they are exploring, and they bring these pieces together in the new world of their dance. Watching them in rehearsal for a new dance is like watching a wonderful house being simultaneously designed and constructed. Working with their accumulated raw material, they piece it together, making hundreds of choices and adjustments, just as a carpenter does when transforming a

Things we make in any work of art have more than mundane meaning.

blueprint into walls and stairs. Out of the raw material of previously existing stuff—memory, experience, words, dance movements, images, musical notes—Donna and Andrew construct a new order with some meaning and several kinds of beauty.

The process of world-making is not limited to the arts. We tend to honor it in "the arts;" and that's fine, the arts deserve such celebration. However, anywhere you find yourself fully engaged in making something, you are world-making. Marriages and friendships are vital media for significant world-making; tricky problems in your job provide opportunities and often-overlooked accomplishments, as do gifts and gardens and hobbies and dinner parties. Remember, the work of art lives in the experience, the journey within the process, not in the resulting monument to be presented in a certified art-place.

Cézanne once said that it was the artist's task to become concentric with nature. This truth extends to making any world. In so doing, you become concentric with some aspect of nature: earth's nature, human nature, your nature, the nature of a notion. The word nature comes from the Latin "natura," which originally meant "birth" and came to mean the inherent qualities of someone or something, as in the nature of things; it meant a fundamental order. The work of art is any process of becoming concentric with some inherent truth and pulling things into some order; it is the process of organizing truth around a personal nucleus.

2) World-Exploring

I call the practice of encountering the creations of others "world-exploring" because when we do so, we become investigative reporters on the trail of an important story in a foreign place. We inquire (might we coin the term to outquire?) our way into an idiosyncratic exploratory journey to find meaning in things others have made.

This active perceiving begins with an attraction; whatever catches our interest becomes a possible point of entry. While exploring in our unpredictable way, we create connections of many kinds. We realize and retain these connections through various media like symbols, stories, metaphors, images, ideas, and personal associations.

Marriages and friendships are vital media for significant world-making.

Nature (nā´chər) *n.* a fundamental order

We suspend our disbelief, allowing ourselves to experience another's world "as if" it were ours. We engage and enrich our imagination. Many worlds are so complex in their nature and so satisfying to explore that they invite long-term and repeated exploration. Their "as if" experience invites us deep, and then deeper, inside. They reward us with equally deep meaning.

World-exploring is most familiar in experiencing works of art. We buy a ticket and go see *King Lear*. We become involved with the performance. That is, we find our way into new, nameless understandings and leave the theater more than just entertained, but actually changed. The impact may be subtle, but after the curtain has dropped, we think of fathers and children, friends, and fools slightly differently. The change may keep working in us as we recall a phrase, a moment, a facial expression from the play that haunts us. On the way home, we may begin to shift priorities in the way we spend our time; we may think over a recurrent bit of advice we keep hearing from friends; we may review with fresh attention what a daughter said a few days ago; we may begin to ponder revisions in our legal will; we may pause the next time we use the word "blind." This impulse to make adjustments after exploring a world is a modern-day version of the "catharsis" we studied back in English class, the release-and-change that Greek tragedy aimed to provide. This internal housecleaning through the impact of art is not some archaic Greek emotional epiphany; it is alive, available to those who explore.

The agreed-upon "artistic disciplines" provide optimal worlds, constructed precisely for our enriching exploration, but they are not the only worlds that invite and reward our best perceiving. When curiosity is alive, we are attracted to many things; we discover many worlds. With practice, we become adept at selecting the particular worlds that hold the best payoffs for us.

Any curiosity can take you into a world.

Any curiosity can take you into a world. Say you meet a woman who breeds strains of old-fashioned roses as a hobby. As she draws you into the hows and whys of flower cultivation, you enter her world as surely as you do Herman Melville's whaling world in reading *Moby Dick*. Her images of tiny white roses with the sweetest smell on earth, or strains that were almost lost except for a single bush discovered in an overgrown garden in Wales, may become glowing symbols in you, new constellations in your inner universe.

Falling in love, too—that may be the life event most naturally packed with world-exploring. When in love, we find many attractions—a physical feature, a turn of phrase, a story of a childhood experience—and pursue each to discover more about the hidden nature of the person who has grabbed our interest. It is no coincidence, of course, that we attain our greatest willingness to make changes in ourselves when most in love. While exploring the world of a new love, we see anew, as if the lover's world were ours, and we make deep connections through which we discover alternative ways of being—new thoughts, new feelings, new ways of looking at things—that we want to keep. Our deep response to the world of this new person makes us want to adjust and improve the way we are put together; and in that wholehearted time, we are so filled with courage we believe we can recreate our internal order. This is not to say that we are able to sustain the changes we envision when in "the craziness" of love, neither is an artist able to manifest every world that flashes through her imagination.

Acts of empathy are world-exploring. When you sit with a troubled or ill friend and discover the way she experiences her difficult world, you engage in the work of art. This kind of attention is quite different than the inner work we might do in listening to that friend's problem and then doling out advice or sympathy. These two different ways of attending to a friend are akin to two different ways of experiencing *King Lear*: sitting through the show formulating intelligent remarks to impress other people afterwards, or, in the wholehearted participation previously described. Empathetically entering another's world is entering a complex story as if it were yours and seeing the world as it looks from the inside. It may or may not lead to advice or sympathy—who knows what will happen? But whatever the result, the shared exploration has a transformative impact on you and your friend. World-exploring with a friend can produce a closer relationship; it also can

It is no coincidence, of course, that we attain our greatest willingness to make changes in ourselves when most in love.

provide the deepest experiences of life. I have used my "as if" perceiving with friends who are dying; the result is not sad or consoling—it is inspiring. Michael Schwartz (a friend whose death I participated in the most closely) vowed to die in a way that enabled me and other friends to share some of the experience of dying, so we would understand more and be less afraid for him and ourselves. Day by day, he gave me a chance to grasp his emotional and physical changes by telling me what he noticed, by answering my every question, by just sitting quietly with me. Day by day, I constructed a sense of how it is to be dying. When Michael finally died, the residue of those explorations was the courage and generosity I had discovered with him and the release of much fear from the rest of my life.

3) Reading the World

"Reading the world" is the practice of encountering the ordinary pieces of your life as if they were full of meaning. When this perspective becomes a habit, you see that your life is indeed full of extraordinary commonplaces, rich symbols waiting to reveal themselves to you. This Lewis-and-Clarking of your own frontiers is a critical literacy in reality; it provides a way to read below the surface and tap the understandings you never knew you had. Reading the world is a way of looking at things that refuses to house art only in special buildings, to find art only within gold frames and proscenium arches; it takes the stuffing out of any stuffed shirt the culture industries might put on.

Reading the world puts the accomplishments and habits of world-making and world-exploring into experimental practice in living. This is the alchemy by which ordinary life experiences are turned to gold.

You have had the experience of reading the world. Maybe you can recall it in the kind of attending (which etymologically means "stretching out of yourself") you did in a foreign land. The traveler's curiosity fairly bursts with the sweet work of art. As you take a first walk down a street in Capetown, or through a remote Balinese village, you are actively aware of what you notice; you try to organize these fresh impressions. You notice the small things—the way the South Africans

"Reading the world" is the practice of encountering the ordinary pieces of your life as if they were full of meaning.

greet one another on the street, the way the Balinese place tiny woven offerings on car hoods—because you don't know that these customs are ordinary; they aren't to you. Anything might take on significance. You are a daddy long legs feeling and tapping all that you encounter with the tips of your eight intelligences.

Many of the same skills used in that traveler's reading of a South African street are also used in the different process of a world-explorer's encounter with *A Lesson from Aloes*, Athol Fugard's play about South Africa. The difference is prompted by the terrain explored: a play is an intentionally constructed whole, designed to share a complex truth; while the event of walking down a street is not selectively and coherently composed for our illumination. Fugard's fine play invites our best attention; it draws us naturally toward its constructed center. The disorganized life on a city street doesn't care about the way we notice it and has no pretension to coherent meaning. (It's interesting to note that the more intentionally designed a public street becomes, like a street in Disney World or Colonial Williamsburg, perhaps even Rodeo Drive in Beverly Hills, the more we instinctively world-explore it as opposed to reading it.)

A first-time visitor's perspective may be a particularly vivid and natural experience of reading the world, but most of us notice things and curiously explore for significance on a regular basis. You may have noticed how differently you look at any home you enter the moment you get involved in buying or building your own—overlooked things like window size and molding shape suddenly become grist for your personal mill. Can you recall the way you paid attention to little things on the first day of a new job you were thrilled to have? Also, you read your conversations with friends and colleagues to hear subtle suggestions of meaning; at least you can read them if you choose to attend with your artistic skills. There are texts everywhere, waiting to be read.

Of course, we cannot "read the world" every moment. There is a necessary surface kind of attention that provides essential information about things to avoid, worry about, take advantage of, use, own, grab. However, the availability of bifocal ways of looking at things opens the

When reading the world becomes a mindset we can adopt any time, we attain the ultimate literacy: the capacity to see beyond the literal.

opportunities in the everyday. When reading the world becomes a mindset we can adopt any time, and use often enough that it becomes a habit, we attain the ultimate literacy: the capacity to see beyond the literal. A world-reader celebrates the great works of art and also notices excellence *wherever* it appears, recognizing that meaning may be written in shapes, colors, small odd improvisations and moments, mathematics and science, sound, spices, jokes, relationships, road signs, and roadkill.

These three kinds of world-work do not function apart, discretely; they feed and flow in and out of one another. Practice in one develops the skills for all three. Together, they develop the attitude and the habits that change the content of so many little moments that they transform the experience of a day.

World-Work in Real Life

Let's take world-work out of the conceptual sphere and let it walk through real life.

Meet Jack.

Jack is bustling through a busy Saturday of errands. He is at Home Depot, looking for water seal to brush onto his backyard deck, the wood of which has begun to splinter. Jack hopes to postpone the necessity of a costly replacement deck for a year or two.

He works his way down the display of different brands, trying to remember the kind he used on his previous home's deck. In the aisle, he sees Carrie, his high school girlfriend, buying siding stain just three yards away. His adrenaline rush is filled with excitement and uncertainty. He races through his memory but can't recall who dumped whom. She looks her age but still great: fit, relaxed, smart. Jack can't decide whether or not to say hi, so he concentrates on reading the water seal instructions. Carrie provides the solution by spotting him and coming right over to greet him. She doesn't even have that "Is it you?" look on her face, just radiance. They chat giddily about old connections, about the burgers still served at the Windmill Diner, about the recent divorce of their double-date friends. They wisecrack about water seal and wrinkles and then part.

Jack buys the cans of wood sealant and completes his list of errands in other stores, but his thoughts and feelings linger in the afterglow of his encounter with Carrie. As he drives home, he toys with his impressions, replays the short encounter to notice more, to feel more. Carrie shows some aging signs similar to his own, but she is still so gorgeous. The phrase "wood protectant" replays in his mind, and he pictures his ailing deck: the words "splintering" and "dry" come to mind. He thinks of Carrie again; time has really gone by, but their re-connection was so immediate. He ponders the difference between the bland, slightly selfish female lead in the story of Jack-and-Carrie he has fashioned over the decades of occasional telling and this grownup dynamo he just met. He notes that he himself seems to be the blander, drier, and more selfish of the two. He follows specific recollections into highlights of their dating life: the Saturday fishing expedition hit by a thunderstorm, dancing close at the prom after-party, his first view of her in a bathing suit, the Duster they sometimes went parking in.

He listens to an oldies station on the radio all the way home, humming along with the tunes. He eats lunch with his kids, checks the mail (an L. L. Bean catalog; right, Carrie used to wear chinos), gets Little Jack to sweep the deck and Kara to clear everything off, and he brushes sealant onto the aging surface.

In this story, Jack is doing significant things in a process that develops his understandings about adulthood, aging, time, and love. He is playing with symbols and metaphors, making connections between the unnameable feelings inside himself and external realities he encounters. Jack is trying to make sense out of this inner ferment even as he shops, drives, makes lunch, and now as he brushes the deck. He notices the metaphor pervading his day's events: protecting once-live wood from the inevitable ravages of time, wood that is now more vulnerable and subtly beautiful than when under the carpenter's hand. He lingers on images like water beading up on top of wood and phrases like, "you're not getting older, you're getting better." A song from the drive home, "Mrs. Brown, You've Got a Lovely Daughter" by Herman's Hermits, lodges in his mind.

Luckily, Jack is an amateur short story writer, so he has an active practice readily available to facilitate his *doing* something with his wonderful swirl of emotions. (Jack's amateur practice could be as a poet, a pianist, or a painter, or a storyteller; it doesn't matter. It is more difficult for those without an active world-making practice of some kind to find satisfying ways to make use of inner tumult. Yet, they too find ways, perhaps less immediate or less organized, to work their experiences into new understandings.)

Before Jack knows it, his intuition is busy working on a story about a middle-aged man who is visited by a ghost of his recently-deceased high school girlfriend. That's his current style in stories. In trying to decide the key incidents of the story, he is sorting out Carrie's impact on him. He watches the video of the movie *Ghost* with his kids that evening. More involved than he normally would be, he notes the clever ways the film proposes different influences a ghost might have on a live person. He cries a bit, which he doesn't usually do when watching movies at home. Getting ready for bed, he notices the haziness around the focal couple in the framed photograph of his wife's great-grandparents on her dresser—there is a yellowness and a radiating quality, a ghost-like presence. He hasn't paid attention to that old photo in ten years.

At work the next day, he lunches with a friend, and they exchange high school dating stories. His friend's recollections include incidents of cleverly sneaking away from parental over-supervision. Jack thinks about his own over-parenting—has he imposed too many rules on his kids? Control has been an issue for him at the office too. He is tickled by the impish nature of his friend's solution as a teen. He wants the new short story to be funny, and he works a playful problem into the plot— the ghost controlling the narrator in some way. Next morning, Jack has an idea for a new kind of communication system in his department— the staff won't have to file lengthy reports each week but can add items to a circulating page that covers a topic. This is a more natural way to keep people informed without imposing unnecessary paperwork, and it still accomplishes what the boss wants.

The three actions of the work of art fill this story. Jack makes connections, resonant symbols, and metaphors that he brings together in the complex world of a short story. He also creates a solution to the communications problem at work. He explores the worlds of: *Ghost*, the photograph of the great-grandparents, his colleague's story. He actively reads the events past and present with Carrie; he reads fresh meanings in the deck-staining task, his parenting dilemmas, and the related communications problem at work.

The different actions work together in the jumble of a life yearning toward greater sense and satisfaction. What Jack notices feeds what he makes, which feeds how he listens, which feeds the problems he is working on, and so forth. His yearning bounces him from one engagement to the next, as he learns to love more fully, to do a better job at work, and to make short stories—all while protecting his deck.

Let me finish the story for you. Jack and Carrie never meet again. Jack completes the short story and decides to create a collection of stories about ghosts entering people's lives. He imagines a photo like his wife's great-grandparents on the cover of the collection. He gets a modified version of the new communication plan put in place at the office. He finds himself thinking about another high school girlfriend, Carla. He leaves the half-full last can of water seal in a prominent place on the garage shelf.

A final personal confession about the ways people with a world-making habit look at things: my deck needs water sealant; Carrie is the name of a girl in my high school past; I sometimes write short stories; Little Jack is the name of a character in a play I worked on not long ago; I went to my first Home Depot recently when I moved to the country; and that damn Herman's Hermits song has been stuck in my head for days, and I'd love to get it out.

Back to Basics: The Fundamental Skills of Art

The word "skill" in relation to the arts evokes images of Andre Watts playing the piano with incomprehensible speed and the complexity of ballerinas spinning while balanced en pointe. By a standard definition of artistic skill, Home Depot Jack seems pretty mediocre; maybe he

Skill (skil) *n.* the
internal capacity to
draw a distinction

demonstrates a little in his short story abilities, but that's about it. In the prevailing view, poor Jack is a Yugo on the speedway of art.

However, the word "skill" originally meant something more basic, subtler, than proficiency in performance. "Skill" originally meant "drawing a distinction." It described *internal* capacities, the mental dexterities that enable people to perform those breathtaking external maneuvers. If we use this older view of skill, we see Jack in the lead pack on the fast-track of art.

Of course, the musician's technical ability to sound the notes well is essential to good music. However, a good note-technician is not necessarily a good musical artist, and therein lies all the difference. There are internal skills (of the mind and the heart), and then there are different skills of the body and hands. The internal skills of art can bloom into masterworks through good technical skills of the hands. When we manifest those internal artistic skills through any medium, we perform the work of art. Jack exemplifies many of those internal skills, even though his stories aren't *New Yorker* material.

In this section, we will address the inner skills of art, the invisible basics that make sense of things and construct change. What are those inner skills? The answer is the subject of the next five sections.

Change is difficult. We make things better by working on what we see—we clean up the neighborhood by picking up the litter. But to bring about real change, to reform anything, we must attend to the less-evident basics under the surface. To make a real change in the neighborhood, we must address the underlying problems that make people feel it's OK to toss their trash in the streets. Otherwise, we don't reform but only adjust and cope. Before long, we tire of devoting hours to the pickup patrol, or we start to pay to have others do it for us. Either way, we get angry, and the neighborhood situation gets progressively worse.

This is the sadly persistent pattern in our lives and in our nation as we try to reform things we know are not working—things like schools, workplaces, social problems, and most importantly, parts of our own lives. Again and again, we gather ourselves to bring about change; we bring the best of intentions, we muster enough energy and gumption,

*To bring about real
change, to reform
anything, we must
attend to the less-
evident basics under
the surface.*

but then we go to work on features rather than foundations. Sad but true—*energy applied to the not-quite-basics guarantees a deeper rut within the problematic status quo.* The skills of art are the *basic*-basics that underlie the way it is. If we develop our skills of art, we manifest positive change wherever we choose to work with our hands.

Do we want school reform? Aggressive campaigns urging a re-focusing "back to the basics" of reading, writing, and arithmetic scores reappear every decade or so. But these efforts flop every time because the good intentions never get to the *real* basics, those underlying skills that make the learning difference. When these less visible skills are emphasized, students rediscover the love of learning, the whole school world changes, and test scores go up.

The same is true in business reform. Too often, businesspeople say they wish to rebuild, to "re-engineer" from the bottom up; but they never get to the true bottom line, the workplace basic-basics. These skills appear in the moments when an individual places mind, hands, and heart onto the work, in the quality of the interaction between the human and the tasks. Put one-tenth of the energy now expended on misplaced corporate reform efforts on the true basic-basics and quadruple the positive change.

Our focus in this book is not on school or corporate reform (although I have come to know how much the work of art has to offer those reformation efforts, providing further good answers to *the question* about the practical value of the arts). This book addresses a different, equally complex organization—your personal life. The same back-to-basics pattern applies to you.

This part returns to the real basics—the skills and practices of art that construct our experience of daily life. As with any skill, apply some attention, get some coaching and practice, and you get better.

For a moment, think of these inner skills as akin to the physical movement skills with which you clearly have some competence. With attention, you can learn more about the ways you move, and you can begin to extend and refine what you naturally do in an average day. You now spend a lot of time effectively getting from here to there; you have some specialized experience that has advanced some areas of your movement repertoire. With intention and application, you can readily develop awareness of, and pleasure in, a wider range of movement in your life: when you move quickly (when late for a train) or with precise care (through a crowded formal event); when you float (on a beach) or focus (in stretch exercises or using a power saw). And you can begin to derive satisfaction from intentionally applying your abilities: playfully (in a game), or attentively (noticing how you feel as you move in different ways), or beautifully (in a dance), or efficiently (at work).

Your inner skills of art are as familiar as the way you can move your body. In the next five chapters, we will try to specify and experiment with your inner artistic skills in ways analogous to those just described.

We will study artists as masters of this terrain. These internal skills are artistic trade secrets not because artists are miserly with their goodies but rather because artists are so rarely asked about what they know. Those uninterested in the arts don't take artists very seriously; few would think to turn to artists for serious answers about constructing better "real world" lives. (Also, I must admit that people in the arts have done a perennially lousy job of communicating the underlying importance of what they know.) I spill these beans about artists' invisible skills in hopes that many can sprout and grow in fertile, personal soil. Like yours.

Of course, not every artist excels in every skill we will detail. I am speaking in a general way, about a typified artist, based on the hundreds I have worked with and known. I speak of artists' skills as one might speak of the many skills of a great parent, even though not every great parent is tops in every skill.

I have distilled the many skills of artists down to five basic kinds:

1) Plugging into essential sources
2) Catching and using key moments
3) Wielding the power tools
4) Harnessing the bucking process
5) Structuring the big picture

We will explore each in the next chapters of this part. Together, these five comprise the infrastructure of excellence.

Your inner skills of art are as familiar as the way you can move your body.

Chapter Three:

Plugging into Essential Sources

Sometimes the parents of an aspiring young actor will ask me to speak with their child. They silently pray I will discourage that young adult's career ambitions with warnings about the "harsh realities" of a life in the theater. I look from the concerned, urgent faces of those parents to that nervous, earnest young face and say with all the severity I can muster: "If your heart will allow you to pursue any other path, follow that way." And my subtext shouts, "If you can, be courageous. You won't be sorry!" If that young soul has the passion that demands total immersion in the work of art, despite the obvious hardships of the profession, she has an enormous natural talent to bring to life, even if her acting talents seem too modest to promise a major career.

Artists are not casual about their vocation. Most are driven irrepressibly to follow their work in art, and they learn valuable lessons through their years of dedication to a fundamental source. Artists develop a steady skill we will explore in this section: they keep themselves plugged into the reliable, renewable, sustainable energy sources that keep them turned on, that keep them sharply alive. This skill is more than a luxury for lives of artistic commitment or financial privilege; it is more than a pleasant fluke for an occasional lucky day; it is a practice at the heart of an artist's natural approach to work that constructs a life of vitality.

All people have this naturally healthy, joyful, creative instinct

Artists are not casual about their vocation.

Yearning (yûr´ning) *n.* the fundamentally human instinct for more

beaming in them, even as they try to put together good lives within workaday realities. We all wear the concerned, urgent faces of those parents mentioned above *and* the nervous, earnest face of the incipient artist. We live best when we provide for both sets of needs. The young artist in us needs to create, to push as far as we can go. The parents need to protect, to make sure there is enough safety and comfort. Fulfillment lies in balance, of course; but many people over-rely on the protectors' priorities. When the vulnerable creative impulse is overlooked, or not guided well, it gets pushed, battered, demanded, and twisted into serving a source that depletes it. Sadly, we can end up dancing to every tune except the quiet one that is our own.

The actions of art are driven by an energy that I call yearning. Yearning is the fundamentally human instinct for more. What the "more" is may be approximated by calling it any number of things: more satisfaction, more understanding of unknown things, an enhanced gut feel of being alive, better answers to better questions. It is the feeling that drives our multi-billion-dollar self-help and psychotherapy industries.

Yearning is a force of nature. Biology calls such forces tropisms. Bean sprouts planted in every first-grade classroom and every piece of earth around the world grow up to seek the light and send roots down for water—phototropism and hydrotropism. Similarly, the seeds of every human experience contain the potential to yearn toward the sun *and* into the earth—upward toward the unknown *and* downward into sensory grounding. Yearning keeps us growing up and down. It fuels the curiosity to explore the unfamiliar, to expand understanding, as well as the persistence to dig in and find out what we are capable of doing. Yearning keeps us expanding in the individual ways, through the particular channels, that mean something and everything to us.

Any one person's palette of specific yearnings may not be nameable or even identified. Known or unknown, these impulses demand that we get more of what truly matters to us. If we go deaf to such urgings, make choices that blunt them, or literalize the urge to mean "more stuff," we seriously damage the quality of our living—we go dead in part or all of life. Many of these hard-to-name "mores" are the same experiences humans have yearned to embrace for thousands of years: to love and be loved deeply, to have a more visceral experience of being alive, to connect palpably with the divine, to know more, to feel we understand, to feel in control of the complexity we perceive. Yearning is our heart's desire; the spirit's urge to discover itself in forms. Yearning is as in the title of the Dylan Thomas poem, "the force that through the green fuse drives the flower." I call it the engine that urges us toward our entelechy.

Entelechy derives from the Greek word meaning "to have the goal" or "to embody the perfection," and it means the full realization of one's inherent potential. For example, the entelechy of a foal might be to be a good racehorse. The horse's life is a journey toward that entelechy, which may or may not become fully attained.

A full realization of what we might become doesn't just happen to us—just as Secretariat didn't become the greatest racehorse by having great parentage and then just hanging out with the mares in the barn all day. Realizing our entelechy, yearning our way toward it, takes work: the work of art. There is no other human practice that takes us more directly toward our entelechy. Many other practices are good—religion, intellectual study, meditation, career success—but none is more encompassing, powerful, or flexibly responsive to individual need; none is more effective nor more beautiful than the work of art, and those other good practices all include the work of art as we participate in their traditions. Remember, this does not mean you must become a professional artist. It means you must find and follow the work of art in whatever you choose to do in your life.

We tend to use the words yearning and longing interchangeably, but they are not the same. Longing contains more concrete desire and awareness of time, while yearning has more depth, heart, and soul. Longing is more of an ache to have some "thing"—as a child might long to own a bicycle. That same child, however, might use his bike as a tool to fulfill a deeper passion, a yearning for freedom or autonomy.

Many people are uncomfortable with yearning. They sense it as a

Yearning is our heart's desire; the spirit's urge to discover itself in forms.

Entelechy (en tel´ ə kē) n. the full realization of one's inherent potential

Longing contains more concrete desire and awareness of time, while yearning has more depth, heart, and soul.

deficiency, a lack, an itch to be scratched. But for our greatest growth, yearning must not be satisfied for long, because if it is, it goes to sleep. It must be nurtured and followed—no matter what wanting-and-getting happens on the surface. The language of yearning is uncomfortable for some people, too; it is abstract, ineffable, and always just beyond what we know. There is one way to understand yearning in a thoroughly concrete way—through hands-on participation in the work of art.

Those who lose the skill of yearning get depressed or concretize their entelechy. They ask only for "things": things that will make them happy when they own them, things that will quell the uncertainty of not knowing—works of art instead of the work of art.

Artists do more than just "have" yearning; just as people who are successful do not attain excellence by merely "having" potential. The artist's active skill of yearning is to accomplish the following two challenges at the same time: 1) to keep the force of yearning fully-charged, and 2) to guide this passion into action that gets satisfying results. Artists know that the skill of pursuing good projects in that second challenge accomplishes the first task as well.

Skillfully designed engagements for artistic yearning appear in large and small ways. The larger strokes of yearning appear in the heroic deeds of art: the courage to envision and complete a whole project; the fortitude to seek personal answers to enormous questions no matter how long it takes; the determination to persist in the face of difficulty and frustration; the openness to inquire into every kind of opportunity, even the unlikely and unexpected. Big yearning enables artists in every field to create the masterpieces that fill so many hearts with inspiration.

The grand expressions of yearning are fed by minuscule moments, the almost-invisible applications of yearning. We will look closely at these in the next few chapters, these are the tiny skills that, when made into habits, change the way we experience living. Though we naturally associate the work of art with big projects, like operas and oil paintings, it is these small, undramatic moments of yearning-in-action that I hope to bring to your awareness and common practice. These are the

Big yearning enables artists in every field to create the masterpieces that fill so many hearts with inspiration.

everyday actions of yearning, the modest works of art, that reward us with "more" of what we crave.

Before we play with these fundamental building blocks, we need to answer two questions about yearning: Where does it come from? How does it come to life?

Where Does Yearning Come From?

This is one of the ultimate philosophical, ontological, spiritual questions, perhaps the sixty-four-thousand-year question. I have a theory to propose, based on my experience: Our yearning is alive in direct proportion to our capacity for wonder.

We are all born in wonder. Of the basic emotions that pass through an infant's face—misery, rage, joy, curiosity, the palette of primary colors from which we mix a lifetime of finer-shaded feelings—wonder predominates. One of the great privileges of being with young children is the rediscovery-contact high we get as they wonder at the amazing beauty of pliers and ratty looking puppies.

Artists sustain this lively access to their wonder. Even the worst artistic curmudgeons will explode with it when the work goes right, when they see the beauty of their "pliers" equivalent. A sixty-year-old painter-friend effervesced for thirty minutes one day, marveling to me about a discovery in a tiny four-inch square of a huge canvas he was working on. Wonder releases wholehearted, unsophisticated, pure joy. The readiness with which artists tap into wonder is partly why they are sometimes dismissed as childlike and immature. The more work of art one does, the greater one's capacity for and energy from wonder. The writer J.M. Barrie knew this: "What is genius? It is the power to be a boy again, at will."[2]

Grownup reality can seem far from the experience of wonder. The serious business of the real world seems to be the antithesis of wonder, so heavy it can smother wonder under the concrete. However, wonder lingers just under the crust of necessity, like the seeds that sprout when you crack open a sidewalk. I had an unforgettable introduction to this dichotomy as a sixteen-year-old boy in my first job. I was a summer

Our yearning is alive in direct proportion to our capacity for wonder.

assistant in a small market research department of the paper products division, in the toilet paper subdivision, of the ironically named American Can Company. By midsummer, I had done well enough that they gave me a project of my own: to prepare a presentation of research findings for the corporate vice-president. Irony persisted. The research was about the way women use toilet paper, and I was a painfully shy young naïf. My supervisor suggested I "pep up" the presentation with tape recorded voices. I ended up going to the secretaries in the office and asking them to read the paragraphs that anonymous respondents had written. I knelt by their desks, tape recorder in hand, coaching these women toward more naturalistic readings about the crumpling and wiping, blushing as if my head would burst. I edited the tape to a few highlight performances and prepared some key facts and a chart for the big show.

I was terrified before the meeting, my first immersion into the pressured reality of adult-job life. I grew more terrified when I saw the boss. He looked mean. He wore a suit I didn't see again until Alexander Haig told the nation not to worry. There was no joking around, no small talk. Two frightened men gave reports before mine. The boss asked them sharp questions; I hadn't prepared for that. Just at the end of the presentation before mine, with my terror rising, there was an interruption. The vice-president's secretary came into the conference room and whispered to him. What a quick change in his demeanor as a woman (his daughter) entered with a baby (his first grandchild). He was transformed instantly, utterly, as he focused on the child. Quite unself-consciously, he mirrored the weird faces the baby was making, moving his features like some gymnastic amoeboid mass. He was really good at it, genuinely funny to watch—Jim Carrey could have taken notes. Mostly he reflected that baby's wide-open look of wonder. The boss forgot about the rest of us for nearly a minute, absorbed in the improvised comedy routine with his miniature partner. The room became easy and jovial around this potentate child.

The instant the baby was whisked away, the crack in the conference room world closed, and we went right back to work, seemingly as if this playful event had never happened. Yet, there was a palpable difference in the room; something had changed. I was surprised to find myself relaxed for my presentation. The boss seemed genuinely interested in what I had to share. There were some questions, but they weren't derogatory. They actually helped me tell more of what I knew. There was even a discussion of the ideas I proposed. Although the whole meeting appeared surreal to my teenage eyes, I never forgot the facts of that day: as hard as the covering may seem, there is playful, humane wonder just underneath, hungry to be tapped by serious play, and contact with that personal zone is utterly transforming and strong enough to change the world around it.

No access to wonder means no yearning. Oddly, wonder is both scarce and hard to kill. Fear and survival-mindedness suppress the expression of wonder; addiction and anger bury the experience of it. But wonder is durable and patient, like that seed waiting under the sidewalk you tread. Wonder appears under the most difficult conditions: just recall *The Diary of Anne Frank*, and more recently, Christopher Reeve's joyful face. Wonder witnesses the good truth that can be anywhere, because it is everywhere. As John Cage reminds us: "Every seat is the best seat in the house."

I once worked with students in an inner-city elementary school in which the teachers had to clean excrement off a classroom wall just before class. An hour later, the third-graders were full of wonder at the way placing a mask on a face completely changes the impact of the wearer. Even the rudimentary white paper plates we drew on, with poked-out eye-holes and glued-on sticks for handles, could transform small, sullen Anthony into a beaming hero to his peers. We were fully absorbed by the wonder of art in the dilapidated room with brown smears.

I have been with equally at-risk students in affluent classrooms, whose first question to me was whether they were going to be graded on our creative work together; what would the test be like at the end? They too can push aside the habits of their survival thinking, their fears, to engage in the work of art, which awakes their capacity for wonder.

Wonder is both scarce and hard to kill.

Wonder is more than "oh wow," but not much more. It is "oh wow" with a difference.

Wonder is more than "oh wow," but not much more. It is "oh wow" with a difference. We "oh wow" when we are impressed; that is, when something makes an impression on us. Note the action of the verb—from the thing into us. "Oh wow" receives a new world; wonder is the impulse-in-response to enter it. A child's wonder is an instinct; he wants to inhabit everything that attracts his interest. A grownup's wonder requires receiving an impression (which means experiencing it as separate from oneself), appreciating that it is extraordinary in some way, and feeling a wordless impulse to pursue and grab what is special. We feel "oh wow" at impressions that knock our socks off. Wonder is the impulse to stick our bare feet into that new world.

We say "oh wow" when we see the Grand Tetons for the first time. We experience wonder when we take their startling grandeur inside, when we ourselves feel majestic and inspired and "high." We "oh-wow" the intelligent answer in class from Paul, the lumpy mouth-breather who never pays attention. We experience wonder when we linger long enough to consider Paul in a new way.

Wonder is wordless and utterly personal.

Wonder is wordless and utterly personal. No one can force it on us, do it for us, should us into it, or even know if it happened. In keeping with the common habit of under-acknowledging our personal skills, we usually credit any wonder we feel to the "thing" that creates the impression: e.g., the Grand Tetons. However, the key to wonder is not the impressive thing "out there," but the quality of the experience inside. If we experience wonder, we *do* something inside; we open something, adjust something—that skill is important. We expand our known world through wonder by participating in something larger than ourselves. Wonder is pure participation, devoid of the need to possess.

Even after we forget specific incidents, the moments of wonder have reformed the images we have to work with and have expanded the scope of our imagination and understanding. Wonder is the impulse, the response to the world, that launches the work of art.

It works backwards too—the work of art revives wonder, which is why the *doing* of art is so important. By intentionally engaging in the work of art, we ground our lives in wonder, as artists do. I recall an example of art awakening wonder in a brusque workshop participant who was creating choreography in a short movement exercise. She had grown up in a strictly religious family that forbade dancing or any pleasure in physical movement, and even though she was no longer bound by these strictures, the habits ran deep. I saw no glimmer of wonder in this forthright and serious woman. She had already proclaimed she hated watching dances and glowered as she began the exercise. I had not known about her background when I began the movement game. A few days later, she tearfully told me her story. She had been terrified when I set out the instructions but decided to try the exercise anyway, even though she usually didn't allow herself "to do such things." She had discovered how beautiful it was to dance and her face bore the characteristic wide-open look of wonder. She used the words "holy" and "healthy" in describing it. She told me she had discovered that she had a lot of body-intelligence and was now determined to use it. The action of art let loose a yearning she never even knew she had.

I recall the explosion of wonder across the face of an angry feminist as she realized the elegance of a solution proposed by the pompous male chauvinist pig who was her by-chance partner. It caught her off guard, and the rigid boundaries of her world shifted.

Sadly, many of us spend years apart from wonder. It feels as if "the normal way it is" pounds the wonder out of us, but it isn't so. Our wonder may take a beating, but it lives. We cannot teach people how to experience wonder. Do we teach plants to grow toward the sun? We can drive someone to see the Grand Tetons, but we can't make him become wondrous at the sight. We can drag a horse to Monet's *Water Lilies*, but we can't make him drink it in. However, we can engage someone in the work of art, and wonder will appear.

Yearning Comes to Life in Response

If *wonder* sparks the impulse to move, and *yearning* is the engine that propels the work of art, then *responding* is the first gear. In our

We can drag a horse to Monet's *Water Lilies,* but we can't make him drink it in.

exploration of basic skills, a person's response is the first action we can actually see and describe.

The word "respond" goes back to the Latin "respondere" which was a compound verb pieced together from "re," meaning "back" or "again," and "spondere," meaning "promise" (which is also the source of "spouse" and "sponsor," words still based in promises). So, etymologically, to respond is to promise in return. Thus, a response is far more than the knee-jerk reflex after a stimulus, more than a witty answer to a question from a talk-show host; it is a small personal commitment, a contract of sorts.

I call the skill to make a committed promise back "response-ability." As used by artists, the skill involves more than a willingness to take whatever comes down the pike; it is more than being sensitive and open. Response-ability includes an eagerness to encounter what appears. It has a dash of the yearner's pizzazz, sensing something of value to be found and grabbed. And with that eager attitude, the artist does indeed discover valuable things almost everywhere her gaze is turned.

The presence or absence of response-ability in a person becomes particularly noticeable in the arts. For example, I have seen many people faced with a complex challenge like relating to a modern painting shrug off their response-ability with comments like, "It looks like a kid's scrawl to me," or, "I don't get it," or, "It doesn't look like anything, I don't like it." Such attitudes may seem benign, but they display the same kernel of disregard for human potential as more overt acts of irresponsibility that we readily decry in the world. The refusal to respond to the new, to discover what value it might hold, is a denial of responsibility.

Clarity in perceiving, ready access to what we experience, and willingness to place a personal stake in a connection are the skills involved in "response-ability."

You see a crying child, and you respond. You hear a favorite piece of music, and you respond. On less immediately inviting occasions, say standing in front of an unfamiliar, abstract painting, your response

Respond (ri spond´)
derivative of *respondere*
(Latin) *v.* to promise
in return

requires an effort, a skill of yearning, to make an authentic connection with the canvas, even a small one. You may have to push past judgments and preconceptions to find an entry point into the artist's world. And, having found a way in, you must also find your genuine response back. That response need not be admiring or even fully clear, it merely needs to spring directly from what you perceive.

This is the response-ability we all have: to set aside our history and prejudices, to genuinely perceive what we encounter, and to connect back truthfully. Responding in this way honors the connective link we have made with our artistic skill. We *make* those connections; they don't "just happen." Even if the connection is only a question, even a small one, it is an accomplishment. Once we have responded to a Mark Rothko painting, for example—even a little—we can never again claim that we "hate modern paintings" or "don't get it." The promise requires us to build upon that connection, however frail it may be, in the next opportunity we find. If we return to a dismissive judgment about modern art, we have broken our promise; we have been irresponsible and have killed a little part of our potential.

We complain of a lack of responsibility among people today, particularly among the young. We are quick to point at the many examples of offensive and damaging behavior and lay blame. If we attend to the true basics, we see that the real deficiency is the ability to respond; that is, to notice well and to make-and-keep a personal commitment back. This skill is learned and developed in the work of art. I have found that developing the capacity to fully respond does more to promote "responsible behavior" than a long list of "behavioral requirements" one tries to impose. A healthy habit of response-ability leads naturally, enthusiastically, to the positive conduct we usually try to legislate.

This is the kind of response-ability we need in the nation. The skill to create small, personal connections to new things and to be committed enough to honor them with a promise back—a promise we keep. Politicians and preachers, New Agers and Far Right Wingers are correct when they demand that we teach responsibility—except they

This is the response-ability we all have: to set aside our history and prejudices, to genuinely perceive what we encounter, and to connect back truthfully.

don't really know what they mean. They intend a set of generalized, adhered-to behaviors. They ignore the source of the mature, committed, positive conduct they demand. They overlook the basic skill of response-ability that lies at the heart of the actions they demand. They overlook it in themselves. People take the skills of responsibility into their lives when the work of art, in its widest definition, appears in their hands.

Do you recall that feeling of putting forward something you invested your heart in: a gift you made, a speech or song you were about to perform for the first time, an exciting idea you were harboring, a town-meeting statement of conviction? It can be frightening. Grownups learn to mask the vulnerability of those moments, whereas a child looks like he might explode or expire. Such tension indicates that you have invested your yearning in what you are offering. It takes courage to put it out there. It can even take courage to verbally put forth a sincere response to an unfamiliar challenge like an abstract painting.

The practice of response-ability develops courage, which grows in the work of art. Until the seventeenth century, the word "courage" meant more than bravery; it covered the full range of the heart's passions, including rage and inspiration, awe and humility, hate and love. The work of art uses and develops that broadest kind of courage; it opens up the range of battlefields where we can be courageous to include the home, the office, the political arena, the Internet, the classroom, the school board meeting, and the conversation in the kitchen. Courage is overcoming disengagement in all its guises. It is the commitment and the skill to participate.

The work of art provides the courage to try, and it reminds us how to take responsibility for what we make. Many of us are great blamers and excusers. Yet, he who makes excuses is seldom good at making anything else. The painting in the gallery does not bear a label with excuses for why it is not better. The jazz drummer may critique his own performance afterwards, but not while he plays "Take the A Train." During the action, all the players take full, courageous responsibility for their preparation, their skill, their choices; they boldly put forward their

Courage (kûr´ij) n. the full range of the heart's passions, including rage and inspiration, awe and humility, hate and love statement, unexcused, to the very best of their ability. They play their hearts out.

The active yearning embodied by jazz, by all work in art, has boldness in it. President Kennedy often told an anecdote about Frank O'Connor, the Irish writer, that conveys an artist's bold attitude of continual yearning: Kennedy told of O'Connor and his boyhood friends making their way across the countryside; and when they came to an orchard wall that seemed too high, and too doubtful to try, and too difficult to permit their journey to continue, they took off their hats and tossed them over the wall—and then they had no choice but to follow them.

Chapter Four:

Catching and Using Key Moments

Those bean sprouts we met in the last section grow up and grow down. So does human yearning. It naturally reaches up toward many ineffables and down to root in small tangibles.

The most basic of life-transforming skills, the closest to the ground we get, is noticing things. Sounds simple? Don't we notice things all the time? Yes we do, but how, and why, and how can we do it better? Artists have much to teach us here. They honor their attention for its fundamental role, and they can wield their noticing like a delicate tool.

If our experience of being alive is the most valuable thing, then what we pay attention to becomes a critical choice, and developing *how* we notice becomes the most important thing we can do.

In workshops, I am always struck by how hard it is for participants, of all ages, in all fields, to notice they are indeed *having* experiences. They do the activities, do them well, and have fine insights, but they resist considering what happens inside them during the experience as if it were important, worth noticing. Many have an ingrained bias that dismisses those inner events as inconsequential because they are intangible. (This tendency is similar to the way we ignore the invisible skills of art, because the overt ones are easier to see and name.) As workshop participants are prompted to start noticing their experience, their awareness flashes in fragile and ephemeral glimpses. Slowly, participants get a sense that those inner events are full of important,

If our experience of being alive is the most valuable thing, then what we pay attention to becomes a critical choice.

surprising information and accomplishments. They learn that it is actually possible to become adept at experiencing and to create habits to open up those inner resources that make such a palpable difference. They come to respect experience-awareness as a skill that directly taps the feeling of being alive.

Philosophy professor Jacob Needleman describes a similar moment of discovery in his experience: "I had a colleague who professed an academically respectable stance that there are no such things as mental images. He was willing to argue and defend this philosophical position because he wasn't even aware how to put it to a test. At a party one evening, after a few drinks, I suggested he assist me in a card trick. I said, 'Take a card. Now, without looking at it, guess what it is and don't tell me.' He took a card and an instant later exclaimed, 'My God, I just had a mental image!' That one moment of internal observation completely refuted his whole philosophy. He had never bothered to look into his own mind; he hadn't known how to."[3]

Artists know how to. They attend to those inner events carefully—to the mental images and the many other internal events that comprise experience. Artists know their creative work begins there and that their authenticity remains grounded there. Their years of practice in noticing experience build proficiencies to clarify experience in subtle, multidimensional ways and to *do things* with their experience—to recreate it in interesting forms. But how can we follow their lead in experience-awareness? How do we learn to notice and tap the rich content of the moments we make?

I have been working on this challenge for a long time: in the arts, in business, in education, in myself. I've studied Eastern approaches, productivity theories, and any number of arcane disciplines and practices. When I worked on noticing in my business, it was not for etheric reasons; if my workers could notice more strategically, they could work more effectively, and we all stood to make more money.

I've come to some conclusions—not final answers, but ideas with enough weight to sustain my inquiry. I have come to know that the work of art is an effective way, perhaps the best way, to develop productive noticers in Western culture. And the skills involved provide rewards in every arena of life, not just in artistic satisfaction.

Noticing is to experience as listening is to music. If a man sits in the concert hall thinking about getting his car's carburetor fixed, he may have pleasant sensations, but he's missing the music. We engage similarly in the performance hall of our experiences; we can choose to notice or not. In that choice lies all the difference. Attending to experience is actively responding, which, as we know from the last section, is always grounded in personal yearnings—it speaks directly to the heart. Artists instinctively attend to what they encounter, inside and out, and experiment with what they perceive. They hear the music; and anyone who hears the music is engaged in the work of art.

Noticing may be a common action, but it is hardly inconsequential. The word "notice" was born in the Latin "noscere," which gives it powerful sister-words like "knowing" and "cognizance." To know—this enormous human capacity and mystery—is the subterranean aquifer from which noticing springs. "Attention" comes from Latin, meaning "to stretch out"; attending is the active effort to stretch out of oneself. This effort costs us something, which is why we must "pay" attention.

Attentive noticing is an accomplishment in itself—especially in a culture in which we are bombarded with stimuli and options for our attention. Over one thousand advertising messages (the average number we are exposed to) shout for an American's attention each day, dozens of screen viewing options are available at every moment. As a survival mechanism, we train ourselves into a kind of callousness within which noticing becomes an act of significance. Artists live in the numbing swirl too. They develop the discrimination to ignore the empty and attend to the worthwhile on a moment-by-moment basis. They remain able to notice naively where they choose, without interpreting or judging; they notice both in general and in specific, back and forth; they work to notice things that are not readily apparent; they notice the odd and eccentric aspects of the obvious— the pattern of veins on the tomato's bright red surface, the subtext of rage in the polite hello.

Noticing may be a common action, but it is hardly inconsequential.

Notice (nō´tis) *v.* to pay attention

Attention (ə ten´shən) *n.* to stretch out

My teaching-artist colleague Randy Williams gives a nectarine to each member in a class of thirty. He asks the students to study their nectarines well. He then puts the nectarines in a paper bag, shakes the bag gently, and opens it. He then asks the class to find their own nectarines. How many common objects do you attend to daily with similar exemplary noticing? The answer needs to be "some."

How Does Noticing Work?

Noticing is not a single kind of act. A range of noticing goes on constantly, beneath our level of awareness. We put out a low level *scan for danger*: erratic driver up ahead, weird color on that piece of chicken. Sometimes this effort doesn't even make it to awareness, we just *monitor*: the sounds around the house to make sure there is nothing amiss while we read in bed, sounds from the children's bedrooms even while we sleep. We have *automatic pilot* noticing: driving "lost in thought" for three minutes on the highway. We have *trigger* noticing: wake when the baby coughs, attend to a vague new pain somewhere near the lung. We have *anomalies-attending*: sensing something odd today about a person we see every day. We have *shelved* noticing: specifics we did not notice at the time, but pull off the shelf to consider later in hindsight. We have *evidence-gathering* noticing: "Are they thinking about changing my job"; "Am I gaining weight?" We have *neurotic* noticing: "She looked at me in a funny way"; "I'm fatter than three people in this room." All of these are manifestations of noticing carrying on beneath awareness, all the time.

Additionally, there is the noticing we are all aware of. We notice the obvious: Elaine looks great in her prom dress; the wall needs painting; what a gorgeous day. There is an entertainment noticing, for pleasure: following the garden year's progression, repeating the words of a favorite song. There is more intentional noticing when we are in some sort of dialogue: making a quick sketch of a flower, chatting amiably with Peter while we try to figure out what is bothering him. There is engaged noticing: deep in one of those "great conversations" with Isabelle or when completely engrossed in work.

There are also other kinds of noticing, beyond those we can scientifically confirm. Whether you believe in the paranormal or not, you must admit there are ways we know things beyond those that meet the eye—intuition at the very least. You probably have a sense of your own subtler, unmeasurable capacities. I'm sure you have relied upon your intuition to make a decision that turned out surprisingly well. You may have felt odd taking credit for it afterwards. Some people prefer to deny these inexplicable abilities. It doesn't matter—there are sixth and seventh senses, still-unproven capacities, whether we widely accept them today or not. Artists are remarkably skillful in this subtle domain.

We can learn to use all these different ways of noticing strategically, like tools, as artists do. To get a sense of how we can train our skills of noticing, meet Skinnylegs.

Skinnylegs

When I was young, my mother would take us three kids and her mother on wonderful, odd travels on alternate summers. To Lapland, around the Mediterranean, through the South Pacific. One of these trips began with three weeks on a German freighter and included a trans-Atlantic crossing and several stops in Europe. I was only eleven and had glorious run of the ship, of which I took complete boy's advantage—from playing cards in the crew's bunk rooms to helping engineers check instruments.

There was one sailor my family began to notice. He had the skinniest legs we had ever seen, so among ourselves, we called him Skinnylegs. He seemed to be everywhere, doing everything. When I would snoop into the engine room to see how things worked, there was Skinnylegs fixing a broken generator. When the hold covers needed securing—Skinnylegs. Even when the stove broke in the officer's galley, guess who was called to fix it? It became a running joke. He never seemed to speak but simply received instructions from the Captain and got right to work.

As we neared Europe, we caught the tail end of a hurricane. The seas

We can learn to use the different ways of noticing strategically, like tools, as artists do.

and we Yanks heaved tremendously. Against strict maternal orders, I snuck up to the open deck above the bridge, the very top of the ship, and experienced the power of the elements all over me—drenching waves, wind, pelting rain. As the ship fell in a wave trough, I would look up at a forty-five degree angle, and there was water way above me everywhere. At the peak of a wave, I could hardly see any water anywhere, and the ship shuddered as the propeller churned air. I had to cling to the rail for life. Needless to say, I was incredibly dumb to be up there, and I loved it. (I never told my mother I did this; she will not be happy when she reads this paragraph.) As I hand-by-handed my way back down, I passed the control room on the bridge. In this bashing, dangerous storm, who was at the wheel? You guessed it—Skinnylegs. Serious, indefatigable, unimaginably hard-working and earnest, he figures prominently in the metaphor of the way noticing works.

Picture Skinnylegs as the first mate of your mind, sitting at an enormous console of panels of dials and screens and controls. (I imagine movie scenes of sci-fi control rooms.) He is monitoring all the input from your different kinds of receivers: what your skin feels, what your eyes see, all memory and intuition, all the scanning, plus those paranormal ways of attending. Skinnylegs' task is to follow all the information coming into the console and select things to bring to your awareness. He is utterly dedicated to your instructions—hey, you are the Captain. He follows all the input from all the screens as best he can and sends a highly-selected stream of images, thoughts, and associations up to your single screen called conscious noticing.

This is no Mom-and-Pop shop, mind you, with Skinny as some secretary passing along phone messages. This is a huge, high-tech operation (the most sophisticated compact system in the universe as far as we know); the input is vast and fast and complex. An appropriate analogy might be that Skinny is an overworked guy who tries to keep on top of everything of significance that is happening in all fifty states to make a constant distillation for the President so she can decide what the nation should do. If the President were dealing with all this input, she would not be able to function. She'd be endlessly sorting out what is of consequence. However, the endless, thankless work of Skinnylegs makes it possible for the President to be effective and maybe even to have fun every once in a while.

If you would like to get a feel for Skinnylegs at work in you, try this exercise. Sit privately in a relaxed position and speak aloud what you notice for two minutes in a steady, fast, stream-of-consciousness monologue. Include everything, no matter what it is. Sounds easy? I think you will discover two things: that you jump around into different kinds of noticing from one moment to the next and that you notice so much, so quickly, that your mouth can't possibly keep up.

Skinnylegs has access to kinds of information far wider than we consciously sense. The screens carry more than visual images of what the eye is seeing and lists of thoughts from the brain. There's data from all the senses, most of which we become aware of only when it deviates from the control panel's set of norms. There's an endless ticker tape of "almost-thoughts" lobbying to be forwarded to awareness. There are emotions (their action seems to me like a series of colored fluids that seek to tint the lenses of awareness). There are individual proclivities: your likes and dislikes, your training, your neuroses, your habits, the phases of your life, your genetic influences, your areas of particular interest; they print out a command sheet that Skinny has posted on the wall to keep particular lookout for. And, of course, there is what is going on in your life at a given time. For example, if you just fell in love, Skinnylegs is going to send very different data to your awareness than if you have a sinking feeling that your job is in jeopardy.

There is also that series of paranormal screens that Skinnylegs knows and uses that we don't yet know much about: the intuitive powers, extrasensory perceptions, spiritual and psychic communicators, and more—as if Skinny monitors a radio that tunes into a far wider range of wavelengths than you, the Captain, can hear.

And dreams. Collectively, we humans still don't agree that dreams are serious attentive work, but it's clear that Skinny is on the job twenty-four hours a day. During sleep, his assignment changes. The Captain doesn't want to be awakened for information-type issues except in an emergency. However, dreaming is another kind of attention Skinny is expected, instructed, to provide. It is the arena in which he can play. The Captain is not a total drudge. He has instructed Skinny to go wild with images and narratives and connections during dreams. Those who attend to their dreams know just how brilliant Skinny can be. Dreams are dense with symbols to feed into waking attention. Artists rely on their dreams and have the skills to make use of them in overt and subtle ways that nourish their work.

Speaking personally, I sometimes directly apply a dream image to a project, but sleep and dreams serve in less explicit ways too. For years, I noticed that sometimes the solution to a vexing problem would suddenly appear "in my head" one morning. I have come to rely on this capacity of sleep. Sometimes as I go to sleep, I review an intractable problem, assigning my sleep time to give rise to new options. In the morning, I see the situation in new ways, with new options available to explore. Thank you, Skinny.

Training Your Noticing

Skinnylegs is a doer, not a thinker. He is devoted to doing everything to run your ship exactly the way you communicate to him you want it run. You can *train* him to send different kinds of messages to your awareness. Indeed, you *have* to train him if you want to receive different kinds of data in your conscious attention. This is what artists do. They keep Skinny informed about exactly what they are interested in, and so they get a stream of relevant, fresh, juicy information and impressions to drink in.

Experience trains experiencing.

But remember this: Skinnylegs gets trained only by actual experience. Experience trains experiencing. You can't send him a wish list for new experiences and expect him to respond by sending up new data. For example, tell him, "Skinnylegs, I would like to notice how the themes from *Hamlet* apply in my everyday life." He won't understand what you want, and you will get nothing new from him. Well, he might send you coincidences like noticing a copy of *Hamlet* on a friend's night table, or noting the several copies of *Hamlet* available in the video store, but nothing that feeds your yearning because you sent him only a vague memo of intention.

What trains him is authentic experience, that which really happens inside you. These are the only instructions he understands. If you wish to find real connections to *Hamlet* in your everyday life, you have to have your yearning, your active curiosity, engaged in the world of *Hamlet*. This notifies Skinny to start sending you *that* kind of data, to let him seek new attractions for you. To get into *Hamlet*, get into *Hamlet*. Dig into it, find what you care about in that world, and Skinnylegs starts receiving your instructions. He gets the message of your interest and adjusts what he will send up to your attention. Suddenly, lines from the play will appear from many places. Words like "ghost" and "madness" and "obligation" will resonate in many situations you encounter. When your life-action is attuned to your yearnings, what you notice weaves into a pattern.

I am often surprised and delighted by valuable things that appear from "nowhere"—the "how amazing you should call right now" moments. Coincidences in my life rarely prove meaningless. I have come to trust that things I notice are there for some reason, and if I seek a connection between seemingly disparate occurrences, I will find some deeper pattern worth attending to. Accidents may have meaning. Louis Pasteur said to a faculty of science in 1854: "Where observation is concerned, chance favors only the prepared mind."

We must take great care with what we attend to, because we are, indeed, shaped by it. Skinnylegs carefully notes what actually happens in your conscious awareness and takes his instructions from that. He is trained by the quality of the objects and experiences you extend yourself into. Early computer pioneers said it well: garbage in, garbage out. I add, conversely: quality in, quality out.

The ramifications are profound. Skinny doesn't respond if you *think* you would like to be involved in something; he responds to the actual experiential data. Intention is pleasant, but participation is all. So just dig in. Follow the things that attract you, and you will begin transforming the way you experience. Praxis makes perfect. You have to

When your life-action is attuned to your yearnings, what you notice weaves into a pattern.

Intention is pleasant, but participation is all.

do the work of art (not just appreciate art objects, not just *want* to be more artistic) to create change. You must practice the skills to become more skillful.

Phonies of the world, take note: Skinnylegs is oblivious to pretension or duplicity. You can't make him think you are actually engaged in inquiries if you are not. Let's say you go to a museum and stand in front of a Rembrandt self-portrait with a fascinated look on your face; he can tell if you are extending yourself into it or not. If you are actively engaged with the Rembrandt work, he gets the message: "Take a note: the Captain is excited by complex emotions of wisdom and pain captured around the eye." Or "Take a note: The Captain is interested in the different colors in a shadow. Keep an eye out for related input to send up to awareness."

On the other hand, if you are not truly engaged in the Rembrandt, Skinny will attend to what *is* going on and will think: "Take a note: the Captain is attracted to the sensation of tiredness in his feet; he's working on strategies to ease up on those doggies—send attention to sitting places or museum exit signs." Or, "Take a note: the Captain is interested in the jacket on the woman who just came into view, leather. Keep an eye out for leather jackets in shops."

Where we invest our attention, that is what we become. So we need to notice our noticing and guide it into inquiries that fulfill our yearnings—things that attract, challenge, and satisfy us. We all do this fitfully, but with a little effort, we can train ourselves to do it strategically, as artists do. Just as we all know how to move, we can learn to apply movement elegantly in a waltz, efficiently in a game of touch football, comically like Charlie Chaplin, or playfully in a tap dance. That's how artists can apply their noticing.

Here is an odd truth about noticing experience: the looking is more important than the location. Worthwhile experiencing happens throughout your life, and the habit of actively attending will spark insights and reveal worthwhile truths wherever you look. If you aren't feeling lively or challenged, don't be so quick to blame it entirely on dull surroundings, like the teenager who complains that everything is

We need to notice our noticing and guide it into inquiries that fulfill our yearnings—things that attract, challenge, and satisfy us.

boring. Sure, there may be some truth to your critique, but adjust your attending as well as your entertainment. It is the skills of noticing that consistently produce the rewards that you crave. A little tale recounted by Roger von Oech in *A Whack on the Side of the Head* captures this truth about noticing:

"There once was an Indian medicine man whose responsibilities included creating hunting maps for his tribe. Whenever game got sparse, he'd lay a piece of fresh leather out in the sun to dry. Then he'd fold and twist it in his hands, say a few prayers over it, and smooth it out. The rawhide was now crisscrossed with lines and wrinkles. The medicine man marked some basic reference points on the rawhide and presto, a new game map was created. The wrinkles represented new trails the hunters should follow. When the hunters followed the map's newly defined trails, they invariably discovered abundant game. Moral: By allowing the rawhide's random folds to represent hunting trails, he pointed the hunters to places they previously had not looked."[4]

Edges

Anyone who has ever paddled a canoe on a lake knows there is more to see, more action, at the edges.

The original parent-word for "edge" meant "sharp" or "pointed." With lively sibling-words like oxygen, acute, and urge, "edges" offer a natural wake-up call. We automatically pay attention to expectations unmet, changes, novelties, state lines, surprises, nudges upon our norms, pressure on the outside of the status-quo envelope.

Limits make things visible. As soon as we know the limit of something, we can begin to form distinctions. Remember that the word "skill" originally meant "drawing distinctions." Making distinctions is essential to perceiving; we begin to know what something is when we get clear about what it is not. The fish doesn't notice water until it has had the gill-flapping experience of not-water. It may be a paradox, but boundaries make for growth.

We tend to resent limitations, succumb to them, or fight to overcome them. To artists, limitations are not liabilities, they are

Edge (ej) *n.* sharp or pointed

To artists, limitations
are not liabilities,
they are opportunities.

opportunities to find fresh, inventive solutions, to clarify key questions, to prioritize and go deeper. Shakespeare was encumbered with near-overwhelming limitations: a five-act structure; requirements for short scenes and regularly interspersed comic routines (even in his heaviest tragedies) because the crowd got restless; pre-cast (and demanding) actors to write for; a sponsor to please; no lighting; no big scenery; loud drunks near the stage; men acting the female roles; and many more. Yet he created some of the greatest accomplishments of human history within these constraints, perhaps *because* of them.

Likewise, the shape of the canvas frees the painter; the specific set of instruments in a quintet awakens the composer's inventiveness; the specific framing of a question launches the researcher to do her deepest work. Creativity is sparked by boundaries and finds satisfaction in new connections across boundaries. Many psychologists agree, as David Perkins writes, "The creative business person, dancer, or engineer needs curiosity about boundaries, restlessness concerning their limits, and toughness in tolerating the ambiguity that inevitably appears when boundaries are challenged. Here, more than anywhere else, psychological traits emerge that differentiate the more creative from the less creative individuals within a field."[5]

Of course, not every limitation is an opportunity. Shakespeare would not have festivals named for him today if he had been prevented from using words. Artists learn which limits to fight and which to use.

There is a catch-phrase among acting coaches, their standard advice when actors find difficulty doing a scene because of some circumstance: they are ill; their scene partner has bad breath; they dislike a phrase the character says; they are upset recalling a bad childhood incident of which the scene reminds them. The good acting teacher listens to the problem and simply says, "Use it." That means take whatever you think is blocking you and apply it to the creative improvisation ahead—whatever manure you've got, plow it in. Even if the reality of the situation is unwanted, unattractive, or upsetting, use it as a solid ground from which to work. Make a blessing of the curse. This is the work of art.

Creativity is sparked by
boundaries and finds
satisfaction in new
connections across
boundaries.

The Artist's Noticing

Driven by yearning, artists have a voracious appetite for noticing, which they feed with a lively habit of attending to what they encounter.

As simplistic as this may sound, doing it is radical. We are generally very lazy, passive noticers, while artists are athletic, almost aggressive with those skills. They don't "just keep an eye out for interesting things" (although they do that, of course); they *do* things with their noticing, like getting better information, new insights, new ideas, and fresh perspectives on the problems they are interested in.

Artists have six other skills of noticing worth emulating for the rewards they provide.

1) Back and Forth

Artists maintain a fine balance between noticing *in* and noticing *out*. They attend to events in their inner life with the same interest and purposefulness as they do encounters with objects and occasions in the tangible world. Their attention shifts back and forth, making connections, seeking better answers between those two kinds of reality. This back-and-forth can become so deft (usually in the thick of creative work) that its speed almost blurs the distinction into a single kind of attending. This feels like a kind of ecstasy. While it takes years of dedication to become that adept, we all can practice the balancing act by remembering to notice our inner experiences rather than just having them.

Artists maintain a fine balance between noticing in and noticing out.

2) Following Attraction

I was not joking in the first paragraph of this book when I wrote that artists live an endless intercourse with attractive things. An individual's complexity is written in, and can be read in, personal attractions, the fingerprint of the inner life. We are what we are attracted to and become what we yearn toward.

We are attracted to all kinds of things in life (within the safety parameters we establish): to beauty, to interesting people, to novelties, to challenges, to pleasure-promising opportunities, to idiosyncratic

We are what we are attracted to and become what we yearn toward.

things that draw us for our own oddball reasons (e.g., my friend Madeline is fascinated by the indentations that too-tight socks and cuffs make on the skin).

Attraction appears in many ways. There is, of course, the purest form of skin-deep attractiveness that spins your head around in a double take. But there are subtler, more frequent expressions: curiosity and interest, admiration and concern. There are even subtler levels that the work of art trains you to notice, like *resonance*. Artists notice when they are hooked by something; the way you might notice a song or phrase repeating in your mind; the way you rehearse a thought through the day; the way a word or image or name or feeling hums. Artists frequently use the word resonate to describe this subtle vibration-connection; they feel attuned to something, an indicator to pay particular attention to discover what linkage lies under the surface.

We might think of noticing as two pieces of Velcro catching. The more adept we get, the fewer tiny hooks have to link between us and the other side's loops before we stop and attend. Master noticers feel the most delicate connections, they are "hooked" as soon as just a few delicate loops have been snagged.

Less-developed yearners notice only more obvious things, and they have a limited repertoire of attractors. They repetitively seek the same kinds of things, surface things, usually those that provide quick gratification. In a gratification-oriented person, a known set of reliable gratifiers exert attractive force—junk food; jazzy tele-vision with sex, violence, or quick jokes; video games; etc. This is a simplistic interaction, expressed in a basically binary vocabulary of want-get. Basic yearners are not able to increase their curiosities with each exploration; they cannot rebound toward greater satis-faction but only toward greater stimulation. They are stuck in one way of noticing, in an experiential rut. They cannot respond (promise back) but can only grab the quickies. If this is the only intercourse they enter into, it is the only experience they can beget. Getting out of the rut is entirely possible, but it requires that one actively work-of-art one's way out.

With practice in attending, we become attracted to the subtler qualities in things, to things that are not immediately evident, to intangibles. We become curious to explore ideas, possibilities, and beliefs. Anyone who has been involved in a long-term relationship knows this becomes an important skill. Sustaining a relationship requires the skills of subtler attraction and ever-deeper discovery. At the beginning, you were attracted to your partner's face, smile, rear end, who knows! To keep rediscovering that mate over time, you need to add new, subtler attractions: to cuticles, to comic turns of phrase, to ways of drying the dishes.

3) Noticing Clean

Artists can detach from the mucky stuff that usually clogs clear seeing. We will look at two particular aspects of this: their skill at separating observation from interpretation and their mastery with expectations.

People are generally sloppy perceivers. We lump all kinds of data into the same sack of attention, undifferentiated. As we face a Diebenkorn painting we hadn't seen before, a typical mental ticker-tape might read, "pretty blue…what the heck is that in the corner…I don't like all that blank canvas…there is a doorway, nice…I think he lived in California…these are bright sunlight type colors…what time is it?…it is a landscape I guess." We jumble aspects we actually observe together with things we think, judge, ask, and interpret about the observation. There is nothing inherently wrong with this habit, but such experiential-jitterbugging is a lousy way to discover what is really there. The less-skilled noticer does this incessantly in the face of everything he meets.

Artists learn how to separate the different kinds of reacting. They have the ability to "just observe," just see what is there for periods of time. This kind of vision is powerful. It increases their appreciation of things they encounter, their storehouse of information, and their understanding of things. Sure, artists judge and interpret, often with zeal, but they do it *after* they have taken in what is there (or they should). Their interpretations, however passionate, are based in the facts of reality, not in swirling explications based on opinion.

People are generally sloppy perceivers. We lump all kinds of data into the same sack of attention, undifferentiated.

The separation of perceiving from interpreting is a key challenge for participants in my workshops. It is hard, and it takes some getting used to—the slam-bam of opinion is tough to hold off. I sometimes impose a nickel fine for every time someone starts a sentence with "I like" or "I don't like"—we usually collect enough for a pack of chocolate chip cookies in just a couple of days. However, when we can adopt the artist's skill of strategic non-judgmental perception, the bounty of the world begins to open to us.

Here is a little activity to try that may reinforce this point. Sit in front of a good painting (or even a print of one). In a relaxed way, just have a conversation about it for a few minutes; do this aloud, even if you are working by yourself. Now turn to another painting. Take another few minutes to meet this one too. But this time, strictly limit what you say to things you can actually see. Try to hold off even natural assumptions like "it is winter"—instead, say you see white paint with gray and brown splotches. Try to avoid all fancy or interpretative words—slap your own hand if you say "impressionistic" or "stylized." Then, after those minutes of careful "clean" noticing, relax the restriction, and see what kind of interpretations appear.

You will probably find a difference in this second experience. I find that the latter way of perceiving produces more complex understanding, more appreciation and empathy for the artist and the painting. At the end of the first, you might feel smarter or more sophisticated; at the end of the second, you will probably feel happier and more alive.

A grace-note about this latter kind of perceiving you just tested: it makes artists and scientists comrades in practice. Common thinking places the choreographer and the chemist far apart, but in truth, many of their most basic practices are very similar, for example: their precision of observation; their detachment from assumptions; their ability to extract significant, subtle linkages, from massive amounts of data; their use of intuition; their ability to identify the best problems to address, and to find precise questions; even their need to communicate their discoveries through the use of metaphor. Try to share some of the respect we have for the practical value of scientific work with the next artist you meet.

4) Using Expectations: Anticipation vs. Expectancy

Another part of artists' "clean noticing" skill lies in the way they can use expectations. In Latin, the word meant "to look out." Expectation grew up in the eyeball family, amid flashy siblings like spectacle, spectacular, spectrum, and specter. Humans expect. We can't help looking out in this way. We are wired to produce expectations, but that doesn't mean the wiring always serves us well. Expectations can assist the work of art, but they can also undermine it. They can help form a rich understanding or deform our experience of reality. For clarity, we will divide expectation into two parts with different names—anticipation and expectancy.

Anticipation. The downside of expectations is that they can turn into prejudice, pre-judgment, a pre-fabricated mold into which we pour our noticing. The Latin root of "anticipate" is "to take beforehand," to grab something before it is there. When we anticipate, we judge experience before noticing what is actually there. Anticipation eliminates discovery and the potential for growth; it leaves us with insubstantial almost-truths, phantasms that seem solid but are not. Anticipators have "done" France before the plane touches down at Orly; they have decided "I hate modern painters like Jackson Pollock" before they enter the museum.

"Don't anticipate" is a common refrain from acting teachers. The mistake of anticipating is obvious in rehearsal: the young actor flinches before his scene partner moves her hand for the slap; the actress begins a scene beaten down before the argument begins. Acting teachers remind students that even if the *actor* has done the scene a hundred times, it is brand new to the *character*. And if the actor skillfully detaches himself from expectations, experiencing moments as they unfold, the scene can be new to him each time as well.

This noticing skill requires a discipline to attend moment-to-moment without zooming off into the past or future and a capacity to read those moment-to-moment experiences for what they actually contain, in increasing complexity. That discipline and inner dexterity is something one *has* to learn to keep growing in a play that runs hundreds of performances. Good actors in life—that is, those who take

Expect (ik spekt´) v.
to look out

Anticipate (an tis´ə pāt´) v.
to take beforehand

This noticing skill requires a discipline to attend moment-to-moment and a capacity to read those experiences for what they actually contain.

effective action with the artist's skills in life—also learn not to anticipate and to read experience with complexity. One of the secrets of artists is that they actively remember what it is like to experience things for the first time. They remember because they do it so often.

Expectancy. The upside of expectation is an optimistic reaching toward the future. This is also evident in acting training. This is the "readiness" actors speak of, the eager, informed openness to receive whatever might appear. As an acting coach, I called it the mindset of the energized zero. You may have seen actors close their eyes and get still for a moment before they begin an audition or a speech. In those few seconds, good actors can set aside the extraneous intrusions of life (nerves, relationship worries, sore back) to become ready and begin. This mindset puts aside what is known and opens new, wide-open possibilities for discovery. I call this state expectancy, and it is the attitude that provides for wonder. Anticipation starves the work of art; expectancy feeds it.

I found the ultimate example of expectancy described by a blind World War II French resistance hero, Jacques Lusseyran. In his autobiography, *And There Was Light*, he describes how, after being blinded in a childhood accident, his sensitivity to touch grew marvelously. His heightened sense of awareness culminated when one day he reached to set his hand down on a table. As he lowered his hand, he actually felt the table rising up to meet it. One may wish to argue the physics of this case, but the experience was undeniably real to him. This kind of expectancy maximizes the richness of what we can experience. This attitude assumes there is an equivalent openness in us and in every part of the world, that both sides of the connection game seek to find rewarding contact.

5) Writing and Revising the Scripts

Some expectations are quite necessary, of course. After we have sizzled our digits a time or two, it is useful to expect that those flames on the stove will be hot. We all develop templates, sometimes called "scripts," that describe the norms of our surrounding world.

Using scripts is essential. If everything were a surprise—the fact that water boils, that toilets flush, and that people smile back when we smile at them—we would begin the day gawking and never get out of our pajamas. But the opposite extreme is also life-threatening—setting rigid expectations and imposing them on daily experiences. It may be safer to be carefully scripted, but it squeezes the life out of life.

Scripts usually work under the surface of our lives, as geological contours work under the soil to form landscapes. Many people become aware of their scripts only as a result of earthquakes in life: when someone dies; when hitting bottom in unhappiness of some sort; in illness; in love; in a peak experience. Others never become aware of being scripted and would deny it loudly and long.

Our scripts hold our expectations of everything—how people should dress; what people who dress like that guy over there are like; all the shoulds, all the beliefs, all the prejudices, all the templates that allow us to feel we have a handle on what is going on.

For example, how do you know if someone loves you? Well, you *feel* that the other one does. What makes you feel that, other than the fact that you hope it is so? It finally comes down to a set of necessary signs that fit into your personal "I am loved" script, which you wrote out of early observation and experience and many other influences, including genetic and cultural. The particulars of each person's "I am loved" template are different, but let's take an imaginary example of a man and a woman who might be falling in love. The woman's "I am loved" script might require: regular moony looks on his face, evidence that he thinks of her throughout the day, indications of willingness to spend freely to please her, his telling what seem to be painful and deep truths, and so forth. The man's "I am loved" script might include: limitless attentive listening to whatever he feels like talking about, efforts to handle particular tasks like ironing, admiration, etc.

Such scripts are not good or bad per se, but yours has an enormous impact on the way you will experience love in life. The narrower and less examined your script, the more *it* runs *you*, and consequently, the more limited and conditional your experience of love. The more you are

Many people become aware of their scripts only as a result of earthquakes in life.

aware of your script, the more you can open it and adjust it, the more love you will notice and feel. If your script, like our male example's, demands ironing as a key indicator of love, and neither you nor your mate knows that, then you will be upset every time she skips the ironing, never noticing that her love is evident in a dozen other ways.

Think how much time and agony that couple could save if they were aware that having shirts ironed was a critical part of the "I am loved" script. Instead of years of emotional ups and downs neither partner can explain, with bitterness and retribution, all determined by the shirt-wrinkle variable they never see, they could handle the shirts-script well: iron them himself, budget to get them ironed, or buy wrinkle-free. Or get skilled enough to rewrite the script, like a screenwriter.

The work of art is the most effective practice for the noticing skills that bring scripts to the surface and for the skills of script revision. We tend to believe that scripts are carved in stone rather than made and remade. But no Broadway play ever plopped onto a page fully formed; each scene is worked and reworked. Indeed, playwrights write a draft and then gather actors to read it aloud. The author can then perceive the life of the script, and she goes right back to work, moving pieces of action and changing words to recreate the order of that world until she has just the right picture. These are good reasons we still spell the word as play*wright*—one who can handle the raw elements of living (words, actions, behavior) to construct a thing that works—akin to a wheelwright who crafted a wagon wheel.

We forget that we are allowed to go inside and revise our personal scripts if we wish. When you perceive or revise a personal script, you are doing the work of art. Joseph Campbell argued that it was the artist's responsibility to re-invent the great human narratives based on present realities—this was the required and designated task of artists in a society. Similarly, it is every individual's responsibility to undertake the work of art, to recreate her scripts of reality, so that she can live an ever-more complex, satisfying life. In a later section, we will detail the ways the artistic skill of revision can enable you to rewrite your personal scripts.

6) Listening

Artists are great listeners. This may not be true all the time—don't test it with the leading man backstage on opening night—but when that same actor is on stage engaged in his art, be assured that he hears with tremendous skill.

All art is made in dialogue, and good artists are masters at both:

1)   expressing exactly what they intend, and

2)   listening.

Much art is made in overt collaboration: a group creates together, or partners co-create, or there is some bouncing back and forth between people. The most evident kind of dialogue is the live exchange between a performer and a live audience.

Yet, even the solitary artist, a poet or painter, works in active dialogue. She engages in dialogue with her imagined audience—how will it feel to receive this phrase? Also, she may question teachers, critics, or colleagues for guidance. These exchanges may be aloud in "real time" or may be imagined conversations inside her head.

The key challenge is for the artist to hear the voice of the emerging work. Even in the early stages, a work of art begins to have a voice about what *it* needs and wants to be. The artist must be able to hear its demands, what it requires for its full realization, not just what the artist requires of it. You will hear novelists swear that a character demanded that the plot take a different turn. This is not schizophrenia, it is a sign of great listening skill. Worlds take on a life of their own, develop their own rules and requirements, and artists have the sensitivity to attend to such subtleties. The most critical comment, and the one often hardest to hear, is the moment the work says, "Stop, I am done."

Artists can astonish with the depth of their hearing. One summer, I took voice lessons from master teacher Kristin Linklater. In the first lesson, she listened to me breathe and speak for about two minutes. Then she instantly analyzed my life history as she had heard it in my

All art is made in dialogue.

Worlds take on a life of their own, develop their own rules and requirements, and artists have the sensitivity to attend to such subtleties.

voice: "You had lung problems when you were young; you grew up in New York but studied how not to sound like it; you usually play heroic roles; you hate to sing on stage," and more, all true. She actually heard all that, as a doctor hears a hundred related bits of information in the thumps of your heartbeat, as a therapist hears an underlying truth in what you do not say. These professionals are all practicing the skills of art in their various media.

Beyond the Ordinary

Artists' skills of noticing open up the secret life of all "things." I brought an unexciting, normal voice to Kristin Linklater, and she noticed a world of distinctions that she generously shared back with me. I brought beige, and she reflected back a spectrum of color that was actually there.

Ordinary (ôr´dn er´ē) *adj.* following the beaten path

The Latin word "ordinarius" grew from the word for "order." Originally, "ordinary" meant "following the beaten path." Right up to the nineteenth century, "ordinary" was a common noun with a range of mundane meanings from daily mail, to allowance, totavern, to the priest who paid the final visit to a condemned prisoner. The adjective, born in the fifteenth century, has stayed close to the Latin meaning, "following the usual course." Look it up today, and find it denotated as common, usual, average, second-rate—the plain pieces of commonplace daily life.

Extra- (ek´strə) a prefix meaning outside or beyond

The Latin prefix "extra" meant "outside" or "beyond." We readily notice things we deem to be above the ordinary. One might argue that the very act of noticing itself confers the personal stamp of extraordinariness. Many people are parsimonious with their award of extraordinariness, reserving it only for a few "big ones." Not artists. I urge you to become as generous as they are with their sense of the extraordinary, applying it accurately and enthusiastically to many worthwhile things that, like Jacques Lusseyran's table top, are uncannily reaching toward you. This generosity occurs quite naturally as your skills of noticing expand; you see many outstanding aspects that you would otherwise miss.

When we put these two words together, ordinary and extraordinary, we describe the main goal of this book: to perceive the extraordinary in the ordinary, and when we get good enough, to live vice versa, in the ordinary extraordinary. Franz Kafka wrote of this experience: "You do not need to leave your room. Remain sitting at your table and listen. Do not even listen, simply wait. Do not even wait, be quite still and solitary. The world will freely offer itself to you to be unmasked, it has no choice, it will roll in ecstacy at your feet."[6]

Our goal should be to perceive the extraordinary in the ordinary, and when we get good enough, to live vice versa, in the ordinary extraordinary.

Chapter Five:

Wielding the Power Tools

The psychologist Abraham Maslow said, "When the only tool you own is a hammer, every problem begins to resemble a nail."

Any artisan is only as good as her tools and how she uses them. Artists carry exemplary kit-bags, full of life's real power tools, which they use inventively and often. Artists have such skill with them that they need not hammer-thump every challenge that appears; they can transform, redirect, understand, use, and extract value from the sequence of opportunities called daily life.

As noted earlier, our basic tools are amazingly good, so effective that we haven't had to upgrade them in several thousand years. All of us have used them, still use them at least sporadically; artists construct their lives with power tools like: intentional noticing, making connections, making symbols and metaphors, imagining, and story-telling. One could write a book-length description of these basic instruments (many such books have been written) and another book detailing the ways artists use them (we would find another shelf of these good books). In this section, we will merely touch on each to recall its value and feel. We begin by exploring the underlying fundamentals.

Yearning is the energy source we plug into. Without any yearning, we can't create anything we genuinely need with the tools. Once attached to the juice, all the power tools perform the same basic action: making connections. They all provide ways to link ourselves to something else.

Any artisan is only as good as her tools and how she uses them.

Yearning is the energy source we plug into.

Obviously, there need to be two separate things before we can make a connection, which is why art ("putting things together") begins in noticing, as we saw in the last section. First, we notice, which draws a distinction. Where, before, there was one undifferentiated something, we notice, and then there are at least two separate entities. And where there are two things, there is the potential for a new connection. So when our yearning prompts us to try to get a solid grip on something interesting we notice, we use our power tools to *make* a connection.

Artists are exemplary connectors in several ways:

* They keep their renewable supply of yearning fuel fully charged, so they are poised, ready to make connections.
* Their skills of noticing feed them many specific and interesting opportunities, so they have an abundance of raw material to work with.
* Their life-work is to make things that hold their best connections, so it is a top-of-the-mind priority in their daily lives.
* They are dedicated to making things that share their efforts with others, hoping to spark worthwhile connections for many; so they are quintessentially generous.

The fundamental act of connection is matching: this is that. It begins in the crib—this thing (a breast) is that (cessation of hunger). It develops with language—this furry, bouncy thing (Spike, the poodle) is that (a dog). It grows in complexity—this piece of food (a cake with candles) is a celebration of me. The binary simplicity of matching is what gives it such strength—enough to keep building with these I-beams of understanding for a lifetime. It is matching that makes symbols. Their effect can be lasting—we carry that symbol of a candle-covered cake with us for the rest of our lives.

We match both from the inside out and from the outside in. More specifically, we work from our inner sense to make a link to outside things (we try to find a way of saying what we feel, and we know when we finally have it just right); and we click with things that already exist (we connect to a poem's phrase that matches what we feel). The work of art itself, world-making and world-exploring, is just a grander expression of these most basic ways of connecting to the world.

Humans use the simple tool of matching to make sense of complex things like experience, feelings, or the unfamiliar. When we encounter something new or hard-to-decipher, we match its elements with previous knowledge until we can identify it: "that is a groundhog," "that couple over there is not married," "this problem is like the one I tackled a year ago." We use matching on a more simplistic, instantaneous level too, as we identify things: bar of Ivory, salty, red.

Matching may take some verbiage to describe, but it's not an abstract concept; it is the very biological mechanism the brain uses to see through the eyes. The eye has 125 million photoreceptors that provide an information-carrying capacity of over one billion bits of information per second, each bit being one binary piece of data. This potential is far greater than the optic nerve can process. So, for efficiency's sake, the retina registers and sends bits of data to the visual cortex in the brain, which "decides" what it is seeing as soon as it can—by matching. Portions of the object's characteristics are registered, the brain recognizes the pattern, and calls a gestalt to the process to save time and effort. Neuro-scientists tell us that the brain is so good at identifying partial images through matching that only a tiny percentage of available neurons need to register in the cortex before you can recognize the gestalt called "house." The more complex and unfamiliar the image (if you saw Old Mother Hubbard's three-story boot for instance), the more retinal cells have to be processed, and the longer it takes before the brain can call out the match in this ongoing game of charades. This process is essential, or we'd spend a decade trying to decipher a bowl of vegetable soup.

If we grow well, our capacity for matching expands over time, we learn to work on more sophisticated levels, with ever-greater ability to discover the similar within the dissimilar. Artists spend their lives

Humans use the simple tool of matching to make sense of complex things like experience, feelings, or the unfamiliar.

becoming adept at the subtleties, and they also have one other matching-skill that is crucial to their success: they know how and when to hold off that impulse to match.

Mastering the Gestalt Default

To make connections as artists do, we must master one of the skills of "noticing clean" we met in the last section. This is the capacity to hold off the urge to interpret, to delay long enough to really drink in what is there. This skill goes against the efficient neurobiological gestalt mechanism the eye and the mind rely upon.

By definition, a gestalt is a collection of pieces unified enough in some pattern that they require viewing as a whole. In practice, it is an instinct to grab a name for something, to find a known category to hold the new. Left unattended, it can become snap-judgment and bias. I call this impulse the gestalt default because we naturally fall into it unless we develop the skill and habit of intentionally delaying it.

The desktop publishing program Pagemaker, which I have used extensively, has a fascinating feature that works like the eye's gestalt mechanism; the feature is called "snap-to guidelines." Say I wish to line things up for a column in my computer page layout. I drag a vertical guideline into place on my screen image of the page. Then I use the mouse to drag a paragraph of text around on the screen, trying to find just the right spot to make the layout look good. The "snap-to" feature of Pagemaker grabs and yanks my block of text into alignment, so as I get close to the guideline I placed, the block jumps right into perfect columnar alignment on the guideline. I can't place the block close to the line but not on it, because the snap-to feature grabs anything within reach and pulls it to the established line.

That's how the gestalt default works in us, too. It grabs something we notice and snaps it onto a previously placed guideline. As I mentioned before, that is often very useful and efficient—but not always. The Pagemaker program lets me turn off the snap-to command, so I can work freehand if I like—I can make something that is just a bit out of expected alignment. Unfortunately, our

Gestalt (gə shtält´) n. a collection of pieces unified enough in some pattern that they require viewing as a whole.

The gestalt default grabs something we notice and snaps it onto a previously placed guideline.

personal gestalt default program never turns off; if ignored, it can strangle our response-ability. The work of art requires the awareness and skill to hold off the gestalt default.

Artists learn to delay the mind's snap to a previous guideline long enough to perceive the specific features of what is really there. They can intentionally disrupt, postpone, surprise, and challenge the matching process to allow for new understandings. They know that the longer you can drink in a Seurat canvas before deciding whether you like it or not, the more you learn about pointillism. They know that inspiration, insight, and delight leap into the unpredictable, playful time in between judgments. Artists can tolerate, even enjoy, not-knowing for a little while, so they can form new and subtler connections.

Many artists try to share this in-between experience by making worlds that intentionally disrupt our snap-to mechanisms. They braid or spiral our expectation guidelines to draw us into their worlds, where they create playful havoc with our existing gestalts, rearranging them to enable us to see afresh. For example, Magritte's cloudy sky raining little men in bowler hats uses our known gestalt of a dreary wet day and surprises us into attention to his drops and their implications. Arthur Miller uses familiar gestalts of selling and family ties to lead us into complex views of American life in *Death of a Salesman*. Artists are master strategists with audience gestalts, seeking to maximize what we can perceive.

This capacity to govern the gestalt default (as opposed to being governed by it) is more than a pleasant embellishment, more than frill in life. Unless we can delay, challenge, and revise our guidelines, we are stuck; they hold the way it was. Without guidance, the gestalt default tendency allows our old understandings to commandeer the fresh experience of everyday life. In small, the script guideline "I don't know much about nature" will diminish your experience of walking in a forest; "I dislike modern music" will kill your chance to exult with Stravinsky. The power of a complicated script like "I am a middle-aged middle-manager in a small unimportant widget-making company" will hijack an entelechy.

Artists can tolerate, even enjoy, not-knowing for a little while.

Unless we are attentive noticers and revisers, we will snap to judgments about many things and never really see them.

Unless we are attentive noticers and revisers, we will snap to judgments about many things and never really see them. We will tag people as readily as we do paintings—with labels that categorize individuals according to racial, personal, or cultural types. It takes the same work of art to really see an unfamiliar painting as to see an individual.

The more we can learn to hold off interpretation and judgment, tolerate the uncertainty, and openly explore what we encounter, the more we expand our capacity to grow with new connections and find delight in our surroundings. The gold lies in-between.

Not-Knowing and the Unfamiliar

Humans like to know and hate to not know. This simple fact underscores the power of the gestalt default, with which we snap out of not-knowing as quickly as possible. Not-knowing is uncomfortable and unstable, so much so that most people simultaneously translate all new experience into the known. As the philosopher and art critic Arthur Danto writes, "We tend to reject that which does not fit into our spontaneous hypothesis of things."[7]

In anxious or turbulent times, this tendency is exacerbated. The fast pace at which new things appear in our days precludes adequate evaluation; we become more wary, more reliant on our existing scripts, quicker to slam doors on unusual input; we get less open to exploring the new with our response-ability.

Knowing provides great satisfaction, and not knowing can be downright dangerous.

The need to know is partly natural. Knowing provides great satisfaction, and not knowing can be downright dangerous. But if our habits of thinking don't allow us to not know at all, growth is not possible. The capacity to draw clear lines within what we know and don't know, and to be at peace with both, dramatically advances the capacity to experience and learn. Indeed, the moment when we know that we don't know something is the most important step in learning. That insight draws a productive distinction within the vast expanse of things we don't know we don't know. In that moment of clarification, we select something out for investigation, for potential connecting; we create a particular canvas within which to engage in the work of art called learning.

The work of art practices opening the door to the unknown. In the arts, welcoming the unfamiliar is safe enough to rehearse in a wholehearted way, and its rewards are delightful enough that we want to do it again. All three actions of art use this skill. In world-making, we mediate between the known and unknown and bring them together. In world-exploring, we decode an unfamiliar world's messages and thrill to some of our discoveries. In reading the world, we play the "as if" game: the familiar as if it were unfamiliar and vice versa. An artist can not know so effectively that she can live there long enough to construct whole "families" of things that fit together, new worlds.

There is a natural tendency to close up somewhat with age, to become less open to the unfamiliar. Folk wisdom reports this in jokes about becoming conservative on a fortieth birthday and in sayings about old dogs and new tricks. You might call this natural tendency psycho-sclerosis, a hardening of the attitudes. Wouldn't you change your diet to minimize your arterial-sclerosis with fewer fried foods, fewer visits with Ben & Jerry, more vegetables and fruit? Well, you can also change your experiential intake to fight psycho-sclerosis: less time with television, fewer repetitions of your same old opinions about people and politics, a critical review of those favorite stories you tell about yourself, playfully experimenting with disruptions to your routines, more time spent not quite knowing but finding out through the work of art.

Symbols

Here is what we do in that place in between what we know and don't know: we notice new things, and with our yearning alive, we make connections. And *how* do we make these connections? We play with matches until we ignite a personal symbol. Symbols are the building blocks of all meaning. There is no connecting (not only no works of art, no communication, no language) without them, and art is the playground of symbols.

First, let's distinguish a symbol from a sign. They are related—indeed, the same image can serve as either one. For example, the image of a cross on a yellow metal rectangle beside the road means "driveway for a church ahead, use caution," while the same image atop a church or around someone's neck can evoke the mysteries and meanings of the Christian faith.

A sign refers to something more literal than itself, while a symbol refers to something more abstract. The physical image of that cross can be either a more-literal sign ("watch out for humans and cars") or a less-literal symbol (people who share certain profound views sometimes gather in this building). A sign and a symbol ask different things of us. A sign asks us to take in information; a symbol requires that we participate. A sign knows and tells; a symbol evokes and invites.

The word "symbol" derives from an ancient Greek noun and verb. The noun "symbollon" referred to the consummating part of a social occasion. After a particularly successful social event, perhaps a memorable dinner party or an extended visit with a friend, the host would mark the culmination by taking a coin or a ring and breaking off a portion of it, called the symbollon. This piece was given to the departing friend as a token of the meaningful time together. The symbol was a specific *thing* that stood in remembrance of a meaningful experience; it tied together the present and the past; it was a part that held a whole. The part (piece of coin, or today, perhaps a gold cross around someone's neck) is more tangible than the experience it connects to (the closeness of the friendship during a week of visiting, the meaning derived from Christian beliefs).

The other parent word of symbol is the Greek verb "symbollein," which meant "to connect," to "bridge over to." Etymologically, the action of a symbol is to connect. Put the noun and verb root-meanings together, and you get this: a symbol is a specific something that makes a meaningful connection to a less concrete something. A noun-verb that creates the presence of an absence. A symbol invokes our natural skill to make meaning by metaphorically matching the concrete to the ineffable.

Symbols don't really exist until we play with them. Like that famous tree that maybe did/maybe didn't fall down in the forest, symbols don't exist until we participate in their formation or discovery. They only come alive in the present tense, as we actively form or engage with them.

A symbol changes each time we attend to it, because the connection is always recreated in the present moment. Imagine that piece of coin. One lunchless afternoon, our ancient Greek friend might hold it and cook up a recollection of the incredibly great dinner on the last night of his visit. The next morning, he may be puzzling over a problem about raising his son—the symbollon now reminds him that love is the most important thing in his life, and he makes a new plan for dealing with his child.

Aside from issues of technical skill, one of the ways we identify greatness in artistic accomplishment is the kind of nourishment we find in its symbols. The less-developed artist creates symbols that hold smaller truths, that evoke experiences less likely to connect to many parts of many people, that offer generalized insights, that remain vague. Master artists create symbols that open worlds of rewarding exploration, that manage to tap something deep in many people, that activate specific lively responsive chords, that work on subtle levels so that we keep connecting in new ways when we return.

Symbolization

Symbolization is the natural process by which people make bridges between things, between a discernible symbol (Rodin's sculpture of a slave) and something more abstract we want to understand (a feeling of the need to escape constraints). The word "symbolization" covers all three ways connecting moves: creating (the making of symbols), perceiving (the connecting to or discovery of existing symbols), and playing (experimenting with improvised connections).

We readily acknowledge our interplay with symbols in the arts because they offer such power and universality—Yorick's skull, Michelangelo's hands of Adam and God. A seventeen thousand-year-

A symbol changes each time we attend to it, because the connection is always recreated in the present moment.

old animal painted on a cave wall in France engages people in symbolic work to this very day.

However, if our yearning is alive, we symbolize everywhere. The symbols we form include the things we make and keep, as well as the personal images that hold meaning: the plate with images of Yosemite bought because it somehow captured the exaltation of standing at the foot of El Capitan, bronzed baby booties, the cartoon on the refrigerator door, the picture on the desk, a recalled and repeated comment by David Letterman.

Children symbolize elaborately; those feathers and stones they keep are symbols of something they know, even though they cannot articulate precise meanings. The characters in the stories they ask to hear a hundred times symbolize some aspect of themselves they are attending to, as do the characters in the stories they shamelessly and compulsively invent.

Families have symbols a plenty. You'll find them in favorite tales and jokes, "in" words, bric-a-brac on display, and in rituals and routines. Groups have symbols to bind their members; from secret fraternity handshakes to the "double wedding ring" pattern understood in quilting clubs; from political elephants and donkeys, to menorahs and Santa Claus. Nations cohere through symbols, and will, in some cases, send people to jail or kill them for relating to a symbol in an unacceptable way. There are symbols that supersede all boundaries too: flying saucers, infants, Nelson Mandela, JFK, a fist, a hand held close to the heart.

We live in an abundance of symbols. We are surrounded by worthwhile things waiting to be discovered, to open what they have to offer. Every home already has enough to keep you busy for ages; even a single great book on the shelf—the Koran, the Old Testament, an anthology of modern verse—can provide a lifetime of symbolic work to a yearning mind. Remember that the quality of a symbol lies only partly within the symbol itself; equally crucial is the quality of the participation you bring to it. There is no scarcity of symbols out there—the scarcity lies inside, in the skills of symbolization.

If our yearning is alive, we symbolize everywhere.

We are surrounded by worthwhile things waiting to be discovered, to open what they have to offer.

I cannot overemphasize the importance of this aspect of the work of art. We construct the quality of our lives with our symbol-making skills. Dedicating their lives to the practices that develop these skills, artists can become exemplary in visceral response, awareness of impulses, fluency with various languages (like images, stories, intuition, emotions, logic) with which connections can be made, and fluidity of connect between languages (words to music, logic to space, body impulses to visual forms, etc.)

Do you recall the discussion of the transformation of the ordinary into the extraordinary that closed the last chapter? Symbolization is that alchemical process. The artist's skill takes in an everyday life interacting with items and signs, and fills it with extraordinary experiences.

Placing Symbols

Symbols speak best when they are set apart in a special or even sacred place to be noticed. This is very clear in the arts—we build special buildings to set apart those symbolic expressions. Within these designated venues, we are in the habit of attending to symbolic issues; we adjust the way we look at things as we enter. (We even place frames around paintings and proscenium arches around stages to set them apart.) We experience a "special," reverential attitude as we enter places like museums and opera houses (and we sometimes pay handsomely for this privilege). We apply this same impulse as we make set-apart places for symbols in our lives: the refrigerator door, the box under the child's bed, the living room wall, the church, the bulletin board, the photo album, the diary.

We tend to confer the sense of magic on the qualities of the special place itself—the opera house's acoustics, the enormity and beauty of Chartres Cathedral. But however superb such places may be, and however effective it is to set things apart, we must remember that the magic resides neither in the place nor in its detachment from the rest of life. To award the power to these alone is to literalize our yearning skills. The capacity to transform the ordinary into the extraordinary lies in each of us. Any space holds the potential to be distinctive when

Symbols speak best when they are set apart in a special or even sacred place to be noticed.

we imbue it with the extraordinariness within ourselves. When we attend to experience with the skill of an artist, we create a "special place" inside ourselves. Museums are inspiring to the degree that we bring the work of art with us and perform it there. Theaters are magical as a result of the receptivity we bring through the last set of doors. Indeed, if our yearning is dead, Chartres becomes just a long bathroom stop on the bus tour, and if our yearning is skillfully engaged, even a bus stop holds the potential to evoke awe.

I have field-tested this proposition in workshops. One time, nearing the end of a week-long workshop, a group was really fired up. Participants were so alive to connections that even the simplest comments—"and there on the table was this box of Life cereal," or "a bad hair day"—launched us into delightful associative journeys. We decided to flex our skills. We made a "stage" in the center of the room with four wooden cubes and placed different objects on it. This was the most rudimentary "special place" imaginable. We placed one object at a time on the stage and spent a few minutes quietly attending to the ways we related to each object as a symbol. Then we would share responses with one another.

Eventually, I placed my grubby New Balance running shoe on the stage, and even this became a symbol with meaning. For me, it symbolized the hard-working, humble tool we use without gratitude or notice, like the chewed pencil or the beat-up filing cabinet I have moved to seven different homes over the years. Some participants found it to be a symbol of things I had sparked as their teacher. Some followed the metaphor of "new balance" to a clearer sense of new ways they wished to bring art into their lives at home. One man tickled us all with his sardonic poem about a group of adults worshipping a filthy shoe—and finding inspiration in the act.

Now, I grant that a photograph of twenty-three fervid sneaker-worshippers focused intently on the altar of New Balance may not be the poster image you want to use for the work of art. It makes the whole endeavor seem pretty silly. However, the key to feeling connected to life is held in the moment. Sneaker reverence may be foolish, but it is wise to work with the tools involved and with a group of individuals committed to attending to the ordinary bits of life as if their lives depended on it.

I should note that symbols that speak to one individual do not necessarily speak to many. If they did, we would have few communications problems in the world. Some symbols do work on a wide scale; they capture and hold collective truths in powerful ways. These become our national symbols, our major works of art, our hero stories and myths, our history. Artists are our primary cultural agents in creating these essential points of cohesion.

Metaphor

We were doing a simple, first-day warm-up activity. This workshop of nineteen teachers in Nashville stood in a circle. We spoke our names one by one. Then I added a wrinkle: this time, as we went around, we were to add a simile about ourselves, one that told a little about us—for example, "Eric is like a locomotive." Again no problem—bam bam bam, very witty and clever. Then I added another wrinkle. This time, instead of a simile that said something about us, we were to make it a metaphor. I reminded everyone of what a metaphor is: a figure of speech in which one thing is designated as another. "Eric is a locomotive." The group shut down. They tried, but many couldn't think of metaphors. I gave practical advice: "Use your simile and just drop the word 'like' or 'as.'" They were still uncomfortable. Some forgot what they had planned to say by the time we got around to them; some could barely speak aloud. One woman was shifting her weight, got her feet tangled, and actually fell down as her moment to speak the metaphor arrived.

There is an enormous difference between saying, "Eric is like a locomotive," and, "Eric is a locomotive." While both sentences contain the same kernel of thought, the first may be true, while the second is literally false. However, while true, the first has little to offer beyond its moment of recognition, beyond the comparative thinking it invites. The second, while not literally true, holds a deeper, more demanding kind of truth. This second truth requires that we slip into the work of art to grasp it.

You can detect the difference if you reread the two locomotive statements. Do you notice an impulse to say "So what?" after the simile? On the other hand, do you detect that the metaphor requires something of you; that it doesn't quite sit still? That's the difference in a nutshell. The literal is flat, an experience devoid of experiment, whereas the metaphor is uncertain, somehow challenging, and invites you to participate.

When we make a match between two different kinds of reality, we have made a metaphor.

When we make a match between two different kinds of reality, we have made a metaphor. If we are stuck in simile, as the teachers in the name game seemed to be, we are stuck in the literal, the single way of looking at things. When you engage in metaphor, you cross a line—a line that makes all the difference. The metaphor line can be called "the willing suspension of disbelief," a phrase coined by the poet Samuel Taylor Coleridge. We choose to suspend the binary mind: the one that quick-judges "true/not-true," the one that serves so well in many of our daily doings. In metaphor, we enter new worlds of the possible, a world in which Eric really is a locomotive. And in the metaphoric mind, we devise a way to hold that locomotive-Eric creation in some image or idea or story. What do you picture right now: A train with a face, perhaps? A locomotive-esque human? The little human that could?

Metaphor (met´ə fôr´) *n.*
a transformer

The metaphoric-mind creates a reality in which a beat-up sneaker holds a network of understandings, a world in which truth has more than a yes-no personality. The word "metaphor" meant "a transformer" in ancient Greek; that's just it, working in metaphor involves the skill of turning (yearning) one thing into another that is richer, more valuable. In his *Poetics*, Aristotle located metaphor "exactly midway between the commonplace and the ineffable." He revered it: "Ordinary words convey only what we know already; it is from metaphor that we can best get hold of something fresh."

Children clearly demonstrate the skills of metaphor. Their work is to play seriously; their mission is to discover things with imaginative boldness; they transform so many things that they touch. As Picasso purportedly said, "All children are artists; the trick is to reclaim this when we grow up."

Imagination and the "As If"

The philosopher John Dewey described the imagination as the capacity to see the world as if it were otherwise. The moment we see that the world we inhabit is not just a sequence of hard, dead surfaces with fixed absolutes, but that it also can be seen "as if" it contains many non-logical truths, many mysteries, we head into a better future. The "as if" transforms artifacts into live media for the work of art. We slip into the "as if" every time we can see "a thing" as a metaphor; when we "as if," we revive the world. Daydreams are impulses from the "as if." Creative bursts invoke the "as if." Playing and joking often flirt with the "as if." Flirting flirts with it. Metaphor requires it.

Artists are very serious about the games of "as if." They live with "as if" glasses propped up on their foreheads, ready to fall into place with just a slight nod. They devise symbols that hold and share their "as if" worlds. They commit themselves. A novelist acts "as if" his characters are real people. He actually feels love for them, fears for them, wants to protect them and sometimes can't. Without "as if," this is lunacy; with it, it is creativity.

In the skill of "as if," we play with certainty within uncertainty. This is more than the arm's length experience of pretending (the root meaning of pretend is to stretch out before you); "as if"-ing is close-in, fully committed experimentation. We experimentally go into a hypothetical world and live there for a while.

We have conflicting impulses about slipping into the imaginative worlds that metaphors offer. We welcome the experience when it seems to be an entertainment that carries us away—transporting novels and diverting movies that "get us out of ourselves" earn quick millions. However, as the work of entering a metaphoric world gets more serious—when we leave the distraction of entertainment and enter the intention of the work of art—the stakes go up because we

We slip into the "as if" every time we can see "a thing" as a metaphor; when we "as if," we revive the world.

begin to change the status quo. It takes courage to suspend our disbelief mechanisms, the very practices that keep us safe and in control, that help us manage our complex lives.

Although imaginative worlds may not be structured according to designs preferred by the literal mind, they are far from anarchic. There are clear lines painted on the asphalt of these serious playgrounds to guide the games. The imagination is governed in patterns and non-verbal forms; it is guided by the intuition, by what we know beyond logic. Indeed, the action of the imagination looks very much like the work of art. When we imagine, we experiment with new combinations. We play with connections between new images and ideas because they seem appealing together, contrast in interesting, attractive, or surprising ways, resonate, seem in harmony, or are funny, or just feel right or look good together. All those phrases are descriptions you might hear from an artist discussing his creative process. The imagination is the intangible studio for the work of art.

"As if" lives in every field of play. "Let's look at the public relations problem as if we solved it five years ago and have developed well since then—now, let's look back on how that happened." "Let's replay that argument we had yesterday, honey; this time as if we were both trying to lose it." "Let's look at these students as if they are completely competent and successful. How does that change the curriculum?" Try those questions for a moment, and notice what they do to your thinking. The good "as if" question is often the one that catalyzes change. It begins the serious play of the imagination with real-world elements and taps the endless solution-play of your intuition.

Having tried those practice questions, now try these: What might it mean to treat your life as if it were a work of art? That is to ask: What does it mean to attend to your daily life the way you attend to a complex masterpiece? What things in your life do you handle and shape as if they were clay? Where do you attend to others as if they were fellow artists? What medium presents you with problems that you find satisfaction in solving?

Stepping into this "as if" changes the way you experience the

The imagination is the intangible studio for the work of art.

ordinary. It doesn't mean you stop paying your bills. It means playing with the notion that paying your bills might contain something beyond literal necessity. It means you engage in bill paying, not merely as a victim of economic reality, nor as a grudging drone who wants to keep the electricity flowing, but as an active player in the external and internal marketplace. The action of paying your electric bill makes you think of the potential of that outlet in the wall, of the current that flows through your house, ready to be used at any moment, and of the electrical gizmos that support your life in the way you have designed it. In an instant of "as if," you can transform the experience of something as mundane as bill paying, by imaginatively connecting the action to its personal implications.

If our "as if" capacity is cramped or suffocated, we flatten the richness of experience. We become trapped in the known, consumeristic, bored, aggressive, passive, depressed. Some people seek an approximation of the "as if" mindset in a bottle or a drug, or in addictions to other things like work, food or the lack of it, television, or sex. I would argue that all are problems of literalization—forcing complex, natural inner yearnings into the literal shape of a liquor bottle or other inadequate, unresponsive answer. Such dependence on any outside support to provide an engaging way of looking at things gives away precisely the skills we need to use as we enter and grow in the work of art.

Narrative

We make a connection, which we express as a metaphor: the business meeting was a jungle. Our yearning puts a demand on that metaphor: don't just sit there, *do* something. We want action from our connections, and a symbol in action is a story. We want to know more about the jungle-meeting—what scary things happened, the ways in which it felt steamy—so we begin to expand the idea into a story. This innate narrative impulse, stringing symbols together with a sense of sequence, is an instinct so simple every child wields it and so deep it cuts to our very core.

Stringing symbols together with a sense of sequence is an instinct so simple every child wields it and so deep it cuts to our very core.

It takes the skill of an artist to discover stories where there was only data. That was the skill that made my company thrive. We could find and tell a great tale obscured within tables of numbers. Many people who looked at the same stacks of statistics asked me, "How do you do it?" They thought I was bragging or hiding a secret formula when I replied, "It's an art." But that was the exact truth. Informed intuition, noticing, and storytelling were our critical skills. We studied a page of numbers and noticed little connections between bits of data. We would intuitively connect and expand, working toward the true story *they* were trying to tell. We found inherent plotlines to make sense of the millions of raw impressions, and our paying audience enthusiastically received the data in more personal, visceral, useful ways.

Narrative is not just a broad-stroke skill for novelists, playwrights, and the occasional trend analyst; it is not only a tool for the work of art; it is a necessary, practical tool we use to function in the world. Narrative informs our tiniest moments. What we notice is determined by narrative, as Skinnylegs compares the mass of input to our story-scripts of normality to determine what stands out from the ordinary, that which in some way deserves our attention.

We all use narrative incessantly—we make meaning by making stories. All humans construct sense out of experience by using narrative to fit our random impressions into plausible contexts. There are many psychologists who argue that every level of understanding, all learning and communication are made of narrative—from the way we make sentences, select words, organize our sensations, create and relate to symbols, remember things, to the way we come to have feelings and thoughts—all done with story-making. Stories make the ineffable comprehensible. Without stories we cannot grab things and hold them.

Narrative is a tool used on a wider scale too; cultural and human history are woven of stories. In *Acts of Meaning*, Jerome Bruner writes, "To be in a viable culture is to be bound in a set of connecting stories, connecting even though the stories may not represent a consensus."[8]

The work of art is exemplary narrative-play, and artists are masters

Without stories we cannot grab things and hold them.

at it. All artistic disciplines tell stories: the dancer tells new kinesthetic tales; the actor's subtext can be pure emotion; the musician tells stories in sound; and the painter articulates the visual narrative in such detail that she knows the coherent nuance of every stroke. The stories held in a Chopin Prelude and a Brancusi bronze cannot be told in any other way.

Novelists, playwrights, and screenwriters are probably the most recognizable narrative-masters. However, we all use narrative so intimately that we create protagonists (ourselves) just as novelists do. The psychologist Donald Polkinghorne suggests how: "We achieve our personal identities and self-concept through the use of narrative configuration, and make our existence into a whole by understanding it as an expression of a single unfolding and developing story. We are in the middle of our stories and cannot be sure how they will end; we are constantly having to revise the plot as new events are added to our lives."[9]

Don't Forget This Power Tool of Art

In this section, we have handled some basic power tools of the work of art—noticing clean, symbols, metaphor, imagination, and narrative—suggesting how deeply they pertain to the way we construct the quality of life. In the next chapter, we will look at another set of artistic skills that effectively guide intuitive processes into successful real-world projects. However, before we slip into projects, I want to leave this survey with something for you to remember: even memory itself uses the power tools of art.

Throughout history, scientists have tried to describe the mechanism by which the brain accomplishes its memory tasks—like recalling what the cover of this book looks like. In each era, scientists have relied on metaphors drawn from the latest technology of that era to explain how we accomplish this marvel of memory. For example, for centuries it was described as a kind of storage-retrieval system: we needed a bit of data, we sent a messenger with a request to a part of the brain to find it and send it on up. Later, memory came to be

Even memory itself uses the power tools of art.

viewed as a kind of telegraphic communication system, and then as a telephone-like exchange, and then as a computer: all evolving stages of an electric/electronic retrieval metaphor of increasing sophistication. The latest neuro-scientific understandings describe the mechanism of memory according to the emerging highest-technology of our time.

Scientists acknowledge the awkward fact that memory seems to involve more than mere retrieval system, no matter how sophisticated such a system can be. There is also a creative action involved in memory. Hard-fact scientists now use metaphors like reconstruction, improvisation, and holography to describe the memory mechanics of the brain. The act of remembering is now described like the work of art. Narrative is fundamentally involved, lending structure to memory in an artistic way. In remembering, we seem to retrieve the particular bits and general shapes, yet we recreate the whole at every performance. Your brain's functioning, the most sophisticated technology our world has ever seen, works the way an artist does.

There is a creative action involved in memory.

Chapter Six:

Harnessing the Bucking Process

Artists are superb problem solvers. Many will attest that making art is one long sequence of meeting and solving interesting problems: from the mundane (how do I get this metal thing to stick to that plastic sheet at an impossible angle?) to the functional (how can I knock them dead at this audition?) to the subtle (how can I make that melodic line more interesting?) to the magical (how can I evoke a memory of childhood omnipotence in this single poetic line?). Perhaps the sheer magnitude of practice artists have with problems explains their excellence with the solver's tool kit.

Before you recoil at that unappealing description of the artistic process as mere problem solving, let's take a quick etymology break. According to its Greek root, a "problem" is not inherently good or bad, neither pleasant nor unpleasant—a "problema" was something thrust before you. It was something in your face that required attention, but it held no implication of things amiss that needed fixing. And the Latin "solvere" did not tell you to take out tools and start a repair; it meant "to release," more like "dissolve" than "dig in." Artists balance these two energies in their approach to problems. They release their preconceptions, scripts, and gestalts to encounter the "thing thrust before them" afresh; and they dig in with their tools in reaction—to re-organize and re-present it.

In this chapter, we will examine the skills artists develop to "run a

Problem (prob´ləm) derivative of *problema* (Greek) *n.* something thrust before you that is not inherently good or bad

Solve (solv) derivative of *solvere* (Latin) *v.* to release good problem-solving process." We do well to emulate and emphasize these practices in our own lives. As with the other skills we have been identifying, these will be familiar. Artists become adept at managing time, asking good questions, pursuing quality, employing multiple perspectives, making choices, using intuition, handling the all-over-the-place feelings of process, and dealing with waste and constructive selfishness. Those skills can handle the raw energy required and released throughout the artistic process, which can get as wild as a bucking horse. Artists learn how to get a harness on that powerful beast, and take one heck of a ride toward their entelechy.

Managing Time

The work of art transpires in a different kind of time from ordinary activity, more elastic and variable. (In the next chapter, we will describe this time frame as "flow.") The duration of the inner work of art is measured not by clocks but by the feelings and thoughts of the artist, by the evolving nature of each process itself; it takes as long as it takes until it is done. How do you know when a kiss is over? It takes the artist in you to find a good answer to that question on each occasion. Inside the work of art, the usual MTV rhythm of life changes to what I call MVT: Maker's Variable Time.

It gets fast: when opening night nears and the energy snowballs. It is sometimes slow: when you are working out a stuck place, or reflecting, or refining details. Fast and slow can happen almost simultaneously: when you take an hour to perfect the light cues for one tiny moment in the play during the speedy technical-rehearsal energy of opening night's approach.

The artist works big (dealing with large blocks of material) and works small (down in minute details); and she works fast or slow within large or small. The choreographer spends a whole day without creating a single new step, as she invests time in detailed work on the placement of each finger during each turn (working small), and she perfects the whole dance of the hands in a single day (working fast). On the last possible day, the ad agency executive decides to revise the storyboard of

The duration of the inner work of art is measured by the evolving nature of each process itself. It takes as long as it takes until it is done.

the pitch to new clients (working big), giving herself a day to refine what turns out to be only a small change in a single frame (working slowly). Each of these artistic women invested the time because she knew the whole event would go better, and she would be more satisfied, if she could make more pieces be just right.

Artists learn to use both deadline and MVT time frames. How good is the time management of artists? Imagine this. Imagine that you work for a company that makes a really complicated product. You are in charge of the new products division. You are required to create six new products every year, with all the innovation, research, re-tooling, hiring, purchasing, budget-management, and scheduling involved. Even worse, you have to announce the day, hour, and minute at which each of those new products will be launched a year in advance. If you screw up, the company will shut down. Sounds impossible? It certainly sounds brutal and miserable. Well, every theater, ballet, symphony, and opera company in America does that year-in, year-out, without a break, without fanfare for the accomplishment. And to make it more difficult, their products are the works of art that are produced in variable rather than manufacturer's time.

Artists create time-frames for themselves that serve the work and the world, and then they guide the work to fit the frames. Artists are time's contortionists. This is not to say they do not feel crammed into a box sometimes. Indeed, they get frustrated, feel hurried, waste time, and have to overwork sometimes to get things done—but they do get things done.

Good Questions

Artists love the questions without single correct answers. People sometimes mistake this proclivity, thinking it means that artists cannot handle a hard right-wrong edge. This view underscores the false impression of a fluffy-minded anything-goes artistic mentality. That's not it. It's that artists seek the best possible questions, the challenging, effective sparks that ignite the answering-engine that moves things forward. As the famed physicist Niels Bohr said, "The opposite of a

Artists are time's contortionists.

Artists love the questions without single correct answers.

shallow truth is false. But the opposite of a deep truth is also true." Right-wrong questions are just too shallow for the work of art.

Good questions are themselves creative accomplishments. Of course, there is more to a good question than just its invitation to produce a lot of right answers. For example, "What are some kinds of trees?" has a lot of right answers, but the work involved in producing them is rather unrewarding, so it is not a particularly effective question. However, if you were designing a landscape, your problem-solving might take you into the arena of tree-recall, except that the work of art requires a more sharply focused question, like, "What are various solutions that trees could offer to that empty part of the backyard?" The formulation of your question determines the way you look at things. Each of the two questions in this paragraph evokes images of trees in the answering process; however, the first invites a recall-and-drop mental game (very useful for taking tests and playing *Jeopardy*), while the second uses images of trees as part of a process you have a personal stake in. If you pose those two questions for yourself, you can probably distinguish the different feel of those two kinds of answering: eliciting a string of nouns versus using nouns in the service of verbs.

Creative people know that the quality of their products is entirely dependent on the quality of the questions they ask.

Most artists would trade five good answers for a single great question. Creative people know that the quality of their products is entirely dependent on the quality of the questions they ask. Skillful inquiry includes seeking and trying good, and then better, questions, as well as the ongoing answering. This is the most direct route to understanding. The actual skills involved in inquiry are a microcosm of the work of art, including:

* *yearning*—to drive persistently toward a better grip on, more satisfaction about, personally meaningful things; why do you suppose it is called a *question*?
* *drawing distinctions*—to create the exact question that enables us to see what we don't know
* *analytical thinking*—to formulate those clarifying questions precisely, allowing us to jump into specifically focused answering-action

* *flexibility in making connections*—to try different kinds of answering (emotional, visual, associative, off-the-wall) to good questions, to see many kinds of patterns, so that we are not stuck with single-path inquiries
* *adopting multiple perspectives*—to disrupt the status quo intentionally, to adjust the existing understandings of the way it is, in order to look for answers through different, inventive, "as if" ways (or in fancier terms, shifting paradigms)
* *tapping many aptitudes*—to use many intelligences, various modes of inquiry, beyond just the logical and verbal (like intuition, body impulses, tapping the subconscious and playing) to extend the range for questioning and answering

When you enter the multiple correct answer game, you find that each answer offers distinct kinds of potential to be assessed and possibly selected for pursuit. Try this exercise. Jot down a quick list of four or more answers to the following question—try to get as many answers as you can without dwelling on any of the items: What is something that you made that you keep available around your house because it means something to you? Make a list of four or more answers.

Once you have made the list, circle any one of the items near the bottom. Now, focus on just this one item, ignoring all the other objects on your list. Can you tell the story of you and that thing? Take a full minute or two and tell it out loud. Be sure to include a beginning, a middle, and an intentional end to the story.

I would bet that you opened a world worth exploring. The circled item probably retrieved some significant part of your life you had forgotten for a while, one that offers fresh relevance as you attend to it now. How does a simple question lead to a surprisingly relevant result? You followed two artistic inquiries. The first was a scanning question that invited you to imaginatively scope through your home to identify any active presences of past world-making. It served as a lens of a sort through which you peered at your life to see what you saw. The second question—Can you tell the story?—launched the work of art to explore the potential held in that symbol of yours.

I often pose a multiple-right-answer question to students and then ask to hear only the fourth answer. I watch the peculiarity of the request sink in. I can see layers of standard "good student" thinking fall away: that there is only one right answer; that first answers are better; that answers you kind of stretch to find are probably weak. With just a bit of attention to that fourth right answer, students begin to recognize just how much value, how much unexpected understanding and cleverness, those less-obvious answers contain. They soon realize that the contents are particularly interesting not in spite of, but because of, the stretch they made to come up with the answer and the following inquiry to uncover what it holds. The stretch beyond logic, outside mere correct-retrieval, launches the work of art.

The only way to evaluate things underneath their veneer is to find and follow the hows, whys, why nots, and what-ifs. Good questions peel back surfaces, push past pat answers ensconced in yesterday's certainty; they create paths of inquiry into the I-don't-known.

Human nature responds only to the questions we put to it.

Asking good, and then better, questions is a work-of-art skill we must develop for a lifetime. Indeed, human nature responds only to the questions we put to it. If we pose simplistic questions to our consciousness, our growth will be equally limited. If, however, we develop the habit and skills of pursuing personal interests with good inquiry, our possibilities for growth become infinite.

Artists are unabashed about their endless questioning because they admit how much they don't know. They speak to one another in questions (I've even seen artists trade them like baseball cards); one hears them mumbling a question over and over to themselves as they work. Because they know that answering is a long slow process, they jump out of their chairs in excitement when they discover the right next question. Artists follow the advice that the poet Ranier Maria Rilke gave in *Letters to a Young Poet*: "Have patience with everything unresolved in your heart and try to love the questions themselves."

In addressing a problem, if you can focus your attention on seeking new and better questions, asking them "as if" the questions themselves made a big difference, you will have taken an artist's giant step toward a good solution.

The questions we overhear an artist mumbling while she works might sound like this: Is there a better way to do that? What is going to make this work? What is the key to this? All questions about quality. The word "quality" goes back to the Latin "qualis," which meant "of what sort?" Quality began with a question, and it still does. However, we have lost the question mark, added an exclamation point, and allowed Madison Avenue to use it to sell things. Quality is more than a binary judgment of whether something pleases or is worth the cost. Put back the question mark, and we become participants in distinguishing the inherent characteristics of the things we encounter, in determining the essential nature of things, in perceiving the attributes that count. Put back the question mark, and we slip into the work of art.

The value of questions is grossly overlooked in the high-demand, quick-fix nature of our lives and our nation. We are answer-oriented everywhere, having been trained to this through schooling that is almost entirely right-answer driven. Scant notice is ever given to the quality of our questions. The rebellious anger of many young adults is (and perhaps always has been) fueled by the inattention or weak answering they encounter to their good hard questions. No wonder some make habits out of their bad answers; no one attends to developing their inquiry skills, through which we all learn the artist's self-sustaining habit of seeking more satisfying answers.

Using Multiple Perspectives

Try this. Here you are: sitting (probably), reading this book. Switch your point of view for a moment. Imagine you are the book. You are pretty flat; you are looking up; you see this human face. What does the world look like to you (the book) at this moment? How do you feel? You just accomplished a mind-feat that artists perform all the time. They intentionally shift the way you see things to gain a fresh, more

Quality (kwol´i tē) n. judgment used to determine the essential nature of things complex understanding of what is going on. As a part of their problem-solving process, they ask questions that require entirely different perspectives of the answerer.

We give lip service to the "importance of understanding different points of view," but we usually do it in a literal way, meaning that we manage to intellectually reconstruct another's arguments. That's flat and doesn't solve the problem. Artists go 3-D. They can stand in another position "as if." They seriously play within that perspective and then return wiser.

Here is another activity I use in workshops to demonstrate the power of perspective. I ask participants to take three small, ordinary items out of their pocket or purse and place them on a sheet of blank paper. I ask them to describe (usually by writing it down) what they see. Then, I ask them to imagine that they are on their deathbeds, and they have selected these three items as the final symbols of their life (like *Citizen Kane's* "Rosebud"). Again, I have them write a description of what they see. Next, I ask them to imagine they are anthropologists in the year 2300, who have just unearthed this page with three items on it. They write this observation too. Finally, I have them imagine they are one of those items and describe what life is like with those other two items. I have invited people to play with as many as ten different ways of seeing those items, uncovering insights about their political, educational, even spiritual perspectives.

Invoking and exploring a variety of perspectives is an essential preparation for the critical moment of choice about which ideas to pursue.

Choice

Making art is comprised of making choices. The word "make" in that idiom underscores the fact that a choice is a constructive act. The artist works to get to the moment of clear distinction and then bravely makes the choice with consequences that must be followed. Again and again.

Some people have difficulty making choices; they are cautious, tentative, stuck between options. There are good reasons for this fear or hesitancy—choice is inherently aggressive and has consequences. The act of choice intentionally kills an option. After years of executing choices, artists develop the maturity to see the consequences of a choice, grieve slightly for the lost possibilities, and then focus full energy on the positive option selected. Artists embrace Yogi Berra's dictum, "When you come to a fork in the road, take it."

The parade of choices is endless: from the tiny (Where do I place this clay strand of hair? Which word works better?) to the immense (Does this story want to be a novel or a screenplay? Do I take the part-time job for money or do I take the risk of not?). When I think of the artist's skills of choice, I picture a sword-wielding samurai warrior. Years of training and dedication on every level, from the spiritual to the physical, culminate in the elegantly simple cut. The master artist can do just that, bring decades of training and experience to the moment of simple choice—"the sequence of notes must go like this." Masters must learn to exercise options gracefully because the questions become so subtle and complex. The less-developed artist dallies and dithers, hacks around a bit, and is unsure in the act, but he learns through practice.

We all exercise our skills of artistic choice: channel surfing, choosing which words to speak in conversation. On a larger scale, we change jobs, select houses and spouses, and pick schools and books for our children. On deeper levels, we make unconscious choices, such as what we notice, who turns us on, and what we think.

Every choice has consequences. The television program you choose to watch shapes who you are; or perhaps you choose not even to engage with a television show, just to veg out on the couch—this too affects who you are. There is no better way to become a good chooser than to practice the series of connected choices strung along threads of personal meaning.

I would argue that the skills of choosing have become critical for a good life today. We already have far more information and activity options available than we could ever take in or pursue. Having five hundred channels available on the living room screen, plus a few

The act of choice intentionally kills an option.

The skills of choosing have become critical for a good life today.

hundred other leisure options available at a moment's impulse, doesn't necessarily make us happy, smart, or popular. Unless we hone our skills of choosing, we become increasingly lost, passive, and stuck in the status quo. With these basic skills ingrained, we can take advantage of this bounty our era gives to us.

Intuition

Artists base their choices on many different kinds of information, commonly including past experience, advice, and logical conclusions. But I have a hunch, a gut feeling, an educated guess—I just know, OK?—that their most important basis for making a choice is the hardest one to discuss: intuition.

Intuition is the process through which you "just know" something, without a logical basis. It is sometimes deemed to be a mysterious talent or gift: the nurse who always seems to know what to do in the tough-call situations; the mechanic who can fix the sputtering engine that baffles everyone else. But the nurse and mechanic have been well-trained in their crafts; they have attended to their previous inquiries, and followed the impact of choices they have made and seen in the past. Intuition is not a supernatural visitation, it is a skill; one learned best in the work of art within a medium you love, be it medication or motors.

Intuition is a kind of sight. Etymologically it means "having watched over." It offers an internal flashlight for you to use traveling in the dark, the unknown. Intuition works, thinks, and speaks in many symbol systems; and your intuitive smarts know far more about your yearnings than your conscious smarts do. As understated as its guidance is, intuition prompts in very practical, grounded terms: "go there, try that." But the voice of intuition is easily drowned out by the mundane, literal voices of fear and demand.

We all have and use intuition. Any time you solve a problem that differs from a formulaic pattern, you use your intuition. Any time you are stumped by a problem, you call on your intuition to begin to figure it out. Any time you make something creative, be it a new kind of

Intuition (in´tōō ish´ən) *n.* the process through which you "just know" something, without a logical basis

Intuition is not a supernatural visitation, it is a skill; one learned best in the work of art within a medium you love.

quiche or a poem about a quark, you engage intuition. Any time you follow a sense of something below the surface—like a friend's upset, the cause of a rattle in the car—you utilize your intuition.

You engage your intuition in reading these pages. When you lift your eyes from the page to think about a sentence, your intuition has joined your logic at work—that is how you selected that particular passage for further reflection. When you allow the flow of this book to spill over into other parts of your life, you will be following your intuition's lead.

Intuition is a necessary guidance tool in any innovative work; it whispers, "Now you are getting somewhere." When intuition is weak or confused, we can lose our way. When this plight persists, or when we persistently ignore these inner promptings, we are in serious trouble.

Mental balance includes a sophisticated intuitive system that directs attention toward appropriate opportunities, an inner Geiger counter that begins to draw our attention by clicking when we are near something that is "hot." An undeveloped intuition leads us into too many dead ends, following anything that catches the eye. Most of the stuff in our lives does not reward inquisitive attending. We cannot, and should not, dig into every newspaper article as if it held a deep metaphoric truth. We don't want to pull off the interstate to ponder what Burger King offers us as a symbol. This kind of porosity is actually a hallmark of mental imbalance.

The words that approximate an intuitive guidance system at work sound vague but prompt us effectively in the direction we need to go: "have a sense of," "get a feeling for," "have a hunch," "just know," "similar to," "somehow reminds me of," "jumped out," "something tells me." These are bad translations of intuition's specific, wordless instructions. When intuition and logic combine to direct our action, as they do in the work of art, we discover our most authoritative individual voice.

Intuition gets educated by experience, as the aforementioned nurse and car mechanic know—anything we do regularly with awareness develops our intuition about it. The Olympic diver has made so many

> *Any time you follow a sense of something below the surface you utilize your intuition.*

> *When intuition and logic combine to direct our action, we discover our most authoritative individual voice.*

dives that he can make intuitive decisions and adjustments down to the micro-muscular level as his foot leaves the board.

The educated intuition guides all the investment decisions we make: with our thoughts, time, money, hard work, and relationships. The intuition for selecting the best problems to work on, the ones most likely to lead to provocative findings, is the artistic skill that separates the outstanding scientist or scholar or detective from the good one.

The educated intuition helps us make the most of what we have got: our particular personal history, genes, our set of intelligences, proclivities and preferences, our offerings to another person in a relationship, our sense of humor, and our luck.

The Wild Side

I wish I could honestly report that involvement with the work of art transforms life into an uninterrupted string of flow experiences. We just pop on the harness and saddle, and off we happily ride on the trail of art. In truth, harnessing can be hard, and the ride can take us all over the map, emotionally and even logistically. The good news I can report is that the skills of managing a work-of-art process will provide mastery for any difficult process we might meet.

The work of art follows no logical plan; it does not, will not, march straight from point A to point B. The work of art moves you like a sailboat heading into the wind; you move forward only by tacking back and forth. You have markers in sight—buoys bobbing atop a sea of unknowns—toward which you head and which guide your choices. But there is much zigging about en route to the goal.

Let's follow that metaphor. Imagine the buoy as something you yearn to complete, a sculpture of a giant geranium for your backyard. Imagine the changeable winds as the various forces that both get you there and make a direct approach impossible; forces like the eloquence/recalcitrance of the materials you are working with, your inner certainties/doubts, what you do know/don't know that applies, the process of conjuring up/narrowing down the key ideas, the usefulness/imperfection of your technical skills—all the natural

The work of art moves you like a sailboat heading into the wind; you move forward only by tacking back and forth.

resources/difficulties that appear in every creative challenge. Strive as cleverly as you may, you get closer to completing that huge sculpture only by working toward it in the constant adjustment of tacking back and forth.

In this way, the work of art is inherently paradoxical, staked out between contrasting poles. Artists manage their progress by navigating as straight a course as possible, while tacking between the following predictable polarities:

1) Emotional Extremes

Artists tack between feeling: close to fruition and far away, exhilarated and despairing, joyful and enraged, free and trapped, charged-up and tired, hopeful and hopeless, wild and timid, satisfied and starved, universally connected and very alone, fed and fed up.

2) Intellectual Extremes

Those with a taste for abstract thinking might say that artists alternate between: the personal and the transpersonal, Dionysian and Apollonian impulses, the process and the product, logos and eros, form and content, explicit and implicit orders, archetypes and icons, dualism and holism, the known and the unknown. They apply brain-power and other times it fails them; they use logic and other times analogic; they get stumped, and then the full range of capacities we call the mind takes them further than the brain could ever go.

3) Metaphoric Extremes

Poets might imagine the artist's tacking process as between the ordinary and the extraordinary, the edges and the center, the part and the whole, the form and the content, the air and the earth, the horizontal and vertical, the individual and the universal, the heavens and the earth, the male principle and the female principle, yin and yang, the shadow on the cave wall and the sight of the real thing, the eccentric cocker spaniel with bad breath and the universal dog.

4) Practical Extremes

Art workers of the world, unite. You might describe the zigging process as zagging between: the concrete and the abstract, telephotoing on specifics and wide-angling on the whole, the urge to create for yourself and the urge to communicate with others, passivity and activity, driving and floating, finding and seeking, focus on the how and focus on the why; interest in groupings and interest in parts, creating new categories and drawing strength from old, intuition and research, ecstasy in the process and the wish you were an accountant.

Let's set aside the sailing analogy and use another to further describe what happens in the work of art.

Think of Lewis and Clark heading west (please allow for poetic oversimplification of their actual mission). With no Interstate 80, no map, they couldn't keep their goal in sight; all they knew was "West." They had to find their way as they went, constantly adjusting to reality. When the idea of West met a boulder or a mountain or river, the resulting improvisation was their creative problem-solving process. They had times of doubt and despair as they detoured for days trying to find a spot to cross that river or deciding to build rafts. They never had enough information to make the "right" choice, but they used their intuition and available perceptions to make the best choice they could.

Think West, and pick your way forward in a dance of adjustment along the way.

If you find yourself Clarking your way toward a goal, you are inside the work of art. Think West, and pick your way forward in a dance of adjustment along the way. Sometimes you proceed like a Sherman tank, driving over obstacles; other times you bounce around, bumping off every little twig on the road. If you insist on orderliness and efficiency in your process, you will be one unhappy Lewis. The process is inherently unpredictable. Lewis and Clark didn't sit down and gripe that a mountain was there, didn't quit or try to move it; they found a way. Artists know that trying to control a process will strangle their best work or drive them mad. They know to do their best and just succeed.

Constructive Waste

It is a fact of creative life: in the work of art, we make mistakes and waste time. I like to think of this phenomenon as constructive waste. There are times when artists are very efficient in the wrong direction for a while—a novelist may write a hundred pages before getting to the page that will become number one—but the work is not wasted, and the pages are not thrown away. Artists have the fortitude to be inefficient on their way to opening a new frontier. They have the skill to accept the waste, recognize its constant possibility, even embrace it, and shed no tears (well, maybe just a few) when it is recognized.

This is still a killer for me personally. I adore efficiency and pushed for it tirelessly in my own business. Inefficiency makes me squirm. Yet, there are times when the work of art just refuses to be efficient, and there are times when I do my efficient damnedest and still end up having to lop off a whole chunk of work.

As we grow up, we are told not to worry so much about making mistakes. And then we get clobbered when we make one. The work of art avoids the binary thinking of right vs. wrong; it focuses on more effective/less effective; it views the dealing with waste ore as an integral part of finding gold. Experimentation advances whether any particular result is positive or negative.

Constructive Selfishness

The first time we snatch an extra ginger snap, we are warned that we must not be selfish. "Selfish" is a nasty label. We try to avoid deserving it (or at least learn ways to disguise its appearance).

But there is an aspect of selfishness that is essential to the work of art. It is the artist's absolute commitment do whatever is necessary to make the work go as well as possible. The composer will give up sleep, proper meals, and infuriate a mate to get the critical part of the concerto just right at just the right time.

The distinction between constructive selfishness and just-plain selfishness lies mostly in intent. Selfishness demands gratification; it is self-centered and self-absorbed. Constructive selfishness demands that

The work of art avoids the binary thinking of right vs. wrong; it focuses on more effective/less effective.

Selfishness fills a hole in the self; constructive selfishness seeks to complete, and then share, a whole world.

Blocked skills of selfishness drive millions into depression, superficiality, or worse.

a particular yearning be pursued; it is almost impersonal and process-absorbed. Selfishness fills a hole in the self; constructive selfishness seeks to complete, and then share, a whole world.

What makes constructive selfishness a skill is its strategic, occasional deployment, far different than a lifetime habit of ginger-snap hogging. Indeed, we can be, might well be, usefully selfish in our work when it needs it and remain generous in every other part of life.

The skills of constructive selfishness are not limited to the arts. They are a gift, for example, to any workplace. In my company, I gained respect for the employee who came and told me she needed a quieter place in the office to do her writing; for the worker who said she had found that the way I suggested she do things was not working for her and proposed her own preferred method.

Constructive selfishness is similarly essential in a long-term marriage. The capacity of both partners to know what they individually need, and to insist on getting it, is a linchpin for long-term mutual growth. Remember the man in our earlier couple who needed shirts ironed to feel loved? He gives far more to his marriage by selfishly insisting on an agreement that resolves that particular issue, and then reciprocating wholeheartedly, than in a polite denial of his need. His partner, in turn, is entitled to find a way for her own constructively selfish yearning to find fruition with her generous mate.

A lack of ready access to our skill of constructive selfishness appears as self-absorption or self-abnegation, as passivity or aggression, as ambivalence or doubt. Blocked skills of selfishness drive millions into depression, superficiality, or worse. When in flow, at natural play, we are inherently constructively selfish, pushing into that which attracts us, turning away from that which feels empty, just like children.

A Skill Called Maturity

Just like children, anyone who regularly engages in the work of art develops a life filled with wonder, yearning, flow, and serious play all over the place. Is that childish? To me, it is the definition of being mature.

Maturity is not the sagacity to know the "right" answers or to appear unfazed by the ups and downs as much as it is the capacity to tolerate paradoxes and complexities, to grow within them. Such maturity provides the strength to hold onto long-term goals throughout the jitterbug of ongoing process, to adhere to overarching themes even as we are engrossed with details. Maturity allows us to hold conflicting values and ideas and at the same time, combine them in productive, innovative ways. Maturity enables us to do two kinds of work at the same time, and with sophistication, to go deeper into the complexities of the subparts as we concurrently check those developments against the status of the whole. Artists learn this maturity though their work, and they apply it to problems throughout life. F. Scott Fitzgerald nailed it when he wrote in *The Crack-up*, "The test of a first-rate intelligence is the ability to hold two opposed ideas in the mind at the same time and still retain the ability to function."

Mature people are often accused of being set in their ways. On the contrary, mature artists may have set some knowledge in place, but this basis becomes a foundation for constantly adjusting the scripts of the status quo. Artistically mature people are adept at change, and they eagerly delve into the uncertain areas of life. Such maturity is earned, it is learned, and experience in the work of art may be optimum way to develop it.

Artists recognize that the world is inherently paradoxical. We all confront and cope with the intolerable, the irreconcilable, the impossible in life. Holding two different realities at the same time requires a metaphoric or disbelief-suspending point of view. If we can use the metaphoric mind to accomplish this, to find a way in which a slip of the tongue is both accidental and intentional, we get a much deeper grip on life. Artists, mystics, teachers, and religions have always used paradox as a tool to expand the status quo, to dislodge entrenched viewpoints, to explore other ways of thinking. What is the sound of one hand clapping? How does Yorick's skull feel about Hamlet? Paradox frustrates logic and catapults us into analogic, creating the possibility of new and deeper connections.

There are guardians at the gates of Buddhist temples, two ferocious-

Artistically mature people are adept at change, and they eagerly delve into the uncertain areas of life.

looking statues of demons who protect the delicate business of enlightenment that goes on inside. These demons stand there to frighten people off, to prevent those without courage from entering the temple. Even for those brave enough to enter, the guardians must be encountered at every entry and exit. They never go away and never look less frightening. Their names are Paradox and Confusion. Take courage; pass by.

Attitude

The mature artist develops an attitude that opens the work of art in an everyday way. It's not a chip on the shoulder, it's a skill of the heart and mind.

Etymologically, attitude designates an artistic aptitude. The Latin "aptitudo" was adopted into Italian as "attitudine," which meant posture. English borrowed "attitude" in the seventeenth century as a technical term in art criticism to express something artists were studying in oil painting at the time—the placement of human figures in landscapes. The "attitude" of a figure was a choice made by an artist, a physical position crafted to communicate a particular mental state. Among the many possible options, the artist created a specific attitude for a particular invented world.

In the early 1800s, the English language began to develop the current metaphoric sense of attitude as a description of off-canvas behavior. The particular setting of a figure in an artistic landscape came to mean "a particular mindset" in regard to the world. We still occasionally use the word in reference to its original artistic context—to describe the physical placement of things like an airplane's or spaceship's tilt in relation to a horizon, or in the ballet term for a specific position. But now, we mostly say: "Don't give me that attitude, young man," "She has a good attitude towards her job," or "Those supermodels really have attitude!"

Let's consider attitude as a truly super model, as a useful metaphor rather than as chin-lifted behavior. Imagine a mindset to be a chosen position one assumes in relation to a particular world. That is to say,

Attitude (at´i tood´) n. a mindset to be a chosen position one assumes in relation to a particular world imagine a person's attitude as if it were an artistic choice, like a figure placed in an oil painter's landscape. Think of attitude not as something one "has" or "is" but as something one "tries" as an experiment. Just as the oil painter can remove or adjust the way the figure looks in the scene, imagine that people can readily adjust personal attitudes in the scenes they inhabit. It requires an artistic perspective to assume this metaphoric point of view. It is an artist's skill to keep this attitude available at all times and to use it often.

In these pages, we have had many small occasions in which this sense of attitude has been invoked: throughout Jack's Home Depot adventure, while paying an electric bill, in seeing the metaphors of a New Balance sneaker, while looking into Pagemaker's "snap-to guidelines." Let's work with a more complex example.

Imagine you are waiting in line at the post office to mail a birthday present to a friend. You notice that the clerk is surly and rude; he has a "bad attitude." What do you do? You can try to ignore or minimize it, perhaps feeling a little annoyed at the unnecessary rudeness, but thinking, "It doesn't really matter, I'll be out of here in a few minutes." Or you can shift your energy to become an arts participant: view the clerk as having made a particular choice to be surly, in this setting, on this occasion. Ask the questions you would ask if you were deeply engaged with an oil painting: Why did he make that choice? (What is the artist trying to say?); What can I see or imagine as the elements of this post office landscape that would lead to this arrangement? (What else is going on in this painting that informs the choice of the figure in it?); Are there clues of other ways the clerk might behave differently in other environments? (ornaments?, photos on the wall?, word choice?— are there subtle hints, details of other kinds in the painting?); What response do I have to this rudeness, and why? (What does this painting evoke in me?). When my turn in line comes, what choice might I make that could change the attitude, the particular position of this clerk? (What line of inquiry would I like to experiment with?).

Those questions engage the work of art. By inquiring into a mundane situation as if it were an intentional construction, we choose to engage in a different way of seeing. Use the everyday perspective, the literal mind, and the clerk is an annoyance; any contact beyond the perfunctory is a waste of your time. But using the artistic attitude, the metaphoric mind, the clerk represents a complex series of choices in a world worth exploring. The first approach depletes you (even if you minimize the impact); the second enriches your skills and understanding. Both mindsets get the gift in the mail, but the latter makes the world a better place for you and for the clerk.

The difference lies in the attitude you bring to the moment.

The difference lies in the attitude you bring to the moment. You can choose to be inattentive to the reality, to resist it, or just not to bother (avoid the museum, or stand in front of the *Rape of the Sabine Women* thinking about your weight). Or you can choose to engage with what you encounter (participate in the process of meeting the painting to see what happens). This difference, this attitude you can assume (which I will refer to by a shorthand term "*the* attitude") launches the work of art any time, any place.

This is not to say you must encounter all of life's annoying moments as if Poussin painted them or Arthur Miller wrote them into Act 2. The critical point is your skill with *the* attitude—knowing you have it; being able to adopt it; using it to serve your yearning; having it handy as a tool to make meaning in ordinary life. Artists use *the* attitude strategically, masterfully. They know when to adopt it to serve their work and when to completely ignore the grumpy clerk.

Let's practice *the* attitude with an imagination experiment. Wherever you are, look at a nearby wall that has things on it or against it. See if you can study it as if it were a set of choices made for a particular situation. Here are a few questions you might play with answering: What do I notice most about that wall? Could I say there is a "main idea" about the wall? Are there other details that go against the major choices? What thinking, beyond just practical considerations, is evident in the choices made to create the arrangement on that wall? What does the wall tell me about the artist who designed it? (Remember, you are playing "as if.") If that were the back wall of a set for a play, what would I know about the characters? What might I expect to have happen in the plot?

Here is another experiment you might try. Get a mental snapshot of a moment on a vacation you enjoyed. Make it a very specific moment—picture who is there, where, the weather, the things you would see all around. Now, assume *the* attitude, and explore that snapshot as if it were full of detailed choices made by an artist to tell a very particular story. Here are a few starter questions, but go beyond these: What might be an intriguing-but-truthful title for this snapshot? What are two main symbols in it? What are three things the artist is trying to say? Is there a tiny detail that could be viewed as a microcosm of the whole?

Do you feel how it feels to use *the* attitude? Do you sense the shifts of perspective you made while assuming it? Did you notice the differences in experience while you engaged in those activities? Those small shifts and differences are important to note; they are markers, reminders for you as you learn to take the intentional assumption of *the* attitude and make it a habit, as artists do.

Habit

Aristotle wrote in *Nicomachean Ethics*, "We are what we repeatedly do. Excellence, then, is not an act, but a habit." Habit is a good word with a bad rap. It carries negative connotations—being stuck in a rut. Habits are dull, unspontaneous, anti-expressive, and it might seem anti-most-of-the-ideas-in-this-book. On the contrary, I'm all for habits.

We all have habits. Even the most spontaneous, unpredictable people I know have their particular mental habits (ways of looking at things), verbal habits (reliance on certain phrases and sentence structures), and maintenance habits (daily routines). Thank heavens—who would relish a fresh exploration of tooth brushing every night on your way to bed?

I am endlessly fascinated by the odd and clever ways people work out systems of doing things. Habits are an eloquent self-portrait of who we are, of our creative idiosyncrasies. We met this idea earlier in this book at the restaurant, as I encouraged thinking about the methods we develop to order from a menu. I am intrigued by people's dishwashing systems, personal dance improvisation patterns when in

Habits are an eloquent self-portrait of who we are, of our creative idiosyncrasies.

Habit (hab′it) *n.*
an attitude in motion

full boogie, problem-solving procedures, what they do just before making a speech.

The word habit goes back to the Latin word meaning "what one has," and it developed into "habitus," which meant "how one is"—your personal state or condition. Etymologically, as well as practically, a habit is the recurrent outer pattern of a personal inner state. (Using both word histories, "a habit" could be thought of as "an attitude" in motion.) Your habits announce how you are, the ways of doing things you have put together that weave the fabric of your life. A friend asks "How are you?," and you might answer with a list including which sock you put on first, the ways you make time to read. Your habits are metaphors for who you are. Francis Bacon wrote that, "Habits are the daughters of action."

Artists do more than just observe habits for their content. They use them to further their work. Habits have some wonderful attributes.

Habits are efficient. Once a habit is set in place, we no longer need to negotiate that action repeatedly. (In fact, if one is still having an internal discussion about an action, it isn't a habit yet. Until all inner discussion ceases, the activity is on probation, requiring further investigation, comparison to other choices.) If a practice passes scrutiny enough times, it earns its way to habit status. At this point, the action becomes smooth, even elegant, and energy-efficient. Such habits express your natural aesthetic, some of your skills in the work of art.

Every artist I know has developed clever habits to be a more effective creator. One writer works at the keyboard from 7:00 until 11:00 every morning, even when the inspiration is not there and when the flu is. Graham Greene wrote exactly 250 words every day, and he counted. A choreographer I know warms up and reviews previously set bits of dance for four hours prior to a single hour of making new choreography. I used to fast all day before a performance as Hamlet, because the edge of hunger produced a quality of energy that was just right (not a habit you want to get into for a show that plays eight times a week).

Habits are authentic. When we develop a habit, the behavior is in tune with our inner condition. We may not like this fact because we

When we develop a habit, the behavior is in tune with our inner condition.

may not like some of our habits, but they are our creations—they are honest announcements of inner states. If you have a habit that you deem bad—say, eating four hot dogs every morning for breakfast—it is a perfect expression of something in your inner condition. Don't judge yourself or others too quickly. It takes time to understand any particular habit as a metaphoric creation, to uncover the underlying reality it expresses. Habits tend to grow from very good impulses.

Artists can be eccentric. Their habits express their dedication to the work of art, placing "what is normal" in a secondary priority to "what works." They align their lives toward their greatest satisfaction and reward; they develop habits that support that arrangement.

That last sentence may sound simple, but the impact can be dramatic. Try this: name, in one phrase, the specific type of experience in your life that reliably affords your greatest satisfaction. Now imagine ways you might change your life to put everything you do in service to that experience of satisfaction. Do you get a sense of the courage in the choice to be an artist? Can you sense the brilliant effectiveness of some of those eccentric habits that you might see in a person dedicated to the work of art? And artists still manage to pay the bills, have families, and get to the movies every now and again.

Habits can change us. We may think of habits as monuments of the status quo, but they can be a tool for revolutionary change. To a significant degree, what we do is who we become. Thus, we can transform an inner condition by establishing a new outer habit. We might call it working from the outside in. (As opposed to American inside-out "method" acting, this is the way Laurence Olivier worked, perfecting the overt characteristics of a part he played and allowing those choices to settle inside to create the character.) I'm not saying changing through habits is easy or reliable or even always wise—as anyone who has ever tried to diet can attest. The diet becomes permanent weight loss only when the whole eating style changes, when the imposed behavior is matched by a successful inner adjustment.

Not all habit changes are launched to dump the bad. The sweet impulse to make resolutions on New Year's Eve is a testimonial to the

Name, in one phrase, the specific type of experience in your life that reliably affords your greatest satisfaction.

What we do is who we become.

positive side. So is the bestseller status of so many personal improvement books. Most of us carry inner lists of things we might change that would bring about what we want to be. Unfortunately, the yearning must be strong. New habits, like marble statues, don't emerge casually. The work of carving out new habits can be as tiring and discouraging as finding the new sculpture inside an old block of stone. Artists experiment with habits and practices to test out results. My friend Victor Mecyssne started to compose music when he broke his arm and couldn't play the guitar, and now he is completing his second CD as a result of his new composing habit. My friend Carl found his writing too wordy, so he set himself the task-habit of penning a haiku a day. More important to note than the particular creative habits artists devise to redirect their work is the attitude they take toward their lives. They play, seriously, until they get things working.

Habits can support us. Any long-term project has its ups and downs. Habits keep us in balance—they can ease us through the downs and keep the ups from becoming too uppity. When the going gets tough, we don't have to agonize daily over whether we should continue or not—*if* the work is a habit. When the going gets tough, we don't have to "get going," our habits just keep us going.

Making works of art is the hardest work I know. People usually have only a vague sense of all that goes into the process of making an important work, all the problems, all the wild forces that provoke good solutions. With a little hands-on experience, people realize the enormity of a single artistic accomplishment, the magnificence represented by a large body of works. Without effective habits of process, such accomplishments would be impossible.

The physicist Arthur Zajonc reminds us of the importance of work-of-art habits. In his book *Catching the Light*, he writes, "The artist and the monk both know through a disciplined practice they can internalize nature so that they can realize new capacities of mind. Personal growth is not only a matter of memorizing sacred texts or of academic artistic analysis, but it requires praxis, daily labor, to fashion fresh, hard-won, soul faculties. Every action of the hand and the eye sculpts the soul."[10]

When the going gets tough, we don't have to "get going," our habits just keep us going.

Chapter Seven:

Structuring the Big Picture

What makes a day great? What is the key experience that happens in a day of yours that, when you get to the end of it, leads you to say: "That was a great day"?

I began asking friends this question. I asked artists, teachers, business people, a reporter, a chef, a handyman, a therapist, a student, a poet, a philosopher. Their answers differed: some described making something worthwhile during the day, some spoke of feeling active love for another person, some identified moments of "real communication," some spoke of learning something new, some pointed to playfulness or surprise or fun, some turned to moments of making a difference for other people, some needed to feel spiritual connections.

Mulling over their different responses, and reviewing my own, I found that what they all had in common was flow. Mihaly Csikszentmihalyi describes flow in compelling detail in his bestselling book *Flow: The Psychology of Optimal Experience*. He notes the following attributes as being central to flow: a distortion of the sense of time (seems to pass very slowly or very fast); a sense of discovery; a merging of action and awareness (mind and hand); autotelic satisfaction (enjoyment of doing something for its own sake); the loss of self-consciousness and anxiety about failure; a sense of orderliness to one's concentration with clear goals along the way; separation from consideration of everyday concerns; a sense of adequate control even as one explores new information, or a lack of a concern about loss of control. Flow is the absorption in an engaging process. Csikszentmihalyi graphs it midway between anxiety and boredom, as action within which skills are challenged just right and rewarded immediately.[11]

All the friends and acquaintances I had asked about a "great day" had described a quality of experience that made satisfying sense of the day. Even if the duration of that key experience had been short, it influenced the feel of everything else they did. A palpable experience of flow radiated meaning throughout the day.

I noticed, perhaps not surprisingly, that there was a distinction between the men's and the women's responses. The men tended to cite active doing—making things—as the irreducible element that led to their satisfaction, whereas the women more often drew meaning from relating to others. But whether it was doing or relating, whatever their profession, age, or gender, all identified the same core experience as the one that made a day great: engagement in an inherently satisfying process. This is what we have been calling the work of art.

I also noticed that friends with an active practice in the work of art were the quickest and surest with their responses. Other friends applied themselves to the question, scrunched faces, scanned the ceiling to find answers. Some took minutes, refined, restated, or postponed their answer for several days. But artists of every kind, people with a daily practice of creative work they loved, knew immediately. The question and answer seemed obvious to them because they had asked and answered it so many times; flow is a magnetic north by which they have guided their choices in life.

The Currency of Experience

We have to talk a little about experiencing. That may sound odd— experience just is, isn't it? Why do we have to jawbone about it? Try explaining water to a fish.

In ordinary life, we actively notice the goings-on of our inner world only fitfully; every once in a while something happens—the tuna gets caught in wave and is thrown through the air for a moment.

Phew, what was that?! Then back to water, back to "normal."

Here is a secret from the work of art: experience doesn't just happen to us. We *make* our experience, as surely as we make sense, make a presentation at work, make a collage, make a medical diagnosis, and make love. Experiencing is a skill. With practice, we get better at it.

In its earliest roots, the word "experience" was a verb, and it had virtually the same meaning as "experiment." Remember that linkage, experience-experiment; the gut feel that you are experimenting, testing out something new, is a tip-off that you are involved in the work of art.

Eventually, the action-verb meaning of "experience" dropped away, and the emphasis shifted to experience as the *result* of experimentation. Over time, we gained the noun "expert," a person who has become adept at experiencing within a particular domain. Creativity researchers have confirmed that experts differ from novices more in *how* they process information than in the data they have in their minds.

An expert plumber may not be the one with the most years under his belt; the expert is one the who can take in the whole house's plumbing arrangement from the clues, effectively diagnose the problem, and address it elegantly. An expert is a fine experiencer who takes effective action. And a superb performance by an expert in any field deserves the description "artful," even "beautiful"—whether in pipe-fitting or pottery, we might well call it the work of art.

Artists are nothing more than experts at experiencing. They have developed the skills to sustain and effectively apply their yearning, which enables them to notice well and engage productively with their own experience. And they also know how to make things that invite and guide the experience of others.

To sustain their yearning, artists attend to all kinds of experiences, inside and outside their chosen artistic discipline. They exercise choice about what they experience, the nouns. They guide their yearning into an endless intercourse with attractive and worthwhile things. Artists are good at sensing just the kind of experiences they want and the ones they need; then they go out to get them.

Experiencing is a skill. With practice, we get better at it.

Experience (ik spēr´ē əns) *v.* to experiment; *n.* the result of experimentation

Artists also apply their expertise by choosing *how* they experience. They practice the full range of their skills, using a broad, playful, curious palette of practices to make ever-richer connections.

Artists know it is risky to separate their actions from their yearnings, literalizing the passion for good experiences into a lust for goods. Without a link to personal yearning, the urge to enrich life-experience can only be fulfilled through ownership, requiring a steady diet of new nouns. This becomes the over-consumer's hunger that creates so much of the addiction, depression, apathy, anger, pollution, and lost opportunity we see in today's world.

Here is an example of the ways yearning can get literalized and lose its way. Skiing on the perfect slope in perfect conditions can provide deep joy. Experience that rush once, and you will probably want to have it again and again. But if you literalize that yearning by becoming a full-time skier, you will end up disappointed. The weather changes, conditions are not always perfect; you'll run out of money; you'll lose interest. If, on the other hand, you understand that the real experiencing is inside your skin, not on the slope or in that perfect cloudless sky, you can reclaim the highs that skiing sometimes evokes without having to buy a lift ticket to get it.

Expertise in experiencing provides highs long after your knees get too bad for the moguls and on the everyday days that make a life. Take credit for your accomplishments—it wasn't the slope that created that joy, that exhilaration. Snow motion was the medium in which you chose to experiment, but you *made* the magnificence of the experience. It was the doing, the engagement of your skills in tune with the challenge, the flow that was the high. These occasions fill your life if you have your experiencing skills as sharp as your ski edges. Artists select the way they engage with things; they apply the verbs of experiencing, the hows. If we follow their model, keep our *hows* growing, the *whats* become less important. With the skills of *how*, any *what* can provide satisfaction, and we learn the skills to construct "great" days in the work of art.

Without a link to personal yearning, the urge to enrich life-experience can only be fulfilled through ownership.

Play

We do best when we live by Heraclitus' maxim: "Man is most nearly himself when he achieves the seriousness of a child at play." We are seriously short of serious play in our world.

We seem childlike when we play because we set aside the familiar everyday rules to apply ourselves within imaginative systems. But play is very serious about its rules—try cheating at charades and see what you get. Aesthetics count more than logic in the land of play; pattern and harmony, beauty and cleverness are held in the highest regard. When we play, we step inside an "as if" world. Released from the weights and requirements of "reality," we can try out different kinds of flight.

When we lose the play of play, we let the "as if" slip into "it is." When we play golf "as if" it were important, we grow as people, improve our wisdom even in an over-par round. When golf is just golf, we may improve our scores, but we handicap our inner game.

The *experience* of play has distinctive attributes that sound a lot like those of flow: it is done entirely for its own sake; it is always new; it taps directly into what you know, bypassing interpretation and explanation; it bears no responsibility beyond the moment; it is unself-conscious; it distorts the sense of time; it seeks control within different kinds of order; it tells the truth. While the stakes involved may differ, making any particular game seem risky or silly, play always begins at the spot where what you know meets what you don't know. These are the inner hallmarks; if they disappear from the play experience, you have stopped playing, even though you may remain on the team.

When play finds its way into the work of art, it may be called imagination, invention, improvisation, innovation, getting into a groove, or good collaboration. Every setting—studio to corporate boardroom—requires play en route to success. Work withers without it. During effortful business meetings with colleagues involved in a difficult issue, I have often thought: Could we just be silly for a while here so we could get something done?

Over a thousand years, the word "silly" has developed two near-opposite faces, but we are currently in the habit of seeing only one. We

We are seriously short of serious play in our world.

Every setting—studio to corporate boardroom—requires play en route to success.

are like my mother, who returned from a trip to Greece with a typical souvenir pair of the traditional comedy and tragedy theater masks. She hung the pair on the kitchen wall, and only ten years later did she notice she had brought home and displayed two faces of comedy. The parent of "silly" originally meant "happy" and "blessed with luck." In the early Middle Ages, it was used to mean "holy" and "innocent." This sense of innocence led to its distinct second meaning in English, "helpless and unfortunate," which developed into the current implications of "dumb."

The etymological story of silly suggests a sad ending—it began at "blessed and innocent" only to arrive at "stupid and pointless." This is a particularly poignant declension, because wonder, the source of the work of art, requires a condition of innocence. So the loss of blessed silliness takes the work of art further away from us today.

But I think silliness is making a comeback. Recently, I find more references to the archetype of the holy fool in pop magazines and in intellectual circles. Thanks to Norman Cousins and others, laughter is gaining respect in the public and professional spheres for its healing as well as spiritual powers. Learning theorists now argue for the importance of non-productive play as a critical component of productive advancement. Play is one of the few universal ways in which we test what we know.

The most effective arena humans have devised for silliness is play; and the skills of play, serious play, are best nurtured and tapped through the work of art. As serious a thinker as Carl Jung noted in *Psychological Types* that, "The creation of something new is not accomplished by the intellect but by the play instinct acting from inner necessity. The creative mind plays with the objects it loves."

Success

Our current usage of the word "success" provides that a miserable and destructive millionaire CEO is readily called a success, whereas a brilliant, joyful daycare teacher who barely earns enough to pay the rent could never be. That's not right.

Silly (sil´ē) *adj.*
blessed and innocent

*Silliness is making
a comeback.*

Originally, "success" had no positive or negative spin. It referred simply to the outflow from a situation. In its parentage, "success" was the fortune (good or bad) following anyone in a particular situation; it was whatever succeeded, whatever followed. (The succession of kings had little to do with the monarch's job performance review.) Over time, however, the usage of "success" came to be limited to exclusively positive outcomes. More recently, it has taken on social cachet—being "a success" is one of the great labels people seek to achieve.

This narrowing of the definition has limited our joy in work. I propose that we revive some of the sense of the word's original Latin parent-verb, "succedere," meaning to go under, go up, come close after, go near. Success, as I see it, is the connecting forward from one creative engagement to another. You succeed if your action finds fruition and bounces you into another set of interesting actions. Thus, the opposite of success is not failure, but stasis. In other words, success is not the attainment of a goal, but the continuing movement toward personally important goals, whether the goals are ultimately "achieved" or not. If your life is alive and moving, even if you have not achieved much in quantifiable terms, you are a success.

By this enriched definition, the hard-hearted CEO millionaire is probably far less successful than the creative daycare worker. By this definition, the artist is the model of success.

Few artists will ever make the Fortune 500 list, but they are wealthy in the quiet currency that counts the most. For the work-of-artist, to "dress for success" means being so engaged in your project that you can't remember what you are wearing. A "power lunch" is the apple you grab to keep the body-engine fueled while you keep on with your work.

I have lived through the deaths of several friends in recent years, and I know that on their deathbeds, in their final reflections, they did not draw satisfaction from the amount of stuff they had owned or the number of employees they had bossed. Their last wishes were not to have sent more memos, or to have had better views from their office window. In that ultimate hindsight, we all automatically resort to the older definition of success—to the joy of complete engagement in life.

Success (sək ses´) n. the fortune (good or bad) following anyone in a particular situation

If your life is alive and moving, even if you have not achieved much in quantifiable terms, you are a success.

One dying friend seemed to contradict this pattern; she dwelled upon the first house she and her husband bought as a highlight of her life. But eventually I noticed that she never referred to the building itself, but rather to the feelings it evoked, especially when she entered it for the first time. She repeated a story about being carried in by her husband, a moment that somehow held a realization of one of her deep yearnings. It was no coincidence, I think, that she basked in the recollection of a first entry into a new home, held by someone she loved, as she approached her next threshold.

Success in a Name Game

Earlier, I described a workshop warm-up activity about metaphors and similes that taught me an important lesson. Here is a similar warm-up game I used to teach a different lesson.

I asked participants to stand in a circle. We went around the circle, one by one, saying our names. No big deal. Then we went around again, saying our names plus a sentence or two about who we were and why we were there. Getting a little nervous, each person donned aspects of their public personality, little bits they rely on in awkward social situations. They got a little clever, or flip, or maybe earnest, sweet, flamboyant; some just suffered a little in shyness. After this go-round, I casually asked how many names participants had learned. A few.

Then I switched the rules. We went around the circle again (the other direction, for fairness' sake), speaking only our names, but this time with an explicit goal. Now the game was to remember as many new names as we could. As we worked our way around the circle, there was a very different energy in the room. People were serious, trying to do well. When we had gone all the way around, I asked people to count how many new names they recalled. We took a rough tally of name recollection with a show of hands—how many learned no new names? one? two or three? four to six? seven or more?

We took a minute to share different strategies people had used: "I made word associations with odd images, like Anna-banana," or "I linked them with people I know with the same names," and so forth.

Then we went around again, trying new strategies, with the intent to remember even more names. The effort was palpable now. People's bodies were tense and mouths silently repeated each name. The whole rhythm of the exercise slowed as the group focused on the task. We finished this go-round and took another count of the names recalled. This count was even higher.

Finally, we paused to reflect on what had just happened. In the second half of the game (that is, once I introduced the challenge to catch and hold names), participants had bought into the goal and its rules, as if they were important outcomes. They bent their minds to its work. They "went for the gold," the measurable results that determined: Had they succeeded or failed? Were they better or worse than others? How had they measured up? Their actual experiences within the game had been subsumed by their efforts to succeed within the rules. And every participant felt some genuine satisfaction that the group as a whole got better; we succeeded, we won. Pyrrhic victory. Here's how I see it:

1) In the first go-rounds, we were seriously playing with the raw material that makes meaning in life. Our approach was not organized, but it was curious and lively.

2) I imposed a completely arbitrary and useless measurement system on a natural human process.

3) We all bent our natural, creative selves to attain a successful measurement within that system.

4) We readily chucked everything our intuitive, creative selves had started in order to play a dead-end game that resulted in nothing of value. People actively joined the name-counting game because they wanted to be nice, wanted to learn what they thought the workshop had to offer. No one was foolish or bad in following along. This is how we play society's game, too.

Here's a deeper analysis: In the first go-rounds, before we began the name-counting, all kinds of juicy, idiosyncratic, interesting stuff was happening. We were performing an improvisation. We attended to the people around us, checking them out for any affinity. We noted those with something we didn't like, gauged our tastes in makeup, clothes, and personality against those of others; we took side trips to wonder how someone gets his hair to do that; we wandered down memory lane ("Janet reminds me of my second grade teacher..."); sometimes hormones got aroused. We were playing and relating and catching and following our impulses. We were engaged in the discovery of new possibilities—perfect warm-up stretches for the work of art.

Then, when I switched the rules, we bought into an imposed and valueless system—to which we donated all of our creative and playful energies in order to succeed by its simplistic measurable standard. Of what real value is remembering some names of strangers for a minute until tested? The currency of the first two go-rounds was empathy and experience; the second two go-rounds paid a quantitative measure of accomplishment according to a system arbitrarily imposed by a leader who couldn't have cared less about the quality of participants' experience during it. Two value systems, two definitions of success, two entirely different qualities of experience.

Obviously, much of our lifetime is expended in the second kind of high-score game. It begins in school: testing and grading bend our natural playfulness over time to the quantifiable systems that measure "smartness" (which, in fairness, do gauge some legitimate aspects of learning). Over time, we relegate to lower status the passionate, idiosyncratic, improvisation that was our instinctive way of learning and judge ourselves (and get judged by everyone else) in terms of our test scores.

This process repeats like a fugue's theme throughout our culture—success as defined by somebody else's bottom line, usually connected to an "objective" measurement system of some sort. I do not advise that we dispense with grades and with all bottom lines. I have run a business and taught in schools, so I know these measurements can have genuine value. But at present, we overemphasize the bottom line, and we insist that it be flat. We relegate the valuable kind of work represented by the first half of that name game to the periphery of our lives and culture. I believe each of us must devise ways to engage our curiosity, empathy, and imaginative play *even as* we learn the names. You succeed in the big picture only if you do *both*: keep the curiosity bouncing forward *and* do well enough within the measures that assess accomplishment. This is the natural balance within the work of art. Artists can gymnastically sustain this balance as they move down the narrow beam.

Next time you meet a room full of strangers, try to have a *successful* encounter by applying your basics. Bring *the* attitude that drinks in all the impressions it can, encounter the improvisations in the social name game, notice well, explore, ask good questions, acknowledge your opinions and judgments as they pop up, make connections of many kinds, check out people's style of dress and hair, and determine who you might want to know more deeply. And on the way home, you can note how many new names you recall. Probably not too many, but if you recall the name of a single person you will meet again, and remember your connection, you will have succeeded.

Bounce

The second law of thermodynamics describes entropy, the fact that any transformation happens at less than 100 percent efficiency, and thus all systems tend to run down. This law requires that a bounce lose oomph over time, like the tennis ball you drop that rebounds lower and faster until it eventually comes to rest.

The work of art defies this law; the more we expend going in, the greater the energy going out. This may be a secret alchemical law of metaphysics. I call the defiant phenomenon *the bounce*. At the heart of every successful work of art is a marvelous small impulse toward more. Our irrepressible yearning can't resist pushing on; at the moment of completion it says, "and." A good answer begets a good question. Making a world bounces us into beginning the next world. And bouncing along is success.

> Each of us must devise ways to engage our curiosity, empathy, and imaginative play even as we learn.

> At the heart of every successful work of art is a marvelous small impulse toward more.

Bounce (bouns) *v.*
to resound

"Bounce's" etymological lineage springs all the way back to the Latin "bombus," meaning "loud sound," which relaxed into the Vulgar Latin "bombitire" meaning "hum." Old French polished it into "bondir" meaning "resound." So bounce and resound grow on the same family tree.

We resonate when we enter the work of art, when we respond to parts of a world someone made, when we ourselves are engaged in world-making. Personal resonance, ripples on the inner lake, provide a bounce. When we feel that vibration in the viscera, we also feel the spark of curiosity toward new ideas. The moment of success in the work of art occurs when we resonate with something and bounce forward into further new connections.

I would like to identify four final "skills" learned in a successful practice of the work of art, skills that re-structure the big projects of living: lifelong learning, connoisseurship, a taste for beauty, and improvisation. Together these four skills lead to *life jazz*.

Lifelong Learning

I come from a mainstream background in which I got fine grades, revered knowledge as a great good, and honored understanding as a word that should be carved above a school. (It actually was. "With all thy getting, get understanding," a quotation from the Bible, was carved over the entry to my brother's high school—I gazed up at it often from my elementary perspective.) But the more I learn, the more I admit that those things called "knowledge" and "understanding" are not carved-in-stone realities. They don't exist, except in the *acts* of knowing and understanding. (I dally in the mind-game that there may be no nouns at all in the world, just verbs of different speed.)

Understanding sounds great; anyone would want it. But like a gold brick in your safe deposit box, it has no real value until put into action. Until you *do* something with it, your understanding is untapped potential.

The most satisfying metaphor I have heard to describe understanding as it really works is climbing on a rope web of connections. Using every part of yourself, you make a move and notice which cords vibrate, pull, and connect; you lay out some new lines and see how that adjusts the whole. Understanding is a creative act. It is improvised play in making worthwhile connections.

Similarly, knowledge is useful only in the actions of knowing. "Having knowledge" (whatever that means) is fine—that gold brick in the bank. But knowledge serves you only when you invest it in action. Knowing is the ability to effectively apply your past experiences to the challenges at hand. The greater the complexity of your connections, the more knowledgeable you are.

The more I think about it, the less I am able to distinguish between the actions of knowing/understanding and the work of art. I would go so far as to say the work of art is the optimum way to understand and know. Learning is the work of art, and artists do it for life.

Three Ways We Learn

Let me offer a thumbnail description of the three basic ways that people learn in life: by instruction, by experience, and by uncovering what we know. Artists skillfully manage their lifelong learning in a sustainable pattern of the following three modes.

1) Instruction

The basic dynamic of instruction is that someone who "knows" tells or shows someone who "doesn't know," and the not-knower tries to learn it—which usually means to reiterate it on demand. This same dynamic applies in classes, personal interactions, books, and the other media of instruction. In many circumstances, this approach is efficient and effective.

However, instruction also has big limitations: it tends toward exchanges about the surfaces of things; it requires that the learner apply tremendous energy to turn the instruction into real understanding, and in most cases the learner cannot accomplish that successfully; and most critically, effective instruction requires the learner to *want* to learn—a fact that is too often overlooked.

Understanding is a creative act. It is improvised play in making worthwhile connections.

Instruction (in struk´shən)
n. to build with a sense of
equipping and preparing

Etymologically, "instruction" means to "build," with a sense of "equipping" and "preparing." Too often, instruction emphasizes the building part, ignoring the necessary preparation that precedes any successful construction project. Too often in instruction, we say to a novice: "Here are your lumber, nails and blueprints. Go build yourself a solid two-level understanding." Would you want to live in, depend on, that house?

2) Experiencing

We instinctively trust people with experience. We would choose the brain surgeon with twenty years' practice in skull-drilling over the one in her first year of residency. Learning in the artistic disciplines relies heavily on this approach, as do apprenticeships, and the schools of hard knocks and marriage.

Remember our etymologies: experience means almost the same as experiment, and an expert is one who is good at experiencing in a particular situation. Learning by experience is taking in the successful gleanings from standard artistic improvisations between you and the real world.

3) Uncovering What We Know

What we don't know we don't know includes almost everything in the universe. Within that vastness is a small golden area of things we do know, but don't know that we do. The work of art takes us there.

Discovering and uncovering what we know is the most powerful learning; it goes deep and resonates for a long time. Homemade knowledge directly reconstructs our understandings in ways we apply the next chance we get. And an optimum learning situation provides a chance to practice that new way of seeing, to experiment with it right away.

This critical but often overlooked way of learning plays havoc with learning systems and with institutions that promote any particular approach. It cannot be programmed; the best we can do is prepare and provoke. This is the magnificently messy school of human beings that the work of art attends.

Of the three ways of learning, instruction is the easiest to manage, the most orderly. Experience is the most powerful place to enter the cycle of three, with the greatest pull toward personal involvement. Uncovering what we know leads to the greatest change and forward movement.

The best learning does not emphasize one element over the others but slips fluidly among all three. I find the best teaching enters the equation at experience, providing each student a strong first grasp on the subject through personal experience and then guiding the learning to move through all three. The best learner is able to use all three approaches in a self-guided stream of inquiry.

The American schools in which most of us were trained overemphasize instruction (most "schooling" is geared toward testing—the mechanical tail wagging a live dog). Schools take experiencing for granted or use it fitfully (principally in sports, field trips and lab classes, and in the dwindling number of arts programs), and schools are embarrassed, or at least confused, by the process of uncovering what we know. Imbalances such as these in the natural tripartite process cause the learner, young or old, to pull back and care less about learning.

Yearning is essential to all real learning. How do the schools that we and our children inhabit for a dozen-plus formative years develop that hunger to learn? They don't. Some of this critical motivation leaks in, but the system, as it is, seems almost diabolically designed to squelch the idiosyncratic love of learning. Individuals' yearning does evolve to some degree, incidentally, through interactions with parents and good teachers and through a hodgepodge of life experiences. But to develop a sustaining lifelong passion for learning, we must become our own learning coaches because our institutions rarely provide them.

What nurtures the natural desire to learn? Better than anything else I have encountered, it is hands-on engagement in the work of art in its broadest sense. I see it all the time: the work of art opens up something we know. That insight makes us curious to follow, which leads us to hungrily seek out instruction, which we experiment with, and so forth, in a self-propelled learning cycle.

This is the natural pattern of lifelong learning.

Yearning is essential to all real learning.

Connoisseurship

DANGER: The word "connoisseurship" is the flagship of the armada of misunderstandings about the work of art. Its usage carries all the weaponry of pretentiousness, elitism, sophistication, and condescension that has successfully battered most Americans into feeling they have no place in art. It is the word that succinctly represents the view that the arts are special, difficult, intellectual, just for the few, and useless.

From my perspective, a connoisseur (as the term is commonly used) is at best a *partial* understander, an earnest appreciator who has placed all of his energy into one corner of the work of art, and in so doing, sacrificed the potential of the whole. The connoisseur's work of study, analysis, assessment, and critique is important but by no means precludes personal exploration and growth. A connoisseur focuses well, even brilliantly, on parts of the process. However, it is only through his personal commitment to making things and applying what he discovers to the way he lives his life—a commitment to all three angles of the work of art—that a connoisseur might bloom into his full potential.

I've been tempted to shoot down the enemy-word "connoisseur." The word is so profoundly associated with the knotty perspectives I am trying to untangle in this book that it seems almost unredeemable. But I want to work with this word rather than banish it to the ivory tower because, as a word, it's so rich.

The story of "connoisseur" goes back to the Latin "gnoscere," meaning "to know," which picked up a prefix to become "cognoscere," giving it the shading "to come to know." Etymologically, then, a connoisseur is not necessarily one who already knows a lot, but one who is skilled at coming to know things. Connoisseurship is about the encounter, not the ownership, of learning. Rather than one enthroned on the "I know," teacher side of the learning equation, a connoisseur is actually a master learner.

As our sense of connoisseurship edges away from the *action* (skillfully grappling to understand something new) toward the *noun* (one who

Connoisseur (kon´ə sûr´)
n. one who is skilled at coming to know things

owns a lot of knowledge), it edges away from live vibrancy into arrogant deadness with a social label. The label reinforces the false notions of art, connoting a separation between fancy experts with snooty opinions and the rest of us unworthy boors.

I will use the word connoisseurship to describe the skillful process of coming to understandings inside a complex world. Always remember: it is a process, not a pose. A connoisseur in action cannot be full of himself because he is so fully engaged in discovering what is inside this other world. He can't spout impressive information because he is too busy working to discover what is new and worthwhile.

Signs of connoisseurship are neither upturned noses nor nine-syllable nouns. Rather, the signs of connoisseurship are good questions, passion, active responses, courageous vulnerability, curiosity, personal insights springing from artistic involvements, and wondering—the skills of artists.

It is easy to spot true connoisseurs. Stand unobtrusively in a museum and watch people as they "work a room." Notice people's movements, the way they invest their time and attention. Connoisseurs scan the room as they enter, looking for the painting that calls to them from a distance. Sometimes they make a beeline for a painting they know and want to rediscover. Their rhythm around the room is irregular—they spend a long time with one painting and completely skip others. They are the ones who return to a painting in a room after they have already looked at it, "done" it. This is the idiosyncratic rhythm of engaged conversation, of questions and answers.

In contrast, non-connoisseurs tend to hang back and survey from a distance or get a regular rhythm going around the gallery. You can almost time their looking with a metronome. Non-connoisseurs also feel compelled to vote; they leave paintings proclaiming "I like it" or "I don't like it." From my perspective, their opining looks a bit like a dog leaving a mark on each piece. It is a way to "finish" with each engagement. Connoisseurs, on the other hand, want to continue with each piece, even after they move to the next, because they all contribute to a larger inquiry.

You might try this. Observe the action in a museum room as if it were

Connoisseurship is a process, not a pose.

a dance performance with carefully choreographed movement patterns (and very expensive props on the walls). See which dancers suggest which kinds of interactions with the art. Have compassion for those poor souls who have come to the museum against their will—dragged by a spouse or obliged by tourist norms. We have all scuffed along in those dance shoes one time or another.

Being a connoisseur is an engagement in the broadest possibilities of life. Art may be the richest ground for developing skills of connoisseurship, but the resulting inquiries take you out of art into everywhere. As Gertrude Stein declared, "Art isn't everything. It's just about everything."

Making Beauty

Beauty is one of the great marvels, so simple and so profound, evident and ineffable. How can anything so delicious be so good for you? It is an effective answer to so many things that go wrong in life. If your definition of beauty includes the experiencing of beauty (as mine does), it comes as close to being a cure-all as anything I know.

Beauty is neither in the eye of the beholder, nor in a beautiful "thing" itself, no matter how exquisite that thing may be—it resides only in both. Beauty is an invisible skill of experiencing; a kind of dialogue. Like any live-performance work of art, it exists only in the moments when it is happening. Beauty is a seeing, a discovery, of some satisfying whole that is completed by our participation.

For example, you might scrape together twenty million dollars to buy yourself a nice Van Gogh painting of sunflowers. (Don't forget the extra million for a proper security system and insurance.) You hang it on the living room wall and sit down to visit with it. You might get a whopping, transporting sense of its beauty. On the other hand, you might also miss the experience, worrying about the humidity in the room. There will be other times when you sit with it, enjoying its presence but not really attending to it. Your thoughts are drifting; you are tired; something is bothering you—nothing beautiful is there.

Conversely, the neighbor's six-year-old may have sold you a drawing

Art may be the richest ground for developing skills of connoisseurship, but the resulting inquiries take you out of art into everywhere.

Beauty is an invisible skill of experiencing; a kind of dialogue.

he made at school; price, a nickel. Mechanically, you stick it on the wall by the phone. And then you notice it. You start to see what the child has done, you see some clever ideas and accomplishments—beauty is there.

Although there are few ultimate human masterworks (thank heavens for museums and the classic repertoire in the performing arts), there is no shortage of beautiful objects, well-made things that will reward attending with experiences of beauty. What is in short supply is the attending side of the beauty equation—the skills, the habits, the priority of engaging with worthwhile objects to discover beauty.

Beauty is more than nice, more than pretty, more than the opposite of ugly. It is even more than a fully engaged discovery of the beauty in things. Beauty comes to life through the skillful execution of all three actions of the work of art. World-exploring is the action we usually associate with beauty; we connect to the beauty in well-made things. Reading the world seeks beauty in daily life. And world-making is manifesting beauty in any process that makes something more satisfying, more efficient, more effective, more elegant, more communicative, more complex, more compelling—more of whatever you see the project might become. In whatever world-making the skill is engaged—be it writing torts or touting warts, Total Quality Management or massage—beautifying pleases the senses and brings new order to the world.

The power of beauty derives from four inherent truths.

1) Etymologically, "beauty" evolves from the word meaning "the good," "the ideal," "the whole." Beauty is yearning's superhighway, the most direct way to drive toward an individual's ultimate truths, toward ideal order in things, toward entelechy.

2) Beauty lives only in active collaboration between the thing and the perceiver. It requires that we come out and engage. (We may get that pleasant "nice feeling" of something that is beautiful as we let a symphony wash over us, for example, but we are not tapping what it holds, what it was

Beauty is more than nice, more than pretty, more than the opposite of ugly.

**Beauty (by$\overline{oo}$´t$\overline{e}$) n.
the good, ideal, and whole**

made to give.) We often mistake the recollection of beauty for the active participation in beauty—don't ever forget the difference between a kiss and the remembrance of a kiss.

3) At the heart of that live encounter that we call beauty lies wonder. To experience beauty, we tap into and revive our capacity for wonder, and experiencing wonder reorders the world for a while. In wonder: we are not alone; the world has a new pattern; joy and love are the law of the land.

4) In experiencing beauty, we create beauty, and we become beautiful. If we experience the beauty of a dancer, we construct the experience by tapping into things we already knew about dance, about body movement, about life. We bring these understandings together in the serious play of perceiving and make some beauty of our own. In applying those artistic skills, we become beautiful and add to the world's storehouse.

In addition to experiencing beauty, we make beautiful things in the work of art. That last phrase is the main reason artists become and remain artists—it feels that good to make beautiful things. This reward alone provides enough joy to sustain many artists' lives to counteract the difficulties.

My terse grandmother used this verity in reverse as she warned her misbehaving, adolescent grandchildren with a stern look and the peculiar admonition: "Pretty is as pretty does." Elliptical as her approach was (especially to roughhousing boys), it stopped us in our tracks. We didn't care that much about being "bad," but being ugly was a different matter. She implicitly suggested that the actions of beauty formed the basics of a character; she gave me my first sense of behavior as a metaphor. It took me decades to appreciate her points; and she made them beautifully.

The importance of beauty rises with the habit of the work of art. That doesn't mean that we must buy all new designer duds. It means that beauty assumes a more central, active place in daily life. With practice,

> *At the heart of that live encounter that we call beauty lies wonder.*

> *In addition to experiencing beauty, we make beautiful things in the work of art.*

beauty becomes a habit of mind. This mindset becomes an ordinary way to experience life, a celebration of the aesthetics of everyday things, which include the way the light falls across a sidewalk, the ironic graffiti on an advertisement, and the pattern of wrinkles in a weathered face. The habit of beauty is expressed in a thousand tiny adjustments and thoughts within each day, all aiming toward the highest quality.

Beauty develops the mind and heart, but I believe its power extends even further. Studying the writings of modern physicists, particularly of Richard Feynman, I have come to the view that beauty is one of the great forces in the universe. Feynman first glimpsed the possibility of beauty as an elemental force in high school. The story goes that he looked bored in science class one day as his classmates typically took three times longer than he did to solve a problem. His perceptive teacher, Mr. Bader, saw the impatient look on his brilliant student's face and came over and whispered a provocative thought to young Feynman. In scientific terms, he challenged his student with the notion that light, like all things, follows the path of the beautiful. That thought shaped the scientific yearning of one of the creative geniuses of our time. Feynman spent a lifetime discovering the truths of beauty in science, as the actual ways the universe works.

> Light, like all things, follows the path of the beautiful.

Improvising

Serious concepts: learning, understanding, knowing, connoisseurship, beauty. In his poem "Lamia," Keats warned that "Philosophy will clip an angel's wings." Let's restore the angel to full flight with something juicy—life jazz.

Jazz, our uniquely American musical form, is remarkable not only for the magnificent way it wears its heart and soul on its sleeve, but equally for its structured improvisational nature, the depth of its musical intelligence, and its raw life force. Performing good jazz requires profound technical abilities and musical understanding, and a subtle sense of the beautiful, all used to pursue a personal commitment to serious play.

The word jazz gets even livelier when you snoop into its etymology. No one knows its source for sure, but most scholars agree that the

Jazz (jaz) *n.*
**any strenuous
physical exertion**

Jazz was the word for sex.

origins of the word came to America from Western Africa with the men and women who were forced into slavery. The word jazz was born on these shores as a slang term and was used for centuries in early African-American English, the argot developed by slaves. Jazz meant any strenuous physical exertion, especially sexual intercourse.

Yes, jazz was the word for sex. (Few people realize that direct link when they talk about jazz music—there must be millions of slaves chortling away in their graves when they hear about the "Smithsonian Collection of Jazz.") When I write that work of art is life jazz, I hope to suggest the musical energy, the satisfying sound of the word, and some sense of making love with your daily life. Intercourse with attractive things.

One of basic components of jazz is improvisation. The key to improvisation is that you choose to enter an unpredictable arena, well-prepared. You intentionally take your skills away from a safe place to play in a danger zone.

Jazz musicians know some things about improvising. They know that luck has little to do with it—the more background and courageous readiness one brings to the moment, the better it goes. They know one can spend a lifetime getting better at it and that making it a habit throughout life improves the quality of one's music and the quality of one's living. Jazz players know that improvisation is a fast series of technical choices with personal skills. So fast is the choosing, in fact, they can't think or plan, they must rely on educated intuition. They know that improvising happens in the perpetual present tense, and it always comes with risk.

Musicians are not the only ones who improvise. All of us do it every day: when there is traffic on our usual driving commute and we contrive a new route; when we meet someone new who catches our interest; when we dance; when the child asks where babies come from and we stutter a response; when we lie; when we try to express our feelings; when we tell friends an anecdote; when we order a meal in a restaurant; when we make love with a partner for the first or five thousandth time.

The Latin root of improvise, "improvisius," meant unforeseen. This is closely related to the word improvident, describing a person who has foolishly left himself unprepared for the future. No wonder we feel the risk when we improvise; we hurl ourselves into the unforeseen. It takes courage. We gather what we know and playfully apply it to what we don't know. It's jazz. Personally, I think jazz and the Constitution are the two greatest gifts Americans have given to human history.

The artistic skills of jazz are used to improvise a life. We experiment, return, respond, follow intuitions, weave thematic strands together; we play with what is there. Stand-up divine comedy. Life jazz is our yearning cruising the streets to find interesting stuff amid the undeveloped raw material of daily life. It is the alchemy by which leaden life experiences are spun into gold. It engages all the skills of artists we have described in this section to play seriously, to make high quality experiences, in the present tense.

Environmentalist Theodore Roszak described the importance of life jazz in *Common Boundary* magazine. He said: "I see [art] as a new kind of wealth that counts for more than owning material things. I'm talking about art as something people do rather than consume, and do as a normal part of their lives: creative endeavor as a form of profound spiritual satisfaction. I don't think that creative experience is restricted, inherently, to a small group of professionals. It's something you can find in any child. If you awakened it in people so that creativity was an integral part of their lives—if we thought for example, that creativity was as important for children as computer literacy—they would grow up assuming that a certain amount of their life needed to be spent at music, art, theater, writing poetry, dance, or whatever the art forms might be. This would be a part of their life that was not spent consuming, destroying, watching television, doing the things the world now tells them they should be doing with their leisure time."[12]

This section has revealed the trade secrets of artists. These are the invisible skills that lend the art to their work and their lives. Now let's turn our attention to the three kinds of practice within which all of us use and develop these skills.

Improvise (im´prō vīz´) v. to act in an unprepared manner

Jazz and the Constitution are the two greatest gifts Americans have given to human history.

Life jazz is our yearning cruising the streets to find interesting stuff amid the undeveloped raw material of daily life.

Part 3

The Work of Art in Everyday Life

Chapter Eight:

World -Making

My longtime colleague, the composer Ed Bilous, once summed up in a two-word sentence three years we had spent together in Bob, the think tank group, thrashing around ideas akin to those in this book. He said, "So we here are. We have done all this thinking, and what it comes down to is this: *make stuff*." That may sound flippant, but it is no joke. Ed is right. Making stuff is the heart of the work of art. I prefer the fancier term "world-making" because it reminds us of the stakes involved and because the etymological history of the word "world" (connected to human existence) includes the complexity inherent in that "stuff." For the work of art to add dimension to our lives, we have to make worlds. Or, as Madison Avenue might suggest: to make it, you gotta make it.

In earlier sections, we touched on examples of learning experiences in workshops. Those experiences gave participants solid answers to *the* big question about why the arts are important to every single person. The magical ingredient in workshops that produces certainty about the value of the work of art is so simple: participants apply their skills to a worthwhile project; they get into world-making action, even if the result is partial or small. This "doing" provides everything of sustaining significance they are going to take home. After the last of the good things said or demonstrated in a workshop (or any teaching situation) have evaporated from memory, the new connections made in doing the

Making stuff is the heart of the work of art.

work of art remain active and growing. The process teaches more than the products involved; the reach and the reaching supersede any things that are grasped. As Francis Bacon said in his work *On the Advancement of Learning*, "Education is what remains after the facts are gone."

As we saw in Part Two, our yearning provokes us to engage our invisible skills of art to manifest solutions to worthwhile problems. In the process, we form unique, internally coherent, satisfying organizations out of already existing things—worlds.

Rarely is someone watching *As The World Turns* one moment, and making a world the next. World-making is not occasional, not incidental. A world-maker is actively investigating something that extends beyond the hands-on hours. The inquiry leads to the formation of a new "world," which stands as a provisional answer. The poet steps away from the television to catch a breath of night air; she spooks a deer in the yard, but it stops and looks at her. The poet feels something significant in the moment. She has a question about why the long human-to-doe exchange resonates in her; she strives with her best efforts and skills, for however long it takes, and produces a twenty-line answer—which sparks another question. The world-making process is inherently engaging, provides satisfactions, and a bounce.

Let's study three examples of world-making. The first two—storytelling and problem solving—are "normal," "everyday" actions we all undertake. We "just do them," rarely sensing that they involve the same processes and skills that artists, great and unknown, engage in. The third example will describe a small project in an artistic medium to suggest some ways in which the arts offer exemplary opportunities.

Example 1: Storytelling

Are you a good storyteller? Even if you say you aren't, I would wager that when the conditions are right, you are. For example, when you are engaged in recounting favorite moments to a new friend—the moment you knew you were in love, an early childhood recollection, the day you almost forgot little Laurie at the gas station—you are telling a story and making a world. There are many ways in which we apply the skills of art in telling stories.

The word "story" derives from "estorie," which meant "an accurate account of past events." Today, we use the word to mean either an accurate account or a made-up account, a fiction. We tell a friend "the story" of an amazing moment, and a child "makes up a story" to cover something true that is too sensitive or embarrassing to admit. A story can be fact or fiction; and the paradox is that any good story is both. Every truthful story contains fiction, and every fictional story contains real truth.

Fiction does not tell the literal truth, but it tells a non-literal truth, which may be as important or more, thus, literature. However, fiction and non-fiction are both worlds we make to tell the truth.

Let's look at some basic types of stories for a rough sense of how easily we handle those confusing variables with such artistic grace.

1) The Flat-out Lie

It is impossible to tell a lie that does not contain a truth. The child recounts that his pants got torn from being beaten up by older kids. While the excuse may be full of false facts (with some truths mixed in, like where the trouser-tearing happened), it overflows with sincere data worthy of a parent's attention. The falsehoods are constructed metaphors; they are symbolic necessities. They are composed with skill, with clever attention to the expectations and skepticism of the audience, and they are often performed with conviction that rings of the truth.

2) The Intentional Fiction

A child invents a funny and entertaining story about the day the purple elephants ate the puppies. While completely removed from reality in its images and action, the story's plot, symbols, and overall feeling hold very real truths. That child's inner strife and uncertainty present themselves in his concocting of this particular fantasy.

3) The Slightly Exaggerated True Story

You recount the true story of how you saved a colleague from making a big mistake. In the telling, you ante-up the stakes involved, maybe

Story (stôr´ē) derivative of *estorie* n. an accurate account of past events

A story can be fact or fiction; and the paradox is that any good story is both.

fiddling with the strict chronology to make the story better for the telling. You are using the tools of fiction to enhance and focus the true message. And even if you get carried away, using the story to impress someone, as you begin to distort the actual facts, you begin to report other truths about your wishes and needs.

4) The Hard Fact Story

Even a "factual" account of your car breakdown out in the boondocks contains far more than the facts of that rainy day. You cannot eliminate the work of art. It appears in the details you select to use and in the phrases you form to tell the facts. Just by bothering to tell that story, you apply the work of art and move a past experience into a special place for attention. The story immediately begins to do what works of art do, transform the ordinary. In this case, perhaps, the story tells of confronting danger, of fears conquered, of heroic accomplishment.

Think of a favorite personal story of yours. If you were to take ten minutes to tell it to me, and after listening, I were to attempt a full accounting of your artistic accomplishments and the skills you used in telling it, you wouldn't believe me. You would reject my long list as gross overstatement. Yet, I would be accurately deconstructing the artistic actions entailed in telling your tale. Following are a few general aspects of the work of art that we naturally apply in storytelling.

Every story has a dramatic shape of some sort, designed to attract listeners into a world of our making. We have had an experience (or we imagine one) of some significance, comprised of things we noticed at the time or after. In making the story, we craft a verbal world that skillfully captures that experience. This is world-making, pure and simple. We address the same challenges and choices that face the novelist, playwright, poet, Communications Director, political "spin doctor," campfire sitter, and every excited child.

In telling a story, we create a small theatrical-world that listeners enter to share the experience we wish to communicate. The following features apply to every kind of storytelling: a story-world has a

Every story has a dramatic shape of some sort, designed to attract listeners into a world of our making.

beginning, middle, and a chosen end; we "set it apart" from the rest of conversation in some way—saying, "I want to tell you a story," or, "You won't believe this," or even, "Once upon a time;" maybe we pause before we begin, or shift energy, becoming more animated; and then we draw the listener in, inviting the special attention that the work of art adores. At the end, we probably drop a subtle curtain of some kind, with a finalizing tone of voice.

In the improvisation of telling, we make hundreds of literary choices: which specific details are critical, which are not directly relevant but add good color, which symbols evoke just the feelings we wish to elicit, which elements can be cut. We shape those textual choices with promptings from intuition and memory, from our personal tastes and previous experience.

We don't stop at creating a good text. The storyteller is more than a literary artist; she is a performer too. We use our acting talents to guide our audience into the world of our story. We emphasize the significant parts, foreshadow the key words, adjust to what we pick up from the live audience, and build to the climax. We open a live actor-audience empathy channel so that our audience receives the humor or uncertainty or delight along with us, even on wordless levels.

All of the above is clearly the work of art. And we do all this work for the sheer joy of doing it because: we feel some wonder at an experience and yearn to share it; the making of the story is a satisfying creative act in itself; we can make a connection to others though the exchange. There might also be more immediate reasons for the performance: to teach, to make a point, to impress, to figure something out, to entertain, to duck punishment.

The work of art isn't limited to the teller of the story. The listener, too, participates in the telling, engaging in the work of art by feeling what we feel, imagining the images we suggest, seeing the world through the lens we offer. The listener leaves with those new images resonating, and we are both better connoisseurs as a result of the improvisation.

The storyteller is more than a literary artist; she is a performer.

A Storytelling Example

The making and receiving of story-worlds is so natural as to be unremarkable, yet it is strong enough to change the way you live. For example, a friend once told me a fascinating soap-opera-like story about the goings-on in the real estate office where she worked. She told me who hated whom, the sexual politics, and so forth—all the inside dirt. The next day, as I was running errands, I realized for the first time that there were seven real estate offices within a four-block radius of my house. I looked curiously into each one I passed. I pretended to be looking at the listings in the windows, but I was really spying on the worlds within, filling out the images from my friend's story, extending and grounding the imaginative soap-opera world I had entered through her telling. The impact of her artistic accomplishment was strong and immediate. It changed the way I experienced my neighborhood. This in turn provided me with new insights about the workings of the real estate world and greater empathy for real estate agents. When my wife and I sold our house a year later, we interviewed a number of agents, imagining the situation from their perspective. We were able to readily pick the best one for us, and I'm convinced we got a better price for our house.

Example 2: Problem Solving

Not every problem is fertile ground for the work of art. A foot of water in the basement is certainly a problem, but the solution is literal—a dry basement—and you will do much better with a sump pump than with the impulse to spin a good yarn.

Problem-solving becomes the work of art when the problem connects to an inner yearning. At that point, the tools of art become just what we need to solve it. As we choose to invest ourselves in solving a particular problem, we transform it into a medium for the work of art. The subject of such a problem may be almost anything: a friend's relationship, financial woes, a boondoggle at work. Given significance, personal yearning, and a new organization of the status quo, the actual work involved in creating a solution is fundamentally the same as in the

As we choose to invest ourselves in solving a particular problem, we transform it into a medium for the work of art.

problem-solving that goes into writing a play or a piece for a woodwind quintet. We may not produce "a work of art" in the process, but we get involved in "the work of art" from which we emerge enriched, more alive, and wiser.

The etymology of "problem," as "something thrown forward," catches the feeling about right, because problems are always jumping up at us. Problems are not inherently bad, they simply present new realities with which we must deal. We can approach a problem with the finesse of a river changing course around a fallen boulder or with the brute force of a tank charging enemy lines.

There are seven kinds of action within creative problem solving:

1) gathering relevant data
2) scanning it to find its organization
3) exploring inside the problem
4) gestating
5) experimenting
6) following a process toward a satisfying fruition
7) succeeding

Let's explore these seven stages (which do not occur in discrete sequential steps, but overlap and intermingle in real life) through a case history in which two friends transformed a financial bog into a field for the work of art.

A Problem Solving Example

This is a true story of a problem I was presented with and the collaborative process toward a solution. My friend Gary has money problems. He is a fine writer without much commercial success. He earns some money as a teacher and through odd jobs, but never enough to get ahead of his credit card bill or make his payments on a personal loan from a friend. He asked me for help.

We began with a two-hour conversation. The relevant data included much more than just the balance sheet of his income and debts. I needed to know how he felt about some of the issues involved, whether the personal loan was more troublesome than the credit card debt; how much he hated taking "money jobs" and which kinds were better and worse and why; what sorts of changes he hoped for; what he liked to spend money on. I was interested in the inside story of his craft work, the pots and bowls he painted as a hobby—was he willing to part with them? Did he have any other items of value he was willing to sell? I asked questions and took notes. Just by answering my basic questions, Gary found that the stuck and seemingly hopeless world of his predicament began to loosen.

In our second meeting, I began sounding out possible solutions. "How would you feel about taking a larger credit union loan to pay off all the debts? This would mean that you'd be paying lower interest than you are now on the credit card but more than on the personal loan. But you would be free of the personal obligation." And so forth. We tried out various possibilities, and finally I offered what seemed like the best set of arrangements based on what I had heard from him. We made scrap paper diagrams as I laid out the solutions, showing the specific changes required and their consequences. He said he would give the plan a try.

In the following weeks, Gary held a sale of his painted pottery (except a few favorite pieces he wanted to keep); he told me he had secured the credit union loan. We were closer friends as a result of the collaboration, and even VISA and the IRS came out of this caper happier. A couple of years later, I am pleased to report that Gary is earning more and is happier, is ahead of his debt payback plans, and has completed some exquisite new writings.

In our two meetings we delved into all seven aspects of world-making.

1) Gathering Relevant Data

We collaboratively snooped around for the relevant information— me asking questions and listening hard, Gary answering and offering his own trails of related thought. We each followed our intuitive hunches and natural curiosity. If a word jumped out, like "debt," we would play with it for a while to find its surface and subsurface meanings. Gary told me stories about his history with money, and if I noted a possible connection he hadn't seen, I would try to articulate it.

Artists gather relevant information for every project: an actor cast in the role of a labor leader most probably will devour that leader's biography and hang out at the union hall; landscape painters look and sketch before they touch oil to canvas. Research, however tedious, is never busy-work. It is a habit of the artist in process—for many, their favorite part.

The key word here—gathering relevant information—distinguishes this process from other related-information gathering tasks like comparing dealership prices on a new Taurus. Relevance opens the door to the work of art. The Latin root meant "raised up" (as in "relief" or the later French ballet term "relever"). Something relevant is that which sticks up to our notice. Today, we commonly use "relevant" to mean logically appropriate. A relevant idea is one which clearly connects to the subject at hand. That is fine, but two dimensional. A work-of-art mind works with metaphor as well as logic and hunts for the relevance that lies beyond literal links. To notice which information, among endless surrounding data, sticks up in relation to a problem, we have to improvise, using intuition and imagination. In this kind of data-gathering process, no matter what the subject area, we make symbolic and narrative connections, follow hunches. Indeed, this broader definition of relevance is a hallmark of a creative problem solver.

Relevant (rel´ə vənt) adj. something that "sticks up" to our notice

2) Scanning

Scanning begins as the information is being gathered (information gathering continues, often up to and past the solution to any particular problem). When we scan, we seek forms, connections, patterns, clumps of data.

Just by choosing the words to answer my questions, Gary made fresh connections, which began to form new understandings that adjusted his status quo. As he answered more questions, he discovered pockets of information that surprised him. More than once he said, "Wow, I can't believe I forgot to mention this…" He kept scanning his internal landscape for overlooked bits as I scanned from my perspective to see any patterns of organization in what spilled forth. We sought better, sharper questions through our provisional answers.

I did note a repeated pattern: every time he stumbled over a "forgotten" piece of information, it proved to be important. Three "remembered" items eventually became the focal points in devising an alternative financial world. When I discovered this pattern, I felt as elated as when I conceive a central metaphor for a new poem. This was inspiration; this was a visit from the same muse who visited Wordsworth, lying on his couch, remembering daffodils.

Some creativity theorists claim that categorization, the meaningful match of two previously unrelated things, is the fundamental act of creativity. As we scan the arena of a problem, we are devising new ways its elements might fit together, making a new world out of the pieces of the old. We pull together a new organization of that problem; we seek an order where there was disorder or chaos.

3) Exploring Inside the Problem

As the existing pieces of Gary's problem-world clarified, I ventured into the landscapes and looked around. Had I not listened empathetically (which means *as if* I were in his world), but only sympathetically (feeling for his plight, but not really stretching myself out, not becoming concentric), I might not have been able to catch the subtle clues of discomfort or surprise or interest. Such understated data provide evidence that is crucial in creating a profound solution, one that will grow and enrich rather than quick-fix and die.

One can enter the challenge as a technician rather than as an artist. The technician deals only with the logically relevant information and ignores the subtler surrounding data. The functionary can impose a technical solution to a problem, as a loan officer or an accountant might, but it takes an artist to make something with meaning out of this exchange. (Let me affirm that accountants and loan officers can be artistic in their professional milieu. My financial advisor Michael Berg is one of the most creative problem solvers I know, and his solutions to my money muddles are often nothing short of beautiful.)

> As we scan the arena of a problem, we are devising new ways its elements might fit together, making a new world out of the pieces of the old.

This kind of committed exploration applies to all creative problem solving: we try on various perspectives to perceive the problem as it actually is, and then we begin to play "as if" with it. We ask all kinds of questions about the ways it holds together ("Gary, can you tell me the history of this situation in five snapshot moments?" "What would change in the final two snapshots, if we made this adjustment to snapshot three?"); and we explore the world as if it were different ("Imagine you just won a thousand dollars, what do you feel like doing with the money?"). This is metaphoric thinking of the highest order. Artistic problem-solvers go into that problem and look/feel/think. They improvise until intuition gets a feel for the blockages, and then their imagination offers alternative possibilities.

4) Gestation

Gary and I took a beer break during our first session, but our real gestation period happened in the time between the two meetings. We chatted on the phone once or twice in the interim, making occasional mention of our "project." I would share a thought or a related incident and Gary might advance a few recent insights of his own. But we were letting the soup simmer down on the stove.

I sometimes thought of Gary during my day, mulling over possible solutions to his problem as I grunted at the gym. Sometimes I noticed with a start that I had been thinking about him without even being aware that I'd been thinking about him. Over the interim, I felt the dust of detail settle, and I began to see the forms of the solution I wanted to make with him. As sometimes happens, he called to make a date for a second meeting just about the same time I too was ready to get back to work.

There is a gestation period in every kind of world-making. We reflect, wisely step back from action, to allow intuition and other wordless inner processes to perform their roles. Gestation occurs mostly under the threshold of our attention, in our subconscious, while we sleep, daydream, fantasize, take a walk, exercise, doodle, put it on the side and go dancing.

There is a gestation period in every kind of world-making.

Daydreaming is among
the best exercises.

Let me put in a plug for the importance of daydreaming; it is a serious mechanism in the work of art, the Rodney Dangerfield tool. that gets no respect. It may not be "productive" in the overt sense of leading directly to a definable result like an insight, but it delivers essential goods nonetheless. Dreams (of the day or night variety) do not travel the way the crow flies; they zigzag like a butterfly. These tools of gestation go to deep places our intuition would like to tap, to worlds we know, unbeknownst to ourselves. The child staring out the window is often doing important work, training essential muscles, practicing her world-making. Adults must attend to their inner fitness too, with regular workouts in imagination's gym. Daydreaming is among the best exercises.

5) Experimentation

By the second meeting, I had designed a provisional solution I wanted to play with. The meeting required that I share my view with Gary and that, together, we improvise with ideas to create a new order. This meeting went pretty quickly because we had done our homework. We pursued a few "if-this-then-that" thought experiments. We used various means to articulate and document our choices: we identified key words, we broke the new plan into phases, and we scrap-paper-diagrammed a map of how the pieces fit together. At the end of that visit, I bowed out of my active-participant role, leaving Gary to continue to create the solution with the other players in his life: his friends, employers, credit union, the IRS.

6) Following the Process

We had launched the new world and now Gary carried the process forward on his own. His realization of the scrap-paper diagram did not play out as imagined: his craft sale got delayed; his father fell ill across the country, and he went to visit; he got an unexpectedly lucrative, but demanding, writing assignment. Along the way, his emotions jumped between extremes, but he managed to keep the solution process growing in the right direction.

In Part Two we detailed many of the artist's invisible skills of managing a creative process; I saved one for here: the humble capacity to follow well. The most visible features of world-making are full of leadership: asking, choosing, guiding. And yet, the realization of any new world requires committed followership as well. We become modest and respectful when we follow; we stay focused upon and interested in fulfilling the small moments; we are content to perform the necessary functions, which can be enormous—a single "executive decision" ("I will sell the clay pots I have painted") can have big consequences in follow-through.

Most of the time and energy of world-making is applied to just doing the work, finding and following the sequence of small successful steps that fulfill the "world" vision. Like Thomas Edison's recipe for genius, the work of art is also one part inspiration, and ninety-nine parts perspiration.

7) Succeeding

Gary is no millionaire today. Nonetheless, we succeeded. He has cobbled together a financial life that is organized in a more effective way and produces more satisfying results. Our work reduced his anxiety and frustration, adjusted some of his entrenched habits with money and his understandings of "debt"—we even discovered something fascinating about the way his memory works.

And he bounced. He got new ideas that carried into his next writing project, a novel about a struggling, down-and-out man and woman who find their way back to intimacy on a long trip to her hometown. He changed direction with his pot-painting as a result of feedback in the strong (positive and negative) language of the marketplace; he discovered that one kind of design really excited people, so he found renewed interest in the pastel splotches over white undercoating, and he pursued it. He took a fresh look at his relationship with his girlfriend, through which they determined they needed a "fairer distribution of responsibilities;" and they made some changes in their daily routines.

The most visible features of world-making are full of leadership: asking, choosing, guiding.

The Payoff

The work that Gary and I did together could have been a bore or an upsetting gridlock. He could have complained and raged, and I could have arrogantly tossed him a few idea bones to weasel out of the challenge. This would have entrenched our individual ruts, made no progress on the problem, and made the world a smaller place.

This didn't happen. Instead, because we both brought a courageous, playful willingness to the problem; because he was ready to reveal some unattractive truths and make changes in the status quo; because we were able to hang out in not-knowing the right answers for a while; because we could collaborate in the work of art; we found a constructive payoff.

Holding a delicate balance, in a touchy subject area, Gary and I made something of which we were both proud. The new world wouldn't have existed unless we worked together the way we did. Perhaps the sweetest part of the work of art is the intimacy of working with others in these ways—this is the good life, engaging with people we love to make things that really count.

It is my hope that you can bring the same enthusiasm and intensity to your next problem-solving situation that you imagine "artists" bring to a page or a stage. Take pride in the solutions you make, in their creativity and efficacy, and enjoy the side benefits: a fuller experience of life, new symbols, deeper relationships, and a fresh bounce into new adventures.

Example 3: Making a World in an Artistic Medium

It may seem odd in a section about everyday world-making to offer poetry as an illustration. In our culture today, poetry is thought to be one of the most rarefied, *least* everyday, of the arts. Even stranger, I propose a poem of my own as an example.

But I use poetry because I want to demonstrate that the work of art goes both ways. I've argued that artists use everyday skills; now I want to show how all of us can use our everyday skills to make art.

Art distills. Artistic media clarify. Poetry, for example, takes the very

This is the good life, engaging with people we love to make things that really count.

Art distills. Artistic media clarify.

skills and verbal medium we use to tell a story and solve a problem and focuses them on a specific challenge to bring forth something we know and want to clarify. In storytelling, words shape a dramatic event; in problem solving, words stand in for actions as the status quo is re-formulated. In *Kinds of Power*, James Hillman describes the potency of words in making poetic worlds: "Poetic language intensifies by packing lots of implications and references into the small space of a word or a phrase. A poem miniaturizes. It is like a computer chip or an optic fiber that carries many messages simultaneously. Such are metaphors."[13]

Four hundred years ago, Shakespeare distilled the power of poetry into these few lines from *A Midsummer Night's Dream* (Act V, Scene 1): "And, as imagination bodies forth / The forms of things unknown, the poet's pen / Turns them to shapes, and gives to airy nothing / A local habitation and a name."

In Part Four, I will advocate that you develop an amateur practice to bring the fullest benefits of the work of art into your daily life. This example springs from mine. I use my own poem, not out of arrogance, but out of authenticity. I happen to have the inside scoop on the down-to-earth process through which it appeared. Also, because I will encourage you to be brave in subjecting your work to scrutiny, I feel it is only fair for me to do so first.

I am not a master poet; I'm an amateur with the habit of writing poems to mark the major holidays each year and rites of passage in which I participate. The hobby helps me pull together my understandings of these occasions; it enriches the way I experience each separate Christmas, this wedding, that graduation, my wife's birthday, the New Year. I find I can rely on Adrienne Rich's claim that "poetry can break open locked chambers of possibility, restore numbed zones to feeling, recharge vitality."[14]

I selected this particular poem simply because it feels like a good one to focus on and because it connects to the themes of yearning, literalizing, and symbolization that are central to this book. It is a Christmas poem from a couple of years ago.

As the Light Hits My Eye

In the time before,
Druids and such
humbled and rejoiced themselves
at the birth of the light,
wept and screwed,
making the blue dye run,

smarter Christians
felt the ancient urge
to make the blue dye run,
and figured
the birth of the light
into their system
with humility and joy
of a drier kind.

Centuries have dried out
the star, the tree, the child,
and only by filling
with wild blue urges
does Christmas
give birth to the light.

In making this poem, how did I make a world? I engaged in the same seven steps we laid out for creatively solving a problem.

1) Gathering Relevant Data

I drew various separate bodies of information together to make this "thing." In my research process, I found these areas to be of interest:

* Druid celebrations (which I knew a little about): the spring fertility holiday of Beltane included the pagan ritual of males painting their bodies with blue dye, donning antlers, and going into the woods

to find hiding females. I knew this was a springtime ritual, not a winter solstice event, but so what?

* The metaphor of light: it is a perennial Christmas symbol and eternal verity, and I had just read a book on vision. What did light mean to me that year?

* Protestant Christmas celebrations: I had felt a dryness at recent Christmas Eve services I had attended.

These were the research areas. I did not have go to the library for the research of this particular poem, although in writing other poems I often check reference books. (I always use my etymology books; no surprise there.) Research in this case included reviewing my memory, distilling thoughts and feelings, looking for connections, and exploring the reasons that the subsurface ideas of wet, dry, humility, and joy kept coming to mind.

My research required me to clarify my own current relationship to Christmas: what was "relevant" *this* Christmas? What was I noticing in the world? I looked through journal writings, poems of Christmases past, and scraps of poems to see if anything inspired me. My research required attending to the ways the world was enacting Christmas that year. How was the economy? Were there any publicized cases of manger scene litigation? Did my sister's neighbor place a large plastic snowman among the manger shepherds in his elaborate lawn display again this year? (Yes.) And I listened to Handel's *Messiah*—yes, even that is research.

2) Scanning

While this research was ongoing, I was scanning it, sifting to find the key pieces that resonated, panning for bits that glittered and attracted me. It was the scanning process that brought the main subject areas into focus: Druids, light, Protestant rituals. There were other areas of attraction too, that didn't make the cut. My notes show I was trying to get sand into the poem and that I fiddled around with the image of animal horns.

My scanning was a questioning: What is it I want to bring out as my theme for Christmas this year? The answer slowly emerged as something gutsy. I found I wanted to go below the prettiness, tap into the big, dark, human stuff underneath holidays. In my journal I wrote, "I want to understand this Christmas—to stand under the holiday."

I fiddled around with lines, images, and questions. Why does every religion have light in its cosmology, and what is different about this year's Christmas light? What did Beltane sweat feel like, smell like? Why does "dry" fit with Lutherans—is this Garrison Keillor's influence?

3) Exploring the World

Even before I had the actual words that ended up in the poem, I was poking around in the relevant areas. I imagined being a Druid. I envisioned Christmas as if I had lived a few years after Christ's birth and was being told about it as a recent marvel. I imagined my way through a simple Shaker Christmas, through a raucous Gospel Christmas. I listened to the surround-sound holiday of my time and place: Muzak carols, street Santas, check-out line conversations.

A simple three-part form presented itself: before, then, and now. I was drawn to the idea of focusing on the thread of connection, from pre-Christian, through new Christian, and modern Christian expressions of December urges. This general structure allowed me to explore each of those three areas more thoroughly and to live briefly as if I were in each December across time.

4) Gestation

I usually begin my Christmas poem early, about the last week of November (right after the Thanksgiving poem). From practice, I know the process takes a lot of waiting, and noticing, and being frustrated; I know there are stages in which it blurps ahead. No matter how early I begin, I invariably end up in a panic to complete it by the time my holiday cards go out.

The reflecting is often the sweetest part; it allows me to walk down the street, using the poem as a focal reminder to attend to the immediacies of Christmas. (Each poem-project helps me to notice and make sense of what I see.) That year, however, my gestation's timetable had drifted me past "sweet" right into frustration. The process was not moving along well; friends' cards had begun to arrive, and I was still chewing on Druids.

5) Experimentation

I fiddled with forms. I thought a sonnet might be right, if I could make it hot and loose enough at the end. I kept looking for a sexy beat to suggest the gut-level world I was after. I tried playing mambo music in my head to see what the rhythm did to words. None produced results worth following.

Not every world-making process has a clear moment of breakthrough. This one did. I was vacuuming the basement. I was singing old pop tunes aloud—too loud for any dignity. I stumbled into the refrain in "Only the Good Die Young," a Billy Joel song I hadn't recalled in twenty years. The word "die" grabbed me as a pun for blue dye. In three seconds, the phrase "making the blue dye run" was playing through my head to the rhythm of that old tune. I left the vacuum cleaner in place and grabbed a pen and paper.

6) Following the Process

Thanks to the pop music connection, I was thrust into the hands-on construction phase, pushing and pulling words. I am used to this process and love/hate it. This was the only part of this poem's process that was full of flow. The song's rhythm gave me paths to follow. The three-part structure kept feeling right. The theme areas all felt important, so I kept making word choices, solving the pageant of problems in pulling all of those elements into one whole. My first post-vacuum sitting the next morning (my best poetry time) achieved an almost-poem.

7) Succeeding

I finished it later. I read and revised and tried a few possible adjustments. It said "done," and I had nothing more to offer it. I slept on it one more night before considering it complete and OK'd it the next morning—spell-check, print, copy. I selected my audience, sending it out to some family and some friends in their Christmas cards (I did not include it in the cards for my employees, business colleagues, or Jewish friends, although I now think I probably should have). There were two kinds of bounce in this "success." The audience feedback was strong on the Druid connection, so I determined to follow that for further uses (it has subsequently found its way into another poem). I also found myself curious to follow the use of song rhythms as the spine of poems. This became a new tool for me to use sometimes, and I still do.

How a Poem Is a World

If we were lucky, the poem worked; it drew you in enough, and had images and thoughts that resonated for you in some worthwhile way. The world of this poem is fairly unassuming on the surface with its simple words, accessible images, and that comfortable, perhaps vaguely familiar, rhythm. My hope is that it leads you into a deeper web of less-immediately evident connections if you are curious to explore further.

Poems try to generate subtle, particular fields of attraction that draw us. As a magnet pulls iron filings into an organized field, so does a poem seek to pull loose shards of understanding into a new order. All works of art seek to do this, and the media of the arts provide particularly inviting, multiple-patterned fields.

The world-making process plays with fields of attraction, too. I described my general notions about structure that served as outlines for the initial experimentation. Then that fifties song rhythm appeared like a magnet under the paper that held the pieces with which I had been working. Its particular rhythmic field felt right, which enabled me to make the choices to place bits in particular places, to cut and shape my intuitions into a definite world. The world of a poem must have a unified field: do you sense it would be awkward to mention Toys-R-Us in this world (even though that was the theme of my subsequent Christmas poem)? Do you sense that a long line in the middle would disrupt?

The magic doesn't always work, but it sometimes does, at least to some degree, even for a middling poet like me. The greater the poem, the more it has to offer, the greater the number of visits you can enjoy.

In terms of making a world, what a poem—or any work of art—does reflect back (to both the poet and reader) is who you are, what you know, how your world looks. It holds the mirror up to nature—idiosyncratic human nature—to show the symbols and stories that hold your truths. To paraphrase W.H. Auden, good writing makes us think, "Yes, that's *exactly* how I feel." Great writing makes us think, "Wow, I never knew I felt that way."

The word poem derives from the Greek "poein," meaning to make or create. This led to the Greek words "poema" (something made) and "poetes" (a maker). If you can permit that heritage to color your sense of the word poem, it becomes something more than a greeting card phenomenon or a flashback to high school required reading. Poetry becomes the making of significant things; a poet becomes a maker of worlds. Thus, we are all poets, people who can make significant things in a daily way, to keep us alive.

Other Examples of Everyday World-Making

There are many activities in which we make worlds without acknowledging them for the work of art they invite and the accomplishments they achieve. Let me reiterate that I can't see a lick of useful difference between the orchestration of my friends Alexander and Elizabeth's wedding that I attended and the way Alexander has produced and directed plays. Yet, we unthinkingly refer to the latter as art but wouldn't use that word for the former.

So far in this chapter, we have focused on work-of-art projects that rely on words. Now, let's look at another common project that emphasizes food and social interaction. This artistic medium taps our interpersonal intelligence above our verbal smarts. It's party time.

When you create a dinner party evening for friends, this can be a

Good writing makes us think, "Yes, that's exactly how I feel." Great writing makes us think, "Wow, I never knew I felt that way."

Poem (pō´əm) derivative of *poein* **(Greek)** *v.* **to make or create**

world you make. Of course, a dinner with friends doesn't *automatically* include the work of art. One in which you order a pizza and hope your guests scram as soon as the last slice disappears, clearly does not constitute a work of art. Remember the basic requirements of world-making: it needs to be an expression of your yearning; it is an absorbing process in which you organize an internally coherent expression that has relevant significance to you; it has some kind of fruition and bounce into further inquiry.

Think of some of the work involved in creating an artful dinner:

* *Gathering relevant data.* You check recipes and review available newspaper and magazine clippings; you figure who might be allergic to what or who loves/hates what kind of food; you ask friends for suggestions. This is the time you call to ask if your guests eat lamb.

* *Scanning.* You develop key ideas, a theme or tone that fits the people or occasion; you get focal notions that resonate, which you begin to build around (possibly the news you heard on NPR that the mayors of Athens and Sparta in Greece had just declared an official end to the Peloponnesian War, which began in 431 B.C.; that is something to celebrate); you check the olive supply in the cupboard; what's in the freezer?

* *Exploring the world.* You "go to" the "truce" dinner party in your imagination, as if you were a guest; you picture the visiting area, the light blue and white dining table arrangement; you improvise the ways you might mention the armistice theme, the kinds of conversation it might provoke.

* *Gestation.* You "plan ahead," allowing yourself enough time to think through the food and home-cleanup projects involved; you "get the overview right" before you get down to the brass tacks of

recipes, shopping lists, olive branch centerpieces, and cleaning up.

* *Experimentation.* You try a Greek recipe you've never tried, and you tinker slightly with it too; you listen to possible background music you might play (the score from *Zorba* just doesn't make it); the experimentation continues right through the event, as you improvise along the way.

* *Following the process.* You make choices, adjust and keep going: the store doesn't have the right cheese, one guest thinks the Greek theme is dumb, the electricity goes out during the party (as happened during our first party in our new home).

* *Succeeding.* You feel the enjoyment of your guests and your own satisfaction; you feel the forward bounces in: future dates with these friends, ideas for another kind of party, a recipe a guest told about, an image from a conversation that stays with you.

Flaunting Your Talents

You have been showing off your world-making talents, haven't you? You flash those skills often and not just in recognizable projects like dinner parties, poems, stories, and financial solutions. You flourish your world-making when you:

* create an original image or metaphor, even if it's in casual conversation;
* tell a joke, make a pun, or point out the absurdity of a situation;
* grab a pen and paper napkin to sketch out an idea you have;
* sketch a garden plan, or a flower, or a child's hand, or directions to your house from a particularly unusual starting place;

- try to find an image or description of a religious or mystical experience you have had;
- teach well;
- put together the outfit you will wear to an event;
- love holidays and fully celebrate them;
- write a thoughtful sympathy letter to a good friend whose parent has died;
- make a special gift for someone;
- seriously answer a child's serious question;
- construct a lie for a particular occasion;
- make a prepared speech;
- notice a recurrent pattern in your daily life;
- construct an elaborate sexual fantasy;
- think about the significance of a coincidence;
- imagine what it would be like to live in a particular home, to have a particular lifestyle;
- notice you have been humming the same tune all day and begin to think about what that means;
- find yourself pondering an image from a dream you had;
- make a choice based on your aesthetic sense;
- keep a journal, and especially when you review previous entries and come to new thoughts reflecting on your review.

Keeping Eyes on the Prize

Want to make a difference in life? Make worlds. Make them often and make the making a regular part of your life. Don't leave it to artists. Don't leave it to some other time.

In Part Four, we will deal with practical advice about developing a world-making habit. However, I have to set one essential priority in place right here; forgive me if this sounds harsh. We must always remember what we tend to forget about the work of art. What is important is the doing of the work: not you, not the reception of the work, not the quality of the resulting products, not how you feel about the work or how the work makes you feel, not what others think of what you are doing, or what you are going to tell them about your doings. The engagement in the process is the whole enchilada; everything else is a fringe benefit.

Nice extras do tend to appear, like being a better or happier person, making things you are proud of, feeling more self-esteem, being admired, having more fun at home and work. However, the degree to which the world-making process becomes a handmaiden to the desire for side-benefits is the degree to which the work of art becomes more difficult and less satisfying. Here is the paradoxical truth: the more you make worlds so that you will feel better, the less pleasure you will feel along the way. And in reverse, the more you make worlds just to make worlds, the more the positive side-benefits add up.

Optimism is a relatively new word in English, coined in 1737 by the philosopher Leibnitz who believed that the world is as good as it can be, and getting better. We may snicker at such seeming naivete, but this kind of optimism is one of our most fundamental and productive human traits, too often smothered by necessity, anger, distrust, and fear. Within every committed world-maker—however crotchety he might appear on the surface, however big the personality chip on her shoulder, however cynical the pronouncements on everything—works a happy optimist doing his damnedest to make stuff that is as good as it can be to contribute to us all.

What is important is the doing of the work

Optimism is the belief that the world is as good as it can be, and getting better.

Chapter Nine:

World -Exploring

The last chapter boiled down to the need for you to "make stuff." This chapter urges you to "get into the good stuff others have made."

In practice, the actions of art do not separate into three sections—one action leads into another quite naturally. This inherent blending of "making and exploring" is delightful to witness in workshops. Here's an example. The *world-making* exercise directs pairs of participants (everyone gets a partner) to compose musical duets in which one drummer repeats a simple rhythmic pattern while the other tries three different musical ways to disrupt the repetition. [The *world-exploring* purpose of the exercise is to enable us to respond more fully to a flute duet we will hear afterwards; the flute piece is distinctive for its rhythmic interchanges.]

Everyone goes to work. The sound in the room is the Bellevue battle of percussionists; I can hardly walk a straight line, let alone think. Yet, each pair is fully able to focus on their work and compose. Those who complete their pieces more quickly can't resist peeking to see what others have fashioned—they even try to hide their surreptitious curiosity like kids. When every duo is ready, the performance time comes. There is no anxiety or show-offiness in the room. There is nothing but eagerness to discover what solutions and clever musical encounters others have devised. The focus is total, the involvement complete. Because they shared the same world-making challenge, they give themselves completely to exploring the worlds made by their peers. If a stranger peered into the room just as a clever bit of bongo-and-chair thumping sent us into gales of laughter, he might be perplexed, but he would see the concentration, feel the intensity of world-explorers in action.

World-exploring is one of the great privileges of being a human. It gives us other people's best ideas in the best form they can manage for sharing them. When we direct our attention to exploring masterworks, we borrow the eyes of genius. In a very direct way, the connections we make while exploring a worthwhile world reconfigure our inner scripts; the fresh understandings provide more satisfying ways for us to encounter what we meet in life. For example, the rewards of the workshop rhythm-duets extended into other possibilities: delight in attending to the sounds of two subway trains approaching the station at the same time (instead of cringing at the cacophony); appreciation of the difficulty of the hand and foot syncopation of a teenager on the train who is immersed in his Walkman's music (instead of being annoyed by his aggressive self-absorption); a different kind of interest in the patterns of a verbal argument between two children (instead of taking sides or getting mad).

World-Exploring in an Everyday Way

Artists create worlds that are designed to reward our explorations. However, the skills of exploration apply everywhere, and the rewards accrue from entry into any well-made world. Let's trace three ordinary instances in which the skills of art are used to explore everyday worlds. Then we will take a detailed look at the some of the ingenious ways that works of art challenge, develop, and reward the explorer. The same age-old pattern applies to all kinds of worlds: we are attracted to something, and we follow into an exploration. Imagine:

a) You are watching a history program on television; the commentator refers to the Declaration of Independence. Feeling mildly guilty that it has been so long since you thought about the document (and even then, it was just to pass an exam), you haul down a dusty

When we direct our attention to exploring masterworks, we borrow the eyes of genius.

Artists create worlds that are designed to reward our explorations.

encyclopedia to look it up. Scanning the dull entry, you read that it was only in a late draft that Jefferson replaced the word "property" with the words "pursuit of happiness" as one of the big three inalienable American rights. The oft-quoted "life, liberty, and the pursuit of happiness," had originally been "life, liberty, and property."

This interests you. You have been having midlife wonderings about your priorities, questioning whether all that stuff you own paves the best route to happiness. So you re-read the Declaration in the encyclopedia, along with the entire entry on it, and discover that Jefferson probably based this change of words on the perspectives of the Swiss philosopher Emerich de Vattel, and he may have borrowed the phrase "pursuit of happiness" from the Englishman John Locke. In a seemingly minor editorial adjustment, Jefferson, one of your heroes, switched to a tenet that the nation's good lay more in the pursuit of happiness than in the possession of its rewards. Suddenly, you relate to Jefferson directly, as if in a dialogue with a living person. You envision him speaking passionately to friends about a book by de Vattel he just read (as you might excitedly share a book by, say, Stephen Covey or Thomas Moore). You picture Jefferson mulling over the possible switch of those critical words; perhaps you see him going for a walk to ponder the enormous change, property versus pursuit, noun versus verb. You read more, consider the implications, and think about this as a critical issue in America today—in your life. As you drive to work, the idea of pursuing versus having stays with you. That night you glance at the painting on the living room wall and think that it has probably been a year since you've really seen it. You take a long look. You've owned the oil painting, but you have not *pursued* it for a long time. You compare your old ideas about the meaning of that painting with what you experience now. Your world has changed.

That story contains all the basic elements of world-exploring—a wholehearted application of your skills of art—in exemplary fashion.

b) Here is another kind of world-exploring, one we all do all the time: listening to a story. This is one was told to me recently by my friend Ed Bilous.

Ed had been house hunting in Vermont. One house he viewed had a small pond in the front yard with a big trout in it. He asked the owner about the fish, and the owner rolled his eyes, claiming this fish had become the bane of his existence. He had caught it in a stream, and for some odd reason, instead of preparing it for dinner, brought it home alive in a bucket and released it into the pond. Every few days, the owner would toss in a scrap of bread or some other food. The fish learned to rise to the surface whenever he saw the owner, anticipating a goodie. After a while, the fish developed the ability to leap out of the water if the owner held the snack above the surface. It was a trick, a game. Over time, the trout grew bolder. Now, whenever the fish caught a glimpse of the owner, even twenty feet away, it would leap out of the water. Sometimes, the ravenous fish would leap so fervently that it landed on the bank. It would flop around on land until the owner rescued it by throwing it back into the water. It became a nightmare; the owner had to sneak in and out of his house so the fish wouldn't see him. Any time he was outside, he had to check frequently to see if the fish was flopping desperately on land, having caught a glimpse of him. He couldn't mow the lawn because the fish would hurl itself in front of the mower. The guy described himself inching along the ground in a commando crawl on his way to work. All because of the fish. And whoever bought the house would get the fish with it.

When Ed told me that story, I was fully engaged in my imagination: picturing the house, the pond, and the characters involved; empathizing with homeowner and fish; enjoying the comic situation. Afterward, I thought more about the fish tale, told it to others, noticed that its lessons applied to sections of the book I was writing. In those few minutes of listening to Ed, I world-explored thoroughly: I was *attracted* to his story before he began because he has a reputation as a raconteur. He caught me with a deft little introduction, "I've got to tell you about this amazing fish." My *yearning* was at the ready (I was ready to jump to his offered treat). I *connected* to the fish (as a freelance consultant, I feel the necessity to sing for my supper); and I strongly identified with the homeowner, *noticing* details through his point of view. I found myself thinking about dependent tyrants in my life; two situations came to mind in which I'd allowed myself to be manipulated into a "commando crawl" on my own turf. Through Ed's story, I laughed my way into a new awareness of the consequences of making people dependent upon me.

c) Here is an utterly mundane example of world-exploring. Occasionally, I receive a prospectus from a smart investment advisor, Mike Vulcano. Mike is suggesting I consider an investment in a company, and the prospectus is the official S.E.C.-required introduction to the company and the offering. A typical prospectus is about sixty pages long, dense, almost unreadable. Let's walk through my exploration of this formal, legal prospectus—a world about as attractive as an oil refinery. It requires tremendous motivation to plow into such a repugnant document. However, the chance to make money can sustain a bullish attraction. For an investor of my middling means, a prospectus is my best chance to discover the world of a company and determine if I would like to join it. So I get a cup of tea and put on my explorer's attitude.

First, I skim the document, looking for parts that jump to my attention: price-earnings ratio, risk assessment, capitalization, products under development, debt. I then follow those leads by plodding my way through portions that seem to carry distinctive news: history of ownership, the plans for the future. As I read, I follow my intuition and compare and contrast information with experiences I have had. I am constructing an idiosyncratic, but reality-based, three-dimensional image of the company. Is it a good world in which to place some of my hard-earned savings? After a while, I have made enough connections to get a feel for it. I begin to form a decision and a plan about participating in this world. Invariably, I bounce into reviewing other investments that I have neglected for a while, to recall those plans and see how they have developed over time. After a flurry of investment thinking, I find myself becoming contemplative, making metaphoric leaps into reviewing other kinds of plans in my life and how those investments have paid. I seamlessly follow the thematic threads of value, risk, and payoff from the financial world into the personal, from money-as-currency to time-as-currency.

The actual work of exploring this prospectus includes many of the same skills I use to explore a difficult work of art: attraction to connection to change and bounce. I use my intuition, relating past experience, comparing and contrasting, constructing mental images, working my imagination, getting a feel for that corporate world. It is no fun to read a prospectus; there is little beauty and no flair, but the potential reward is important to me. The world those words describe, albeit in unattractive language and data, makes a difference to me, my family, the financial consultant, and the many people in that company.

The Basic Actions of World-Exploring

World-exploring develops those invisible skills of art we met earlier. The more we perceive, the more deeply we can perceive; the more we accomplish as explorers, the greater our hunger for further adventures. The lifelong explorer gains the skills to accomplish William Blake's challenge:

> To see the world in a grain of sand
> And heaven in a wildflower
> Hold infinity in the palm of your hand
> And eternity in an hour.[15]

This is the paradoxical power of perceiving well-made worlds. By entering into specific, finite, well-made mini-worlds, we discover the universe. Active world-explorers often find Blake's grains of sand, discovering also the truth of the poet William Carlos Williams' quip, "Anywhere is everywhere." Skilled perceivers find symbols in the everyday; they see, feel, and act upon the presence of the universal in the specific. World-exploring is no more predictable than world-making: we never know what the next exploration will be like (even of the same world); each adventure begins anew. In spite of this perennial first-timeness, a basic set of skills apply, whether the encounter happens

Skilled perceivers find symbols in the everyday; they see, feel, and act upon the presence of the universal in the specific.

in a performance hall, the office, or the kitchen. Here is a quick reminder of the ways that some of the artistic skills we met in Part Two apply in exploring a world.

Yearning. We don't just watch or wait for "it" to grab us; we yearn our way into a world. Yearning provides a reaching toward "something" beyond what we already know, something we sense is held in a world someone made. This element is often lacking in Americans' experience of works of art, and it is the one that makes all the difference.

Attraction. The simple experience of being drawn toward something is the beginning of world-exploring. Such inclinations are promptings from your reliable intuitive sense of potential connections. The word attraction reminds us that there is something visceral, almost muscular, and beautiful in engaging with worlds.

Noticing. Once dancing the tango of attraction, we begin to draw distinctions. Certain aspects of the world rise to our notice. We begin to gather specific observations, draw distinctions, and perceive the choices made by the maker.

Connection. This is mostly what we do in world-exploring. We form all kinds of connections, on many levels, using different aptitudes and parts of ourselves, from the logical, to the emotional or intellectual, to the metaphoric. Making connections is the way we gain a grasp of a new world.

Change. We are changed by the connections we make inside a world. Perhaps not in a dramatic way, but in a very real way, discoveries adjust the status quo of feeling, thinking, intuition, and perhaps even behavior. These subtle internal changes do not automatically translate into changed behavior, although they do provide a basis for such growth. A new way of doing things results from experimental action based on those tentative new understandings. Yes, world-exploring requires world-making to fulfill its potential; you have to make stuff in order to make changes in who you are.

Remember this paradox about making a world: If we make a world *in order* to feel happier, we won't feel happier; but if we make a world

If we make a world in order to feel happier, we won't feel happier; but if we make a world just to make a world, we are likely to feel happier.

just to make a world, we are likely to feel happier. The same dilemma applies here: we do not explore a world *in order* to become changed, we explore a world only because we yearn to explore that world. If we read the Emancipation Proclamation in order to become more tolerant, it won't happen—because our intended result precludes the unpredictable, idiosyncratic experience of exploration. If however, we read the Emancipation Proclamation because there is something about it that draws us in a way we can't describe, and we engage with it, we will make connections that change the way we see the world. That expanded vision provides new options to try in the way we act—which changes who we are.

People often feel they don't know "how to get into" an unfamiliar world. They stand in front of a masterwork as if before an impregnable fortress, feeling small and incapable. They would like to be engaged but don't know how to start. It simply requires a little preparation.

We don't enter a foreign country as a whole—we enter through a particular entry point. Similarly, we enter a world through a specific entry point, a personally relevant entry point, or PREP. The PREP to a world can be anything—an idea, a moment, an image, a question, a turn of phrase—anything that grabs an idiosyncratic interest hooks the attention of our yearning. It can be the predicament of a protagonist, the form of a ballet dancer, or a phrase in a historical document. The key to a PREP is not whether it is an "important" aspect of the work as much as the strength of its grab on us. I will sign this guarantee: if something is interesting, it is important enough to pursue.

PREPS are quirky and different every time. Children are natural with them. Have you talked with children after they have seen a performance? They can have the strangest recollections. Six-year-old Alice once told me she had followed the butterfly at the symphony— I finally figured out that she referred to the way the piccolo played throughout one movement. Following one part in relation to a whole through a metaphor is a very sophisticated notion; we would all do well to approximate Alice's strategy.

If something is interesting, it is important enough to pursue.

Adults are usually more intimidated by the challenge of entering significant worlds, particularly artworks. We tend not to trust that our interests are connected to what is really significant about the work. Schooling and growing up have taught us that there is important stuff held in an art thing and that we probably don't know what it is and are likely to screw up and notice the wrong stuff unless we are careful. The encounter with artwork becomes much easier if we doff that knapsack of insecurity and rely on the inherent smarts of our attractions and yearnings—they are entirely competent to lead us to genuinely important discoveries. I tell my Juilliard students: for the mind to go to work, the heart must listen first; and the heart speaks the language of curiosity.

Here is an analogy for world-exploring: entering a new world is like entering a party that is already in progress. It can be intimidating; it can be hard to find ways into the ongoing activity. We have individual methods of coping with this entry challenge: waiting hopefully for someone to come over and speak to us, going to a stranger to make contact, heading for the food or drink, getting very busy with things like the books on the shelf, standing on the periphery and suffering, feeling so awkward we just leave. We enter the party differently on each separate occasion because there are so many variables: mood, the nature of the party, the people who are there and our relationship to them, and so forth.

But if we act as connoisseurs (using the revised definition), we never show up alone at the party, we hope for the best. We have our experienced intuition with us, which, like a wise and slightly pushy guardian angel, urges us across the threshold and into the strange party. We say we don't know anyone; the party doesn't look familiar. Our intuition angel will always help by pointing out specific attractions that provide a way to be in the room (the world) comfortably enough to get into the swing of this party. Once in, we play.

Works of art are famous for their parties. Let's attend one in detail. And let's use its distilled nature to point out some general truths about the exploratory process within any world.

Entering a new world is like entering a party that is already in progress.

First, two key distinctions about world-exploring that become evident in the arts:

1) *appreciating* worlds is not the same as *exploring* them, and
2) world-exploring is not analyzing or judging.

1) Appreciating works of art is a fine feeling to have; the world would do well with lots more of it. However, too often the feeling of appreciation becomes the goal of an encounter with art rather than a pleasant, but incidental, side-result. As a goal, mere appreciation is too soft, too generalized, to deliver the real power of full engagement in a work of art.

The term "exploring" reminds us that the encounter is inherently an active, improvisatory, challenging adventure. Recognition of the positive impact that well-made worlds can have on us—admiration of their excellence, enjoyment of an afterglow—these are sublime bonuses that can accrue from the arts, but they are not what you *do* when you engage within a work of art. We must focus on the actions of the encounter itself, to avoid attachment (detachment, really) to only this one kind of response, however pleasant it may be.

The traditional linkage between art and appreciation underlies the anemic American view of the arts as pleasant and peripheral. If we link art to its essential skills and verbs of encounter, to create positive change, we begin to restore the arts to their rightfully dynamic role.

2) Exploring a world is different from deciding if we like it or not. The habits of quick judgment, of simultaneous interpretation, choke the capacity to breathe in new understandings from the creations of others around us.

This view does not preclude or even disrespect interpretation and judgment—these are powerful tools, essential to the work of art. But left unattended and untrained, they are bullies; they strong-arm the more vulnerable actions of perceiving into submission. Interpretation and judgment can shame our wonder back under cover, will stand between our active receptivity and new experiences, will defend our

The traditional linkage between art and appreciation underlies the anemic American view of the arts as pleasant and peripheral.

current scripts and understandings with everything they have got. They restrict us from the transformative experiences of the work of art.

Exploring Worlds in the Arts

Let's dig into a detailed exploration of a small work of art. Before you read the following poem, pause for a moment's reflection; take note of what is it like to be in your head at this moment. Another way of asking that question is, "What is the quality of your attention right now?" This will provide a benchmark we can refer to later. Now read the poem.

The Pasture

by Robert Frost

I'm going out to clean the pasture spring;
I'll only stop to rake the leaves away
(And wait to watch the water clear, I may)
I sha'n't be gone long.—You come too.

I'm going out to fetch the little calf
That's standing by the mother. It's so young
It totters when she licks it with her tongue.
I sha'n't be gone long.—You come too.

While your poem experience is still fresh, see if you can recall what happened during your reading. Thoughts? Mental images? Feelings? Phrases that struck you? Unrelated thoughts? Associations? Do you recall any events in the reading process: places you paused, skipped, broke away, reread a line?

Let me invite you into a few thought experiments before we continue:

> * Take one of the specific images that came to you
>   as you read. Picture it again. See if you can trace
>   it: Where does it come from? Why did you

select that particular image out of the millions you could have chosen?

- Which feelings were the strongest? Were they tied to specific memories that the poem tapped?
- Did you take any "side trips," short detours in which you followed a personal train of thought, related to the poem or not?
- What phrases lingered? When you recall them now, do any have a particular feel?
- Think about your natural exploratory process, that is, how you proceeded through the poem. What features did you notice about your exploratory style?

Please read the poem again. Take a deep breath or two. Take another moment to clear your mind, to set aside everything extraneous, to prepare for an improvisatory encounter with this constructed world.

The Pasture

by Robert Frost

I'm going out to clean the pasture spring;
I'll only stop to rake the leaves away
(And wait to watch the water clear, I may)
I sha'n't be gone long.—You come too.

I'm going out to fetch the little calf
That's standing by the mother. It's so young
It totters when she licks it with her tongue.
I sha'n't be gone long.—You come too.

Once again, reflect on things you recall from this second reading. Thoughts? Images? Feelings? Phrases that struck you? Body sensations? Unrelated thoughts? Associations?

Did you notice different things this time? Do the differences say anything about the experience of the two readings?

What was the process of reading the poem like this time? What was the quality of your attention during this reading?

Can you generalize about the ways in which your first reading of the poem differed from your second reading?

Reflecting on Your Readings

I hope you found how much there is to notice in exploring the world of a work of art, even one as small as Frost's poem. In a workshop, we might productively invest a lot of time to unpack all that happened in those brief explorations. I might begin by asking, "What did you *accomplish* in the process of those two readings?" (That question often strikes participants as odd. Initially, they doubt they accomplished anything. If you participated in exploring the poem, I think you accomplished a lot.)

At the very least, you changed the way you attended. I had asked you to note the quality of your attention. It probably began as "prose" attending: logical, efficient, up in the head—natural enough for reading along in a book like this. But I would bet that by the second reading of the poem, your attending changed to a more poetry-appropriate style. You took in words in a different way, brought different parts of yourself to the interaction, looked for and created different kinds of experiences than you would with a paragraph of prose. You *did* this; it didn't just happen to you. It is a genuine skill you applied to strategically redirect your attention.

You know how to prepare. You clearly know something about active reception to a world: how to assume it, how to use it. I am sure you prepared for "poetry"—imagine how different your reading experience would have been if I placed the poem's words in a prose paragraph format. There is no such thing as "just reading." Reading is an improvisation of connections and noticing and choices. You have your own exploratory style, which is a totally truthful expression of who you are and how you perform the work of art throughout your life.

Reading is an improvisation of connections and noticing and choices.

You may not be aware of it, but you instinctively brought significant expertise to the task. You hauled some literary-analysis tools out of the old shed to take in the experience of the poem, to notice what the poet had done—even if it has been decades since you used such tools, and you can't remember their names.

Also, you did some imaginative connective work. You recalled images from your immense mental storehouse and put them in place in your reading experience: a particular pasture, a rake, a calf? Exploring those images—where they came from and why—can provide valuable insights. There is so much power held in our personal images that creative arts therapies effectively use them to restore a client's mental health.

Multiple Modes of Exploration

Let's use your reading as a reference point to clarify some aspects of world-exploring experiences. As I suggest some "levels" to elucidate through contrast, do remember that these are not discrete categories of experience, but fluid approximations. Levels of engagement change all the time; we may slip from distracted attention to a deep insight in a moment. Also, try to avoid the self-rating impulse; we *all* participate at *all* levels. The purpose of drawing these distinctions is to enhance our grasp of the optimum work, not to grade ourselves or to inspire guilt or gloating.

No connection. It is possible (in fact, common) to have contact with a world and make no connections at all. It happens a million times a day: among experts, artists, the well-educated, and the naive.

Even when your face looks interested, and you have highbrow opinions to offer at the end, you may have made no connections. Until you pay attention (reach out of yourself) and find your way in, *Swan Lake* may be, as a young student I was working with once announced, nothing more than "a bunch of skinny ladies with eating disorders jumping around in puffy skirts."

I recall a man in the third row one evening at a one-man play I performed at the Kennedy Center. He was moaning in appreciation

Levels of engagement change all the time.

during the show. I sensed that his grunts were signals of profound connections with my performance. Wow, was I changing this guy's life, or what! Well, I thought that until the second act, when I noticed his hand on his ear had a wire trailing into his jacket pocket. I finally realized it was a radio, and he was listening to the NCAA basketball semi-finals. It became clear from his dejection before the final curtain that his team had lost. My work of art was irrelevant to his drama.

In a concert hall (or any room), no connection can resemble the deepest connection. If the music is merely a pleasant background score to your contemplation of personal problems, you are not exploring inside the world at all, but no one else can tell. There is nothing *wrong* with enjoying the surrounding feel of a work of art without really engaging with it (indeed, this phenomenon keeps our orchestras in business), but such an experience delivers none of the rewards of a real exploration.

The lack of connection is equally prevalent in other kinds of world-exploring. You look attentive as the boss presents a problem scenario, while your mind is out to lunch. You keep an interested expression on your face, while you wait for that person to stop telling you his story, so you can start to tell yours.

Entertainment level. Let's call the first level of exploration the entertainment level. At this level of entry into the Frost poem, you might have imagined relaxing, pastoral images. You are likely to have seen the color green (even though it isn't mentioned), a pasture of some kind (probably from a distance), a small body of water, perhaps the cow/calf scene. You explored Frost's world in a flow of pictures, like scenic panning shots in a movie. You may have had other sensory connections too, such as the smell of spring earth or the welcome feel of sun on skin. There can be real pleasure throughout these connections.

The way poems work, you read words, and in response to some of them, you make connected mental images, relying largely on recall from your storehouse of personal history. If you pictured a pasture, you either: recalled one you had seen in life; recalled one you had seen as an image, say on television; or constructed one from fragments of things you knew. Even if the pasture you saw in your mind's eye didn't resemble anything you can consciously recall, it is still constructed from things you have seen in one way or another.

In forming images, your mind makes no distinction between: Aunt Lilly's field in which you got grass stains on your knees, an invented one you could create in your mind right now, the one you imagined when you read *Little House on the Prairie*, or the one you remember seeing on the television show of *Little House*. They are all equally valid in your storehouse of images. (The power of images is so strong that in our latter years, we sometimes can't distinguish if we actually experienced something when younger or only read about it.)

Dialogue level. On the entertainment level, "it" gives to you, and you receive what you like. The poem or other world provides satisfying thoughts, and you go with them. A more deeply engaged encounter produces a kind of back-and-forth quality, a dialogue—you and the poem collaborate.

Things are always less predictable in dialogue, which etymologically means "finding meaning together through words." If you engaged in the dialogue level of exploring Frost's world, you probably made leaps of connection less directly tied to the literal words: pasture, water, cows. The words triggered associations and emotional connections; you may have made leaps of intellect; maybe grabbed ideas or images from your personal experience and tried them out in this pasture world.

For example, the phrase "clean the pasture spring" may have sparked an improvisational riff in your mind during which you pictured a movie-like snippet of that action, relived a memory of doing something similar, or researched your memory for information about how springs work. Any word or phrase might have evoked associations and symbols from your past. Maybe some quality of the poet's tone of waiting to watch the water clear evoked a feeling in you, or something about taking moments for personal reflection, or something about the character's attitudes toward his work.

In dialogue, you are involved in a back-and-forth improvisation, full of specifics, in which you make creative connections between the artist's symbols and your own range of life experience.

Dialogue (dī´ä lôg´) *v.* to find meaning together through words

Metaphoric level. In metaphoric exploration, you slip into the world of the poem: you are Frost's narrator. As you explore in this way, you engage in the work of art as a co-creator with Robert Frost. You become concentric with the poem. The leaves, the calf, and the invitation to come become parts of you, not merely Frost's poetic elements.

As a result, the imaginative connection becomes less direct, less use-a-word-get-a-response. On the level of metaphoric exploration, "as if" becomes right now. You are "going out" right then and there as you go out to the poem, and your creative imagination is sparking a way to discover what that means. The calf is some sweet, vulnerable, tottering aspect of you.

You make connections of many kinds with wild, inventive flashes of association. Mental images are only a part of the experience. There are likely to be unnameable feelings, intuitive leaps, and narrative sprays of thinking.

Metaphoric exploration is almost impossible to talk about because it happens beyond words—before, after, underneath them. It is neither a tidy nor a clear experience. Metaphoric connecting starts things that it does not complete, inquires rather than answers. This level of connecting prompts us to understand many things, even though we can speak only part of our accomplishments. Artistic media provide life's readiest and richest opportunities for this kind of metaphoric connection.

I have tried to offer a few points about this deep level of exploration for you to reflect upon, but in truth, the appropriate kind of response to metaphoric exploration is metaphoric expression. World-exploring sparks world-making. Go make a world.

Other Aspects of World-Exploring

World-exploring includes other aspects of experience:

Feelings. Generally, the more deeply we explore a world, the less predictable the emotional experience. For example, a first connection with "The Pasture" probably evokes relaxing, gentle feelings; the poem is sweet and safe. As we relate more deeply, subsurface connections arise

Metaphoric connecting starts things that it does not complete, inquires rather than answers.

and can bring unexpected feelings. Indeed, deep connecting can be disturbing; "cleaning the pasture spring" could pose a frightening challenge to the status quo. I have seen people burst into tears when I spoke this poem, and they could not say why.

Deeper exploration is more fragmentary, less articulable; it is less "nice," and more "everything else." Entertainment reassures by confirming what we know; the metaphoric stretches us emotionally by drawing us into what we don't know.

Not all artists rely on emotional connections as key paths to enter their worlds; twelve-tone music composers, for example, actively reject emotional response as a tool. However, most artists use the emotional channel to connect to people. The arts use emotions with greater subtlety and power than any other media; humans have yet to exceed what artistic masterworks (musical ones, in particular) can do with emotions. Throughout history, the arts have remained a haven, a gymnasium, a university for the heart.

Exploratory journey. World-exploring is utterly individual. No two individuals would have the same experience of exploring Paris for the first time; even you yourself would have vastly different experiences on two subsequent holidays to the City of Light.

All kinds of things can happen in an exploratory journey. For example, in encountering Frost's poem, you may have flown a quick reconnaissance mission, checking ahead to see how long the poem was. You may have paused during the reading to construct certain images, perhaps the image of cleaning the spring. You may have taken a little side trip to an association or memory. You may have formed an image more than once. You may have skimmed or reviewed. The particular nature and sequence of the incidents of your perceiving journey don't matter, but they are grist for your mill. This is you at work. Your yearning, your intuition, your problem-solving style, your particular intelligences and learning habits are manifested and detectable in this process.

Some readers may have had the whole journey colored by a subtle flash of being in school. The overall assignment of "having to read a

Throughout history, the arts have remained a haven, a gymnasium, a university for the heart.

poem" may have awakened a ghost of English-class past; this too became a part of your reading process. Your past is your prologue, and if your past history leaves you unable/unwilling to explore worlds like poems, your past is your whole story—the book is closed.

Less-invested explorations can be passive, literal, or lateral: passive explorers expect the work to do all the work; literal ones trundle along, dealing with, and then dropping, whatever appears; lateral attenders ramble untethered, jumping from an image, to a noise outside the window, to a shopping list. Deeper reading journeys are, of course, much more involving, but they are not necessarily smooth and even. They may become febrile or uneasy because we ask more, look deeper, make fewer and smaller assumptions, nose around for subtext and connections.

The more deeply you can attend, the more you can accomplish in the work of art—and elsewhere. Imagine that it took one minute to read "The Pasture." When your attending is fit and ready, you can do an enormous amount of meaningful work in a single minute. Imagine that you can train yourself to have that kind of attending at the ready so you can strategically engage it whenever you wish. This is possible through the work of art. It is one of the trade secrets of artists.

There is nothing wrong with the lateral, literal, everyday mind; you would go quite mad without it. It is the mind that figures out how much laundry powder to use and how to avoid the person who drives you crazy at work. It plans well. It does not, however, provide the enrichment that you need to make life rewarding or full of beauty.

The Wide World of Worlds

There are many well-made worlds out there, inviting us to attend. Children handle this bounty with uninhibited appetite, gobbling up any world that attracts them (quite literally when they are small). Their capacity to explore is huge and joyful, and they readily trade their prior understandings for more satisfying ones, based on their exploratory experiences. What they lack in discrimination as world-explorers, they gain in openness.

The more deeply you can attend, the more you can accomplish in the work of art—and elsewhere.

As any parent of a teenager will report, young people go through a long phase of constricted exploration. Adolescents and teens need to dedicate much of their energy to exploring the seismic rearrangements of their inner worlds; they are enrolled in a crash training course in the intentional use of their work-of-art skills. Consequently, many reduce their expressions of curiosity and withdraw overt efforts to make connections, leaving only a narrow range of attractions that they fiercely pursue. I've known many teenagers who stay alive entirely through their insatiable passion for music.

We learn from these expansive and retractive phases of youthful exploration; we inculcate the joy of openness, as well as the power of passionately-selected engagements. Adults need a balance. A well-balanced explorer develops some sophistication in selecting the most productive worlds to explore and carries a good kitbag of skills with which to connect. Together, these lead to a regular habit of satisfying engagements. Imbalanced adults can lose the passion of their world-exploring or get sloppy about selecting the best worlds to explore. So, many are shaped and changed by worlds that provide much less than the greatest possible joy and understanding.

In selecting which worlds to explore, there are no absolute rules about which are empty and which are nourishing. We might be inclined to pass negative judgment on material as seemingly bankrupt as, let's say, Saturday morning television cartoon programs. They seem hollow to me. However, I have spoken about these programs with young people who were able to view them critically, from different perspectives, and to decode the programs' assumptions and worth. Our discussions were deep and worthwhile. Even "the worst" television programming can provide nourishing experiences if authentic yearning is engaged. I have also worked with young people to open up their understandings of the worlds of music videos and television commercials. Young people's visual literacy so far exceeds my own that I stand in awe at the abundance of meaning they can glean in what appears, to my first glance, empty.

There may be no world so vapid it cannot spark profound experiences of inquiry, given a sincerely exploratory attitude. (Let's not waste any

Even "the worst" television programming can provide nourishing experiences if authentic yearning is engaged.

energy testing that hypothesis.) However, the more vapid the world, the more energy it requires from the explorer to find value in the exploration. Conversely, there is definitely no world so magnificent that it can nurture an unwilling attendee. Rembrandt, Mozart, all the greatest artists, fail with non-explorers every day of the week.

There is a chicken-and-egg conundrum involved: Which matters more, the quality of the world or the quality of our exploration? The absolute quality of the world matters less than the quality of the yearning that drives the exploration; and the quality of our yearning is developed by the quality of the worlds we explore. Neither comes first, and they grow only together. To keep our yearning healthy, we must feed ourselves and those we love an ongoing diet of challenging rich worlds.

Let's take a short station break to directly address the world's dominant leisure activity, television. Even that billing understates television's influence—it is the No. 3 time allocation of Americans, behind sleep and work.

World-exploring and television—research suggests just how peculiar the relationship is. Surveys show that television is the only mainstream leisure activity that becomes less satisfying the more we do it *and* at the same time becomes more addictive. Studies confirm that most people turn on the television to find involvement in a story that interests them. Studies also find that 1) the more television they watch, the less involvement they feel, and 2) the more viewing options they are given, the more they skim rather than invest their attention in something they care about. Viewers complain of bad programming, demand more educational offerings, and then mostly skip such programming when it does appear.

Clearly, Americans play a complicated game with the worlds offered through this prevailing medium. For the purposes of this book, we must answer just this question: Can television provide worthwhile work-of-art explorations? Some of my artist-friends have answered "no" and given away their sets; others just say no by using the set only with a VCR. However, most find the tube to be an invaluable tool; they use it carefully and with delight.

> *To keep our yearning healthy, we must feed ourselves and those we love an ongoing diet of challenging rich worlds.*

Looking just at the home-screen viewing experience, be it with network, cable, or other programming, we must admit that television watching is a particularly unengaging medium of interaction. Cinema screen-viewing is enhanced by the dark, the minimized distractions, the collective audience attention, as well as the trip you made and the money you paid to attend. Television requires our sustained energy to engage with programs and to garner any rewards that feed our yearning. It is the rare program that naturally bounces us into generative action or reflection; most viewing pulls us toward passivity—the law of entropy is at work, whereas the work of art naturally contradicts that law.

There are, of course, "good programs" on television (and the occasional vegging out, even with dopey shows, is an honorable pleasure); however, it is only with vigilant awareness and keen selectivity that even the good shows can consistently serve our deeper needs. To find and engage with productive worlds on your home screen, you must be selective, wary, and active with your attention. There is nothing inherently wrong with the restful, passive participation that television evokes; just don't mistake it for something that shapes you well. The work of art requires that you be disciplined in picking precisely the programs that speak to an inquiry you have ongoing. Keep your attention active, even though the medium itself tends to lull. Shut off the set immediately at the end of a program. And most importantly, self-impose a reflective period, even a short one, directly afterward, to discover and grasp what was relevant. You must remember to do this, because the medium itself smothers the impulse to reflect.

So, here is the answer to our question. Yes, you can find worthwhile worlds to explore on television; and yes, you can create thoroughly enriching experiences with them. But be a vigilant, energetic explorer, because there is a powerful gravity involved that will squeeze dimensions out of your experience.

Empty worlds. We are surrounded by worlds that are functionally empty, by shapes (sometimes human) that deplete us if we pour our time into them. These worlds may be highly attractive on the surface,

It is only with vigilant awareness and keen selectivity that even the good shows can consistently serve our deeper needs.

yet they provide no nourishment for yearning or wonder. These are the junk foods of the spirit. Such tasty, fake food does not spark the personal work with symbols, questions, and narratives that keeps us growing and alive; does not offer idiosyncratic entry points; does not provide a glimpse with the eyes of genius, the bounce into new inquiries, the natural reflection within which we incubate our understandings. Empty worlds do not leave us changed or charged.

Middle worlds. Those who are not on a junk-world diet do most of their exploring in middle worlds. These are the works of our peers, the less-than-masterpieces of many fine talents, and our own good work too.

Life is filled with these successes. There are thousands of art shows in America every year. They may not showcase a single masterpiece, but they brim with worthwhile accomplishments. Business people complete important projects every day that don't belong on the cover of *Fortune*. There are significant worlds being made all the time, in living rooms and community centers, in businesses, schools, and universities—even in state legislatures and the homes of struggling single mothers. Explorers don't turn up their noses at middle-level worlds; they seek them out to grab the excellence they offer.

We need to explore these worthwhile-but-not-magnificent worlds with the same attention we pay to masterworks. These works invite, challenge, and reward; they require the same skills of perceiving and provide connections, insights, changes, and a bounce. In many cases, they are easier to enter because they are less complex, so their rewards can be more immediate and palpable. They may not speak with profundity, may offer only a single visit's worth of nourishment, but they have much to teach.

Masterpieces. Masterworks of art are the densest, most complex worlds we humans make. They have provided more meaning than anything else humans have ever devised. They reward entry at many levels concurrently; invite repeated exploration with deepening satisfactions; spark insights; widen our capacity to understand; give us potent symbols and stories with which to grow.

The arts are the most noticeable media for what we call masterpieces.

We need to explore these worthwhile-but-not-magnificent worlds with the same attention we pay to masterworks.

I have dedicated most of my life to the arts, wherein I have found most of the masterworks that have shaped me, and have seen their power to work miracles for many others. The arts belong in our lives as protein belongs in an athlete's diet.

However, the perspective of this book reminds us to celebrate the fact that the arts do not own the copyright on masterpieces. To the same degree that *Hamlet*, *Cosi Fan Tutti*, *Sense and Sensibility*, and *Citizen Kane* are masterpieces, so are the Bill of Rights, the Pythagorean theorem, the laws of thermodynamics, the periodic table, the "I have a dream" speech, the geodesic dome, and the Chrysler building. These masterpieces crafted in "non-artistic" disciplines can have profound impact. For example, the laws of thermodynamics reward my scientific curiosity, my poetic excitement, my systems-thinking, my spiritual interest. A reading of the Constitution feeds my interest in inner government, as well as my curiosity about business organization, pop culture, and trend spotting.

Masterpieces tend to appear in our lives when we need them and reappear when we might learn from them again. (Just today, I heard a baseball announcer quote *Hamlet*; I noticed an unusual angle of the Chrysler building used in an advertising collage; and the evening news referred to the Bill of Rights.)

A masterpiece nourishes any hunger that enters it. This is one of the qualities that makes a work a masterpiece: it is satisfying to enter whether you are a beginner or an expert.

For example, to whatever degree a high school student might yearn her way into *Hamlet*, she will find a world to explore and will find satisfying answers to the personal questions she asks of it. If I were teaching her class, I would be rereading the play at the same time, and I know a lot about *Hamlet*. I, too, would be discovering answers to new personal questions in my reading. As she and I read the same play at the same time, sitting across the same table in the library, or watched a live performance together, from our differing positions of expertise, we would each be having equivalently profound perceptive journeys with the same work.

The arts do not own the copyright on masterpieces.

Masterworks also challenge. Once you are inside a masterwork, engaged at whatever level, it asks questions of you. It challenges you to see and think differently. When I can wangle my way inside a Bach Invention, it challenges me to hear more deeply, to follow two lines of melody at the same time, and then three. Bach raises an eyebrow toward me to see if I can learn more about the relationships between parts and wholes.

I have heard a misleading argument against exploration of masterworks. Some people who are unfamiliar with the work of art argue that engaging with a masterpiece discourages the impulse to create one's own worlds. Their view says, "What the world really doesn't need is another mediocre pianist," or "I'll never win a tennis tournament, even at my club, so why bother?" I would answer: Why bother writing a love note to a spouse? After all, poets, hundreds of years ago, were doing it better than we. But we do it because it makes our world righter; because it provides joy just in doing it; because it builds something in us and our relationships. And, after we have engaged in our own articulation of love, we will treasure Robert Browning's accomplishments all the more. To the connoisseur, a reading of Browning's poems may well prompt an attempt to compose a personal love poem to a spouse, rather than crush the impulse as the skeptic suggests.

Going into a Masterwork

We carry a load of cultural baggage about masterpieces. Our insecure culture of celebrity tends to make demigods rather than respected colleagues of those who create masterpieces. We incline toward worship more than apprenticeship or collegiality. But having a worshipful attitude toward Cézanne does not help you perceive space the way he saw Mont. Sainte-Victoire. Admiring Martin Luther King Jr. is very different than seeing and acting with his vision of justice. Admiration and reverence, however satisfying they may be for all involved, are hands-off and looking-up; the work of art is hands-on and eye-to-eye. When a masterwork is placed "up there," and we are separate, less,

Our insecure culture of celebrity tends to make demigods rather than respected colleagues of those who create masterpieces.

small, here below, the separation inhibits exploration. You cannot be concentric and below at the same time. To perceive is to become a peer, a partner, with the master for a given period of time.

We may revere a great artist, but the masterwork changes us only when we reach through the distance of admiration to move inside the world as a co-creator. World-exploring is a commitment, whether conscious or not, to change daily life through the worlds we enter and to find those worlds wherever we can.

The framers of the Constitution would be far less interested in my veneration than in the fact that I think before I vote, write letters to the editor, and pay my taxes.

What Makes a Masterpiece?

The discrimination it takes to detect a masterwork is masterful itself. We may suspect something is a masterpiece if we have heard society tell us so repeatedly: if we have heard parts of Beethoven's *Fifth Symphony* in a dozen different movie soundtracks; if we have seen Andrew Wyeth's *Christina's World* reproduced on posters and cards. Americans confer authority on experts. We rely on a commercial/institutional art authority system to dole out the blue ribbons. If the "smart ones" deem something to be great, and/or it becomes worth a whole lot of money—it's a masterwork.

While there is some wisdom and efficiency to this system, finding our own masters is a key to long-term learning. A master is nothing more (or less) than a colleague whose abilities and accomplishments teach us important lessons. There is nothing better for us than to revel in the greatness of a master we have discovered, whether famous or not, without "expert" advice.

Masters serve different periods of our lives. I have had a long series of talented people whose works I have hungrily scarfed into my psyche, whose world-making remade my own, and whom I've left behind as I moved on to other masters. My own eclectic collection of masters has included Nikos Kazantzakis, Italo Calvino, the Beatles, Paul Cézanne, William Shakespeare, William Carlos Williams, Doris Lessing, Joni Mitchell, Alec McCowen, Susan Deri, Rupert Sheldrake, and Ken

We may revere a great artist, but the masterwork changes us only when we reach through the distance of admiration to move inside the world as a co-creator.

Finding our own masters is a key to long-term learning.

Wilber. These are hardly all the creative people I have admired or revered, but they are some of those with whom I served a serious apprenticeship (even though I have only met one of them in person). Most of these names are well known, some are not. They reside in my personal Hall of Masters, and I can trace my growth by walking through the Hall.

As a fun activity, I invite you to collect your own Hall of Personal Masters. These are the world-makers whose work has had a significant impact on your work of art, on the way you experience the world, study things people have made, and make things yourself. Let me suggest two stages to this activity: 1) gather the nominees, 2) design the Hall.

First, gather lots of nominees, more than you will finally enshrine. Jot down everyone whose invented worlds might have had a formative influence on you. Consider lots of possibilities: childhood influences, teachers-by-example, local characters, writers or artists who caught your passion, celebrities. Remember, these are not heroes who have had an impact on you, but those whose *created worlds* have had an impact on how you have created your world.

Once the nominees are in, begin the selection process. You will need to create your own specific selectivity question. This will be the test you apply to each nominee to determine if he or she really meets your Master criteria. You might want to think about issues such as: Did this person's creations make a permanent change in your inner culture, in who you are, in the way you make sense of life? Did you completely dedicate yourself for a time to a study of how this person made worlds?

Whatever your final wording, write down your acid-test question so it won't shift around during the final cut. And then select. You can be as generous or rigorous as you want; your number of enshrined Masters is no reflection of your worth.

If you are enjoying this game, go a step further to design the Hall. You may want to draw an actual sketch or perhaps just make a mental model. How is each master represented? By traditional bust-statue or in a more original way? How is the Hall laid out? Who goes where and why? Is the arrangement chronological, or is there a more intuitive design? Do you want to have little plaques or statements about each inductee? What do you want a visitor's experience in this Hall to be like? What would you like us to be feeling and thinking as we move through? How will you encourage that kind of experience? Colors? Lighting? Sound? Location? Do you want to have an induction ceremony—what would happen in that ritual of honoring?

The work you did in that imagination game is connoisseurship in the highest degree. You treated your life as if it were filled with encounters with great masters (which it is); you looked at your personal history as if it were as jam-packed as the Metropolitan Museum of Art's storage rooms, with you as the curator decisively placing the appropriate Masters on display.

A Lifelong Relationship with a World

I have claimed that masterpieces of the arts are the richest worlds humans have made. They invite many visits and provide new discoveries every time. Here is a personal example.

I have been a passionate explorer of *Hamlet*. It was the dominant artistic passion of the first half of my adult life. I read *Hamlet* again and again; I played it several times as an actor, directed it, repeated soliloquies constantly as I washed dishes and trained for marathons.

Every time I took a fresh approach to the play, it had something new to tell me. Say I had ignored it for a year and returned to it on a Saturday rereading—it seemed to have rewritten itself with a whole new meaning in the time I was gone. Now I knew what it was *really* about!

Reviewing old journals and notes, I came to realize that each new understanding was a perfect expression of what I was trying to come to grips with in my life at that time. *Hamlet's* themes were my themes and vice versa.

For example, in my early twenties, I believed Shakespeare had written a play about the birth of a new kind of society within an archaic system (yes, this one appeared in the late sixties and early seventies). In my mid-twenties, I "discovered" that *Hamlet* was the story of simple goodness trying to find authentic expression in a corrupt world (during this time, I was an idealistic actor, angry at the idiocies of the theater business). Then, I finally *got* it. The play was a model for how to be a responsible citizen and a fallible human at the same time (do you detect thirtysomething thinking?).

More recently, in my forties, I have rediscovered *Hamlet* as a whopping-good story about the development of consciousness—the inadequacy of mere logic and the growth toward complexity of understanding. (You can draw your own conclusions about what this suggests about my current state of mind.) The point is that my relationship to this world was, and continues to be, a rich, ongoing exchange. As I enter into *Hamlet* each time, I see my world anew and with greater clarity. This process made me a better actor and director. It makes me a better teacher and friend, a better husband and person. It enables me to make things better.

This ongoing pursuit launched me into many studies to get more information. Of course, I dug into Shakespeare's text, as well as the writings of critics and scholars. I also drank in performances of *Hamlet*—good ones and breathtakingly bad ones. Every one had something to teach me. *Hamlet* set in a spaceship didn't teach me much, but the Ophelia in this production brought the mad speeches to life in ways I had never seen before. Kevin Kline's *Hamlet* had many clever turns of comic mind and fascinating juxtapositions of scenes. Raye Birk's *Hamlet* was full of fresh rhythms and emotional flips. Richard Burton was so sad, and Nicol Williamson taught me how to use contemporary style; Olivier taught me about romance; Gielgud pointed to places where the poetry can be prominent without losing the gut feel; Mel Gibson showed me simple down-to-earth places that I had been too fancy about. Even my twenty-two-year-old Hamlet understudy at a regional theater unintentionally pointed out a few passages I could improve. I say unintentionally because it is "not done" for an understudy to give the lead actor tips, but I hid behind a curtain like Polonius (so as not to intimidate him) during an understudy rehearsal to hear if there was anything I could learn from him. Lucky for me, I picked up two new line readings and an extra comedic turn of phrase. So, all these other people who were pouring their best into *Hamlet* were peers and teachers. I was not comparing myself with Richard Burton, I was working with him. I was not outraged when a wonderful, big budget, high-visibility production had a Shakespeare-novice movie star for the Prince. I was not condescending when a "kid" did a mediocre job. All contributed to my lifelong process, and I "borrowed" at will.

Exploring Our Own Stuff

Exploring our own work presents unique difficulties. Theoretically, it should be the same to explore our own work and that of others. For example, I *should* approach the charcoal sketch I made of the meadow in front of my new house with the same mindset I bring to a Cézanne landscape. But, quite honestly, if I bring my Cézanne eyes to my Booth sketch, I'm disgusted at what a rotten sketcher I am. I know the difference between good and bad, and my drawing is *bad*. Hardly the nurturing attitude that encourages an artist's creative passion!

I am not alone in this tough-guy attitude toward my work. I hear it all the time. I hear people in workshops say the harshest things about their own efforts: "This stinks," "How pitiful," "I am hopeless," and plenty of four-letter words.

The process of brutal judgment usually begins before the work is complete, or even before the work has begun. I hear: "I'm a horrible painter," "Keep a place in the garbage can for this one," "Here comes a waste of a good piece of paper."

Young children do not have this harsh mindset. From what I have observed, it seems to appear at around age nine. (Developmental psychologists suggest that this attitude emerges from the realization of being judged, of comparative analysis being applied to us and by us, and the unpleasant discovery that we are seriously lacking in some areas.) A younger child believes her every drawing belongs on the school display board or in a museum or on the refrigerator door. Pre-judgmental world-makers love their work and have limitless respect for their own talents. I still delight in remembering the six-year-old who

The process of brutal judgment usually begins before the work is complete, or even before the work has begun.

answered my question about her drawing of a house with, "Well, I think it is probably the best drawing anyone ever made." That jig of confidence is up once we reach double digits, and for many adults, the jig is never danced again.

For most of us, the world-maker's jig becomes a tough trek to see the value within our mediocrity, the bits of gold within the somewhat muddy stream.

The capacity to explore our own creations, recognizing the accomplishments they hold, is one of the critical skills of the work of art. To do this, we must set aside prejudice and judgment, perceive with clarity, discover what works, celebrate process, and bounce ahead. If we can engage in an open exploration of our own work, we magnify our artistic skills, our engagement, and our pleasure in living.

We must place each exploration in the context of a journey of improvement. We don't have to show a world we have made to anyone, but we do have to be able to perceive it ourselves with openness, without flinching. My next meadow sketch will be more satisfying.

This ability to perceive the weak parts within a positive whole is also a critical capacity in a marriage. A mistake, a fight along the way, is not the end of it all, but rather an important piece of a process. A failure is full of valuable data if, like artists, we can look at it for its content, take a process perspective that decodes the key information. Compare an artist to a marital partner. If every time she completed a sketch that was not perfect, she contemplated giving up the art, she wouldn't ever get anywhere worthwhile. Same with a relationship; the canvas is an interpersonal dialogue in the mixed media of love—paint and paint again.

The Three-Action Synergy

Have you noticed that the deeper you get into world-making and world-exploring, the more similar they sound? This is inevitable. A significant part of world-making is exploring the world you yourself are constructing; and a significant part of world-exploring is constructing the fresh creative connections inside the other person's world. At their

If we can engage in an open exploration of our own work, we magnify our pleasure in living.

The canvas is an interpersonal dialogue in the mixed media of love—paint and paint again.

deepest levels, these two actions become almost indistinguishable, supporting one another in active synergy. Perhaps the only fundamental distinction between the two is the direction of the energy: making things has an outward energy, applying effort to making a new shape; while the perceiving energy moves inward, making new understandings based on the new shapes you explore.

These two actions also feed one another; get out of the way, and they spring from one to the other. We see this with children. After studying something they love, they instantly want to *make* something. At age three, my niece Darcy was taken to see the musical *Brigadoon* and was already composing her own musical in the back seat on the way home.

If you are a world-maker, you naturally become curious to investigate the worlds of others. Carve a statue out of wood, and suddenly you yearn to re-explore what Brancusi did, what the Dogon carvers in Mali do, how wood grain is formed, how faux-wood grain is produced, etc. Decide to redecorate your living room, and you get interested in what neighbors have done with their living rooms. Extend yourself into a world you are making, and you yearn to experience similar worlds well-made by others.

Extend yourself into a world you are making, and you yearn to experience similar worlds well-made by others.

Review

Let's review some of the key points about world-exploring:

* We are surrounded by worlds that reward our exploration. Some are masterpieces we can explore for a lifetime, but most are not. We dedicate too little of our time to explicit world-exploring, and we would benefit from more.

* The essential components of world-exploring are: a personal yearning to discover, attraction to parts of the world, PREParation, curiosity and specific noticing, an improvised encounter made of connections, change, and a bounce.

* World-exploring is a natural companion to world-making and reading the world; these actions feed, support, and complement one another. To separate them, or omit one, undermines the potential of all three.

* There are different levels at which we can connect, which provide different kinds of rewards as we go deeper.

* Practice trains the ways we can attend, making deeper experiences possible.

* World-exploring is not analyzing or judging. Perceiving is not interpreting. Explorations are playful interactions in which we become co-creators with the world maker.

* We need to be strategic in selecting the worlds that will serve us best. We are surrounded by so many options and so many empty worlds that being passive in our selection process leads to dead-ends and depletion. This is particularly true for watching television, where, to succeed, we must choose carefully, stay very attentive, turn the tube off at the end of a chosen show, and remember to reflect.

* The capacity to explore our own work without prohibitively negative judgment and discover what it holds is a critical skill.

The poet Adrienne Rich writes, "A poem can't free us from the struggle for existence, but it can uncover desires and appetites buried under the accumulating emergencies of our lives, the fabricated wants and needs we have had urged on us, have accepted as our own."[16]

With our personal desires and needs (our yearning) revealed to us through explorations of worlds well-made by others, we can successfully go to work in the ultimately ephemeral and most-precious artistic medium—daily life.

Chapter Ten:

Reading the World

A psychologist from the then-USSR, Alexander Luria, undertook a study of peasants in remote areas of Uzbekistan and Kirghizia in the 1930s. He studied how language influences the way people think. The conditions for his research were difficult, leading to scientifically incomplete conclusions. However, his groundbreaking insights prompted subsequent researchers to continue his studies. Luria's beginnings have led to many discoveries, one of which is stated by Barry Sanders in *A Is for Ox*, "An individualized consciousness forms only in literacy....Reading and writing radically alter perception. There seems to be no such thing as a little literacy. Even the smallest amount of literacy begins to alter perception. Almost immediately it has the effect of lifting a person out of group thinking and setting him or her back down in a more self-centered and abstract world."[17] You can see why a repressive Soviet government was not keen to have Luria pursue a line of research that eventually led to that conclusion.

Luria noticed that people who could not read or write did not fully engage in abstract thought. In their comprehension process, they had to link abstract concepts with tangible things from their experience in order to understand them. For example, a circle could represent a tire or the moon to them. However, they were not comfortable with a circle representing something abstract, like roundness or wholeness. Luria recorded that this lack of capacity for abstraction had nothing to do

People who could not read or write did not fully engage in abstract thought.

with an individual's intelligence or even imagination or creativity. A person can be clever and capable, but without literacy (even just a little of it), that soul is blocked from full participation in thought.

Luria's data substantiate a truth we observe in young children. The pre-literate child is likely to have a delightfully wacky imagination and unfettered powers of symbolization, but until she learns to read and write (which ideally should not be urged on a child too early; let a child create a rich oral world first), she works within the limits of her tangible world. When she becomes able to do things with written symbols, she cracks open another carapace of understanding.

People can get along without literacy. Luria's intelligent but illiterate manual workers made decent lives for themselves, but such lives are unnaturally constricted. Gone are explorations of all the great books, any capacity to express oneself in writing, and, cruelest of all, ready access to abstract thought with which to construct one's own sense of life. Would you call such a life an enviable one? Can a person with such important doors locked shut discover his inherent potential, offer his best contributions to make the world a better place? Of course not.

The capacity to "read the world" is a kind of literacy too, and it shares some features with the literacy Luria studied. Both are complex proficiencies with inherent human skills; the basics of both are usually learned when young and improved for a lifetime; both enable us to grasp the significance of common symbols we encounter throughout our days and to do meaningful things with these symbols to communicate our understanding; both challenge and feed our yearning.

Luria's research sparked the finding that word-literacy opens an entire region of experience; so does world-reading. Literacy in the symbols of our daily lives opens the realm of experience beyond the surface of things; it opens doors to the fullness of being alive. It requires the skills of art to begin attending to the full story of reality.

If we cannot learn to read the world in this artistic way, we can keep life and limb together, but we cannot make full connections with people, overcome the anger or depression that result from the paradoxical, illogical, and upsetting experiences we encounter

Literacy in the symbols of our daily lives opens the realm of experience beyond the surface of things; it opens doors to the fullness of being alive.

everywhere, sustain our lifelong learning, or offer our best contributions to the world. Without literacy in reality, we bury our entelechy.

How to Just Do It

What do you *do* to read the world? The answer is less specific than for our first two angles of world-work; you neither make tangible stuff, nor explore someone else's creation. To read the world, you put on an attitude, *the* attitude we met in Part Two. You might like to picture it as a set of eyeglasses you put on, or a mindset you adopt for looking at things you encounter as you proceed with what you normally do. In other words, as opposed to *what* you do in the dedicated work-of-art occasions of world-making or world-exploring, reading the world is about *how* you apply your work-of-art skills everywhere else. The work-of-art cycle begins to spin its transformative magic only when we ply our skills upon the raw material of daily reality.

A world-making poet discovers a perfect phrase and creates a context to share its impact. A world-exploring reader makes a new understanding in connecting to the line the poet has made. The world-reader notices a phrase in an overheard snippet of conversation and plays with it to see if it offers anything of personal value—which clarifies a perfect phrase as the seed of a new poem.

You can switch to this perspective in a flash, just by choosing to. It is my hope that these pages have prompted you to don those glasses a number of times, to look across your life in "as if" ways—most obviously, looking at the small events of your life as if they were important (because they are). The practice of reading your world means ready access to experiencing your day as if it were intentionally packed with attractive objects and surprising opportunities.

It really works. Change the way you attend to objects and opportunities, and they change before your very eyes. Use a different perspective, and you see more. Adopt *the* attitude, and discover a satisfying world presented for you to read.

In practical terms, the same skills of art apply here as to the other actions of the work of art. Your yearning must be active, prompting

> To read the world, you
> put on an attitude.

Posing questions is
the central act of
reading the world; it
must become a habit.

you to engage with things that attract you, then to inquire into them to make satisfying connections, which bounce you into related action.

Posing questions is the central act of reading the world; it must become a habit. You will ask yourself: "Why is that photo on my bulletin board?" "Why did I hate that hat worn by the lady in the car I just passed?" "What patterns appear in this chatty conversation; where else do I create patterns like that?"

I wish I could give you a handy kitbag of reliable questions to try, but there can be no prescribable set of sure-fire questions. The whole game is one giant improvisation; it is unplannable. Also, the questions themselves are far less important than the habit of questioning.

I have never met anyone who reads the world regularly by *remembering* to do so. I doubt it can be done. We deal with so much activity in moment-to-moment mental, physical, emotional, and circumstantial daily life, we are busy with so many things, that we can't remind ourselves often enough, "Oh yes, it is time to look at this moment 'as if'…" Even if we programmed a watch to beep every hour as a reminder to read the world that moment, it wouldn't work. World-reading requires a habit of readiness to follow attractions as they fleetingly appear, of sensing which grains of sand may offer universes.

Here is an example of one way the world-reading habit might appear in everyday life. Let's say you witness a clothing store dispute in which a clerk requires a receipt with a returned pair of jeans from a customer who says she never got one. You watch it as more than a retail melodrama. In reading the world, you choose to see the dispute as if it were full of relevant information for you personally, and so you slip below the surface altercation (in which you attend to whom you agree, who argues better, who is likely to win) to attend to with this universal drama about individuals and institutions fairness, rights, and trust. Having actively attended with your response-ability, you then transform what you discovered into something more, into things like advice (creative suggestions about how the two might resolve the dilemma), a new understanding (a sense of the criteria that you use to determine fairness in disputes you must manage elsewhere), new kinds of action or influence (a renewed sense that it is fair to ask to see your child's homework, or a new resolve to keep all your receipts collected in one place).

You attend to the ordinary as if it were extraordinary in some way. And then it is.

I have put one of my world-reading habits on display in these pages—etymology. I attend to the words I use as if they were good stories. A word catches my attention, and I dig into its history. In doing so, I regularly find provocative insights. Indeed, for me, this particular habit has prompted some of the deepest world-making of my life. I am in the habit of looking at this ordinary thing called a word as if it held something valuable. Almost every word does. And even when an etymology turns out to be dully predictable, the action of inquiring nurtures my habit for the next discovery.

The word "read" itself holds the secret of world-reading. Etymologically, the verb to "read" includes far more than a capacity to identify and use word symbols. Originally, the verb meant "to advise," "to inform," "to interpret." Add these extensions to our more mechanical understanding, and reading becomes a constructive, creative act. Thus, reading-the-world earns its position as the sister action to world-making and world-exploring; same work-of-art family, merely using different media and playing for different rewards.

Read (rēd) *v.* to advise, inform, or interpret

This expanded definition of "reading" requires that we:

1) *perceive* with clarity;
2) *assimilate* what we perceive (make the impressions "similar to," or "like" something we know to connect with them);
3) *use* the new connection in some way.

The person functioning at one extreme of world-reading is closed-down and completely literal. This individual casts glances across the pages of life, taking in only enough information to pass the upcoming tests. People cannot speed read their way through daily life and expect to assimilate deeper meaning from their experience.

At the opposite extreme of world-reading would be a wide-open, incessant, deep-meaning seeker. I picture this soul walking down a city sidewalk, goggle-eyed in amazement, finding profound messages in the sidewalk cracks, the shapes of the litter. Not a recommended way to live. (Later in this chapter, I will tell the story of an extreme experiment I posed myself: to read the world as fully as possible for a whole day.)

We live best somewhere in the middle, with a habit of keeping the world-reading attitude at the ready, eagerly attuned to delve into those moments that draw us. The middle ground can be very simple. It may be just a single notion rehearsed through the day: noticing the highway sign "soft shoulders" one morning; mulling the phrase over as it recurs in relation to a clothing shop window and a teary friend; and then sharing it at dinner in a discussion of funny ways to communicate risk warnings.

Major events in our lives place world-reading glasses on our faces, whether we know it or not: rites of passage, illnesses, crises, insights, falling in love. We attend differently at such times; we notice with heightened skills and make surprising, meaningful connections. The specifics we engage with may be odd, even inconsequential: the motorcycle roar that drowns out a part of the wedding vow, the elegant sweep of an intravenous tube, the three freckles on a loved one's hand. The symbol doesn't matter; it's what we make of it that counts.

Even very passive, grumpy souls read a word or two of the world on occasion. Who knows when it might hit? A sentimental television commercial might spark a moment's deeper reading; a shooting pain in the heart may shock such a person into attentive sight.

Practice Activities

Here are a couple of short activities to try. Each prompts you toward an experience of reading the world, to refresh your sense of how it feels:

1) Wherever you are right now, assume this place is a room in the Museum of Contemporary American Life. This room has become a popular exhibit, and you are an art critic who loves this exhibit because it is such an eloquent expression of a particular world. Spend a few

The symbol doesn't matter; it's what we make of it that counts.

minutes taking notes on the details you are going to include in your article, which starts, "Rarely have I seen a work of art that so beautifully captures a particular reality. For example…"

You may actually want to write some of that article.

As a second stage of this activity, take another view of the place you sit. The year is 2099, and you are in the Museum of American History. This room is a new exhibit entitled, "American Life at the Turn of the Millennium." You are an anthropologist studying this exhibit for a book you are writing about the turn into the 21st century. Take notes on this exhibit to catch what the artist is saying about America in the late 1990s. What can you tell about America, late 1990s, from this room?

2) Get out your watch. Imagine that the next two minutes, after you begin this exercise, are the first two minutes of a film. Attend to whatever happens in that interval: thoughts, sounds, events, actions. After the time is up, quickly note what happened. Get down as many details as possible, including your thoughts and impressions.

Assume that the whole film is eighty-nine minutes long, and you have just seen the first two minutes. Also assume that those first two minutes contain the seeds and foreshadowings of all the major things that will happen in the remaining eighty-seven minutes of the film. Based on the specific things you observed in its first two minutes, lay out what happens in the rest of the film.

The Stakes

Nietzsche said we need art so that we don't die of reality. But many culturally "smart" people are dying of just that because they are illiterate in reality reading. Some of these people are the very ones who would score high on cultural literacy measurement tests, giving themselves comforting pats on the back as their vitality slips away. They feed on reality gruel, not on the feast of which we can partake. I know many well-off people, even art lovers, who lack the fundamental habit of really perceiving the world, and many so-called "underprivileged" people who are sharp readers of reality. The work of art is truly an equal

The work of art is truly an equal opportunity employer.

opportunity employer, and anyone can get rich in its currency, the quality of experience, the feel of being alive.

I have come to doubt people who speak with great certitude about "the real world," offering shoulds and opinions. Pontificators may spout impressively about "the way it is," but they are usually reading "the way it is" on a Dick-meets-Jane level. Even worse, some distort the truth for particular advantage: political, personal, neurotic. Distortion, whether intentional or not, whether for a good cause or not, precludes participation and kills a culture. Reality is not simple, and representations that make it seem so are false.

Reality is deep, fluid, and complex. Reading reality is a full contact sport that requires the best of every part of us; it is not a spectator event. A reading of reality includes far more than just what you see at a given moment, more than a preferred interpretation of what you see. If you can briefly describe the way the world is, you are choosing to see simplistically; just as you misrepresent the complex truth if you tell me what *Hamlet* or Monet's *Water Lilies* "means." In these cases, you may be telling me a partial truth, but a part is not the whole truth. The only way humans can grapple with the whole truth is through the continuing work of art we perform on its pieces.

Laguna Beach

Let me tell you about an experience that taught me about reading the world. A few years ago, I challenged myself to try an experiment: to live a whole day reading the world in maximum-intensity. It was an attempt to see how fully I could put my work-of-art skills to use. I do not offer this story as a prescription; rather, it is an extreme example that emphasizes the depth of potential held in a typical day.

To be free of distractions, I went away from home for the grand experiment. (I feared I wasn't adept enough to focus my skills on a day that included junk mail, phone calls, and faxes.) Since my wife and I were visiting friends in Los Angeles, I gave my effort two days solo in Laguna Beach: a day to get rid of cluttering worries and get organized, and then a day to play seriously.

Reality is not simple, and representations that make it seem so are false.

Reading reality is a full contact sport.

On the great experiment day, I checked into a near-the-beach motel to be "set apart." On the registration form at the motel desk, there was a line to fill in: "Representing _____." Rather than skip it, which I almost did and which was the appropriate response, I noticed the opportunity it offered. Given the challenge of the day, I decided that I had to fill in that blank invitation because it caught my curious notice. I explored the ramifications of the question asked by the word and the underlined space for my answer. In typical Eric fashion, I had a dictionary in my bag, and so I looked up the derivation of "represent." It read, "to bring before the mind." I pursued the question: Whom do I represent? Men? Americans? Caucasians? People with multiple-ethnic backgrounds? Artists? Businessman-teacher-artists with wavy hair? More precisely, whom did I bring before the mind on this *particular* experiment-day: Poets? People who yearn for greater meaning? People playing hooky from the real world for a day? I took another look at the word—"re" "present." Was this day about being present, again? Or maybe "re" as in "concerning," and "present" as in a gift, or maybe "present" as in present tense? This line of thought zoomed me through what little I know about Zen meditation and its emphasis on "being present." But nothing really connected. I had sped a jet stream of interesting thoughts but was no closer to a good answer for the motel registration card challenge. I stood there, staring fixedly, in jeopardy, and losing.

As you can imagine, the poor motel clerk was getting nervous by now. The young man had a textbook open on his desk, so I assumed he was a student. I took in the situation from his point of view, and it wasn't a pretty sight: a guy staring intently into space with the registration form half full and then looking in a dictionary—a foreigner? I tried to think of some honest way to tell him what I was doing, to give him something to hold, something familiar-and-thus-acceptable, but at the same time true to my experiment. By now I was not only staring intently, I was staring *at him*, as I tried to devise an elegantly distilled explanation, one less alarming than "I'm following a metaphoric inquiry into what I 'bring before the mind' today." With forced cheerfulness, the clerk finally told me it was OK, I only had to sign the form and give him my credit card.

Credit card, wow! My yearning to make sense launched me away again. I represent someone (I don't know whom or what), *and* I have been given credit for something—what? Is there a connection between the two? What do I deserve credit for? Holding up an index finger to tell the clerk to wait just a moment, I looked up "credit." Etymologically, it meant trust, belief. Some part of the world had placed its trust in me. Was I being asked to produce proof that I was worthy? In this day of experimentation, what did this mean in terms of action? To be trustworthy, today, meant to see the fullest possible meaning of every moment.

The moment of grace that the wait-a-moment gesture had bought me ran out. The clerk was becoming visibly uncomfortable. The deeper I saw into the significances available in this moment, the more he interpreted the situation as dangerous. The poor guy must have been running through strategies for how to get rid of a madman. I could see him mentally flipping pages in the motel clerk's handbook to find some paragraph that might help him deal with a moment like this.

Again, I assumed his perspective and began searching for a way to help him out of his predicament (without compromising my own) before he felt compelled to dial 911. The switch in perspective fired off another line of inquiry: Whom do I represent in this moment now? All the threats from the unknown? The scary, undesired, undeserved intrusions into reliable plans to get along in daily life? There he was, calmly studying for his accounting test, and wham, in sauntered a freak.

But the freak was me, and I knew I was working on a worthwhile experiment, for the benefit of people like both of us. I lamely gave him the wait-a-second finger again; he received it as if it came from the adjacent digit. I decided I must fill in the blank immediately. At least that written choice would be some sort of mark on the world, and it would alleviate his anxiety to some degree. (I knew I had to put down something, as I recalled Adrienne Rich's comment, "America is afraid of the experience that leaves a mark.") But what words? At a loss for an elegant solution to the problem, I decided to improvise to get any solution: I would just put down the first answer that came into my head that felt even a little bit right. In the blank space after "Representing," I wrote down "a curious way of seeing." That is the term the muse gave me, that moment, that day.

I could feel the clerk's blood pressure drop as he saw me complete and sign the card. He cautiously eased into the credit card exchange ritual with the care of a parent laying a dozing colicky infant back in the crib. I noticed the sequence of graceful movements with card-in-machine; there was a pattern underneath his confident swipe and release, the stuff of dance. I controlled my impulse to ask him to repeat his actions so I could take notes. Instead, I just swooped my hand through the pattern a little, carefully below the level of the counter, trying to remember it.

As he handed back my card, I wondered if the kind of credit that Citibank conferred on me is one I could actually take pride in. I wondered if that company would be proud to give credit to someone who was thinking my thoughts. As a thank-you gift to the patient clerk, I conformed to the expected norms perfectly for the closure to our improvisation. I smiled wanly, said thanks, really meaning it, and left fast. The clerk didn't look at the completed registration card until I was just outside the office. I have wondered about his response, a dangling thread in my day. But I was too chicken to ask him about the whole experience he went through. Did he pick up a whiff of anything more than a visit from a new float in the freaks' parade? I fantasize that he will read this book and recall that event.

I recall another part of that long Laguna Beach day. I had walked down the beach, noticing small significant incidents I would have overlooked on an average day: lessons from a golden retriever who loved to dig in the sand (not to find things, said his owner, just to dig); metaphors from sandpipers (back and forth with the edge of the wave); symbols in tide pools (tiny trapped fish looking very calm). Every single time I paused to attend, I found something worth attending to. In my notes, I wrote, "There is a treasure under every rock today;

whichever way I turn follows the secret pirate map." I looked up the etymology of "treasure"—same root as "thesaurus." I couldn't miss.

I arrived in the more-crowded town beach area—what a fiction-versus-reality scene. It looked exactly like the television images of California beaches, as if I had stepped into a program that in my den at home I would have clicked past. Tan young gods and goddesses played jolly volleyball; they were particularly impressive from a distance, when I couldn't hear them. As I approached, I was drawn into the vivid paradox of the perfection of their physical bodies and the aggressively flimsy quality of their discussions about whose hair was bouncier and which beer advertisements "really rocked." What image might help me hold this contrasting split? Perhaps they were the gods on Mt. Olympus discussing the 31 flavors of ambrosia?

I turned to the shoreline. More perfect young bodies cavorted in bathing suits measurable in square centimeters. My serious-experiment day of living in maximum connectedness was taking a pleasant turn toward the carnal. Then into this television reality walked two figures completely covered in Day-Glo yellow environmental protection suits. They were utterly armored, from giant rubber boots to helmets with built-in goggles and breathing contraptions. I reviewed my available store of information to comprehend this bizarre reality. Yes, I had heard there was an oil spill just a bit up the coast. That must be it. The yellow-rubber figures ambled near the water line with the relaxed gait of a couple on holiday. They slalomed between the young near-nakeds on their towels and blankets. A Frisbee flew by them. One of the yellow figures bounded over, like another teen at play, and tossed it back to the laughing girl who had thrown it. What a metaphor! In a moment, I saw an assembly of strong, improbable images: a lovely natural coastline invisibly polluted to the point of a sci-fi horror film; utterly vulnerable, perfect-health bodies playing, *giggling* with poison-protected gargoyles; the clean horizontal line of a Frisbee toss connecting the worlds. Everyone behaving as if in a sitcom, except there was this monstrous piece of information in the middle of it, glowing yellow.

I began scanning my life for unmistakably loud messages of major trouble that I choose to avoid by playing out a sitcom reality. There was one "toxic" worker at my office who was horrible, and I was not dealing with it, making the rest of the staff play metaphoric Frisbee amid the problem. I had a friend who had an alcohol problem, and I was refusing to confront her. Another friend had just learned that he was HIV positive, yet we both went through our days as if nothing had changed.

I had happened onto a metaphor at the shoreline, one which could provide a curious lens for looking at things, if I played with it. I tried on the lens, looked at my life, and saw the more complex truth in the situations of the office worker, the drinking-problem, and HIV-positive friends. I had assimilated some messages from the unfamiliar, and now I had an invitation to use the new-familiar in "normal life." Having read a new world, I could now rewrite my own reality.

Those two brief real-life incidents, at the motel desk and the shore, were valuable because of the ways I read the worlds they held. I saw with clarity, assimilated some of the truth they contained, and made use of the new information. The metaphors have significantly enhanced my life, serving as effective tools for grappling with new experiences.

For example, if I am confused in a moment at work or in an interview, I ask myself, "Whom do I represent?" If I am nervous before making a speech, I ask, "Whom do I represent here today, to this audience; what do I seek to bring to their minds?" It calms me. I have used that question often in writing this book: in deciding how to organize it; what to include or cut; to goose myself into another day of writing when I was fed up. I also have a more complex appreciation of my credit cards as a result of that inquiry into credit and the ritual of the card sweep and exchange. Of course, this does not mean I fall blubbering into tears every time I haul out my American Express card. However, it does mean that I don't leave home without an enriched understanding of the connections in my life (American expressions?) that the plastic rectangle represents and holds new understandings that I can tap to apply to poems, to advice for my friend Gary, to find greater satisfaction in my life as a player in the consumer game.

The yellow figures have ambled into other surprising corners of my life. The image has become a symbol for trying too hard to act normal, to the point of overlooking something seriously wrong. There have been situations that looked normal but felt a little off. In those moments, I ask myself, "Am I playing Frisbee with yellow monsters here?"

I recall one specific incident during which the eco-disaster suits shot through my mind. I had been working for a dysfunctional organization, slaving like a maniac for months running my division, trying to hold the important work together, but I couldn't get the boss to pay attention to the range of problems I was coping with. He wouldn't even grant me a meeting. I was frantic. Finally, he grudgingly gave me half an hour to go through sixteen specific items that required his immediate decision. But for the first three or four minutes of the meeting, I just sat there, sharing small-talk pleasantries. The Laguna Beach scene flashed through my mind—the ecosystem of this organization was in disaster, and the boss and I were cheerfully tossing verbal Frisbees. It was sobering and grounding to recall the metaphor in this situation; the recollection transformed the stupid politeness in which I was caught into an effective, deal-with-the-problem mode. A metaphor saved the day.

Discovered metaphors can feed world-making, too. I once wrote a short story like the Laguna Beach incident with beach bunnies (rabbits, that is) and monsters in it. Working on my short story, I went back and reread Raymond Carver, one of my writer-heroes. I noted more fully the way he gets central images to ring out from the text and resonate long after the final sentence. As a result of the beach incident, I went back to my own story and revised. In fact, I went back to revise it again as I was retelling the story here. Someday, I will say—it will say —it is done. This is how world-work works: a bounce from one action to another.

It occurred to me later that the day's two key incidents are closely linked to *Hamlet*. "Whom do I represent?" is a question that plagues the Danish Prince—he has a new blank to fill in. And he, too, is visited by an armored ghost that suggests something rotten in the state. Had I been drawn to these experiences because I had been shaped by Shakespeare's play?

There is yet another, odd benefit from the experiment. I tell this Laguna Beach story to friends. Each time I do, friends immediately begin to share similar events that they say they had forgotten. They recall a moment when they had instinctively looked in a different way and transformed an ordinary part of a daily routine into valuable symbol. In the recollection, they feel—we both feel—elevated by the insight.

The Laguna Beach experiment confirmed the following for me: just how readily worthwhile connections appear when we pay full attention; how much more is going on than we normally bother to notice; how any day's gleanings can pay long-term rewards; how natural the bounce from one part of world-work to the next can be.

My conclusion was that there was nothing so ordinary in that ordinary day that it didn't warrant meaningful investigation. To the passionate reader of reality, anywhere is everywhere.

The Attitude That Reads the World

Reading the world is an improvisation with an attitude. We described *the* attitude in Part Two as a critical skill of the work of art. You read the world quite naturally when you notice something that has always been there, discover a new level of meaning in something routine, make a connection between something new and something in the past, realize that an acquaintance reminds you of someone else you know, make a pun, "see" someone in a fresh way, apply something you read to your daily life.

As we mentioned earlier, you read the world at "special" times like crises, epiphanies, or celebrations. You read the world in sacred, mysterious, historical, or beautiful places. You read the world with friends, mentors, teachers, or family members who foster the attitude in you. You read the world intensely when you are "in love."

You read the world when you are engaged in the work of art. For example, as the painter leaves her studio, she discovers that the street feeds her new ideas to assimilate into the still-life painting upstairs, the dinner conversation is surprisingly relevant to the problems posed by the light on the painted plum, and the image in a dream makes sense

There is nothing so ordinary in an ordinary day that it doesn't warrant meaningful investigation.

*Reading the world is
seriously playing with
the medium of daily life,
as opposed to merely
coping with it.*

for the next painting she will try. When we are actively world-exploring or world-making, the connections spill out of us. Reading the world is seriously playing with the medium of daily life, as opposed to merely coping with it.

Practice, Practice, Practice

Here are four suggestions for developing your practice of reading the world.

1) Make it a habit.

The nineteenth century playwright/novelist Charles Reade is attributed with the observation, "Sow an act, and you reap a habit. Sow a habit, and you reap a character. Sow a character, and you reap a destiny." A habit of the attitude takes you directly toward your entelechy.

There are an infinite number of ways to support such a habit, and you must put together a set that works for you. Here are ten quick suggestions you might try:

* Set aside a dedicated time every day to do one of the many exercises suggested in this book.

* Assign yourself two specific times each day when you stop what you are doing and look at the moment from an entirely different perspective.

* Assign yourself a theme for the day and notice the number of times you can find where it applies (for example, "invisible in plain view" or "animal images" — e.g. computer mouse, someone in the doghouse).

* Propose a movement attribute for the day (like "choppy" or "weightless"), or a quality that

particularizes physical movement, and watch for its appearances in your own movements, in the movements of others, in verbal images and rhythms.

* Play secret "as if," which means to adopt a different perspective and carry on without telling anyone. Experience your day as if you were ecstatic to have the occasions that comprise it; as if you were a saint, a hopeless optimist, a poet, an alien spy from a planet who wants to learn what makes humans so weird; as if you were the person you most love in the world.

* Keep a journal of each day's small discoveries; you may want to carry a tiny pad for quick reminder notes, as I do.

* Imagine you are going to make a short (ten seconds?) film of each day; keep an eye out for the best image(s) for you to select.

* Play extrasensory scientist. Experiment with things like reading people's thoughts, communicating without words, remote viewing, predicting the future, and so forth, and notice any evidence of success–(The purpose is not to become a fortuneteller, but to practice attending in expanded ways.)

* Look for and take note of patterns in the sequence of events in a day, any repeated images you see on the street or in a magazine, in words that recur.

* Get a something-of-the-day calendar for your desk, and make it a practice to do something with its daily suggestion. On the back of each sheet write down something you discovered that day, and keep the pages as your insight-of-the-day calendar for next year.

2) Use people.

Life sometimes gives us freebies—people who immediately offer a chemistry that naturally catalyzes *the* attitude in both parties. I call these people freebies because we don't have to work to develop our subtle affinity with them; we instinctively share a feel for reading of the world and use the skills of art to improvise together. Gather, nurture, and spend focused time with such peers. This may mean little more than becoming closer friends and spending world-reading time together on a regular schedule. Do things with this inspiring friend: travel, have adventures, just go to lunch, work in the garden, talk on the phone, do volunteer work together. Ask. Watch. Discuss. You needn't formalize this relationship or even name it. The advice is to dedicate time to do things with people who evoke the world-reading attitude in you. If you are lucky enough to have this rapport with a live-in mate, don't take it for granted—feed it with your best attending, lest it dull over time. My wife and I discovered one another as freebies with a cymbal-crash of similar seeing. Now, twenty-four years later, we find we must consciously apply an effort to provoke ourselves to read the world together, to pick up the instruments of perceiving anew, to improvise into fresh sight.

Life does not provide a cavalcade of freebies, however, so we need to work intentionally to create relationships that share and use the attitude. Finding playpals like this takes the courage to express what you see, to ask what others see, to offer and provoke in a gentle way. Don't be inappropriate; just gently extend the parameters of what is being exchanged if you hear something that rings true. Offer an "as if" that you think will be useful. The people who respond to your offering

Dedicate time to do things with people who evoke the world-reading attitude in you.

have the potential to become partners in your world-reading habit. You will discover how many people perk up and join an inventive moment in dialogue; many are just waiting for someone to surprise them into a creative exchange.

3) Sustain an amateur practice.

Probably the easiest way to develop and sustain the habit of reading the world is by getting involved in the arts. An amateur artistic practice provides a concentrated focus to steadily develop the skills of art that apply everywhere. This means becoming a connoisseur in the largest sense of the word. While the media of theater, music, dance, visual arts, and literature are the most common disciplines for an amateur, they are certainly not the only effective media for a passionate practice. Any medium that engages you in flow, that challenges your work-of-art skills, and rewards you consistently over time can be perfect. We will discuss this topic in detail in Part Four.

An amateur artistic practice provides a concentrated focus to steadily develop the skills of art that apply everywhere.

4) Attend to base metaphors in your life.

Do you believe the world is a hard, dark place with only glimmers of light? Do you believe the postal clerk is a monster? Is work a necessary evil, or a piece of cake? Is your marriage a desert, or perhaps an oasis? Is the kid down the block trouble?

In reading the world, you can discover and clarify your base metaphors, those subterranean beliefs, scripts, and prejudices about "the way it is" that color your experience. Working with them, rather than just functioning within their dictates, provides opportunities to change them, and thus change the way you understand the world. Practice reading the world as if it were adhering to the pattern of a different metaphor.

How do you discover your foundation metaphors?

Shift perspectives. Perceive your physical world with the poet's eye, the perspective that sees the ideas in things.

You might want to try this story-game:

1) Tell the story of a typical work day of yours. Write it as a paragraph or tell it in just a minute or two.

2) Keeping the basic shape and sequence of your average-workday story, retell that story as if it were a great mythological journey. Be as inventive as you like.

3) Review the mythological story. Find its key metaphors, the specific everyday things or events you translated into archetypal mode (for example, maybe the office water cooler became a magical spring, or secret glade; maybe the boss became a toothless dragon). These are key metaphors for you.

Listen to how you speak. You actually express your key metaphors often. When you are talking seriously about the "way life is" with someone, what do you find yourself saying? Do you describe work as a prison? Do you revert to computer metaphors like programs and software? Are there words you use often, expressions you like, particular phrases that others would identify as "you"? Gather them and see what they say. Are these the understandings you want to base your experience upon? Where did you get them? Do you want to trade them in for new models?

Notice what you notice. There are a million things you could select to experience at any given moment. Which do you choose? Attend to the life of your ordinary noticing "as if" it were entirely deliberate. Are you cruising life for danger, for instant-gratifiers, for sex, for surprise? Ask yourself questions like: What kind of a person notices things like that? What comes next for a character who has spent a day noticing what I noticed today? What are the recurrent images and symbols in what I noticed today?

Give yourself pop quizzes. You can spark your attending with a quick challenge any time. Here are some examples: Take a particular thematic thread, say "control," and reflect on its position in your life right now with the question, "What is the current state of control in my life?" Or you might pick a moment in your childhood and write a small poem about its appearance in your life right now. You might jot down an answer to this question any time: "What *else* is going on here right now that is quite different?" Ask and answer it five times in a row. Ask and answer: "How would this world seem if I were that spot on the carpet, the telephone, the heart at work in that man's chest?"

Your imagination can change your base metaphors. Let's assume that one of the above exercises revealed a metaphor you want to outgrow. Let's say, for example, that your job is a dead end. There are, no doubt, many unpleasant occurrences that have led you to that belief (which underlie the entire experience of the job, even when you have a good day). Our base metaphors are often inherited from our parents' experience of things, communicated to us when we were young. Base metaphors are so firm that they persist—in this case, probably even if you were to change jobs.

How Do You Adjust a Base Metaphor?

It takes the work of art to propose a new metaphor that you think might work better, and it takes imagination to play it out. Let's say you gather your best thoughts and determine to experiment with the new metaphor of your job as if it were not a dead end but a small entrepreneurial business you own. If you can apply your imagination to view your job through that fresh lens, many things will look different. You have a different definition of success (whereas before it may have been not getting fired, or doing as little as possible, now it becomes delivering the best product you can); you will cruise your routines differently (before they were grinding and dull, perhaps now they become full of tricky little problems you can work on); and so forth with the infinite number of new things you can discover by reading your world with a different set of lenses.

It has been my experience that intentionally experimenting with new base metaphors makes a difference. The change is not a sudden switch to a radically new kind of experience; rather, we adjust bit by bit—a small part of the work day will feel different one Tuesday, a conversation

If you can apply your imagination to view your job through a fresh lens, many things will look different.

with a boss will have a different tone. A project as large as fulfilling an entelechy takes the best skills we have and a good deal of time, so we must expect the manifestations of new base metaphors to appear in small, undramatic ways. It is said that the great changes of our lives come not with sound and fury, but on the footsteps of doves.

The Everyday Mind and The Attitude

Artists are exemplary in the deftness with which they switch perspectives. One moment in metaphorical "as if," the next millisecond in solving the problems of getting the blue on the brush just right.

We can emulate that flexibility in our own endeavors, with a readiness to shift between the everyday mind and the work-of-art attitude. The everyday mind can be efficient, smart, and productive; it takes care of business and busyness; it manages, copes, and keeps life together. The read-the-world attitude is subtler, less predictable, and more spontaneous. The everyday mind manages your progress through the world; the attitude shows you where you are, what significance surrounds you, and where you seem to be going.

With practice, these two personae become intimate. They appear in one another's spheres. You snoop for meaning as you perform a mundane task like filling the gas tank. You stumble upon a very practical solution to a what-to-wear-Friday-night problem amid your exploration of an F. Scott Fitzgerald short story.

Mark Twain wrote that there were two ways he could experience the Mississippi River: as a writer or as a riverboat pilot. For Writer Twain, the swirls and eddies evoked rich associations that launched his imagination and feelings that bounced him into literary world-making. For Pilot Twain, those same swirls and eddies were signals of shifting sandbars and dangerous realities that could threaten his boat's safe passage. This practical reading evoked effective real-world action, or else.

The artist at play and the professional at work; same river, same boat, same man at the helm.

The artist at play and the professional at work; same river, same boat, same man at the helm. The Twains must meet. Writing fiction and steering a boat are obviously different, but not entirely different; in what they share awaits a hidden gold mine.

We all write (do the work of art, at least in bits and pieces) and pilot (try to find the best way through the difficulties of life). Most people choose to live predominantly within the pilot's point of view: watching out for problems in order to make a decent living, avoiding trouble, coping with all the complexities of the real world. But a full life is found only in some balance and interplay between the two.

The World of Those Who Read the World

Passionate practitioners of the work of art join a kind of community with many informally shared beliefs, priorities, and practices; I have tried to name some in these pages. We share a bold place in which we participate, take some risks, challenge what we know, and seek to make substantive offerings to the future. If you were an etymology freak, you might go so far as to propose that our shared practices and beliefs comprise a religion of sorts.

The word "religion" derives from the Latin "religionem," meaning "a commitment," or "care for that which is sacred." The tripartite work of art is just that, active care for the most precious part of ourselves, a commitment to our entelechy. In her fine book *Ordinarily Sacred*, Lynda Sexson describes this notion of religion:

> Religions reassure, reacquaint, realign us with the known and keep us safe from the chaos of new perception…. the religion with which these pages are concerned is the religion of picking up the pieces, improvising, making up and making do….It is the religious consciousness that apprehends the sacred without authority to do so….If a religious tradition decrees a particular day holy, then all other days are potentially holy—or temporarily expansive. If a religious tradition decrees a stone holy, then any stone may tell a secret; or if it decrees a story holy, other stories also may conceal themselves in the language, expand the boundaries of knowing. The culture that we know is continually shifting its shape, changing its mind….Changes in metaphor are changes in religion.[18]

Religion (ri lij´ən) derivative of *religionem* (Latin) *n.* a commitment, or care for that which is sacred

Part 4

Engage

Chapter Eleven:

Deep Sight

When I was a boy, blindness fascinated me. Sometimes I would try living in my bedroom with my eyes closed. I would practice walking around the house blindfolded to see if I could remember where things were. In one experiment, I arranged an obstacle course of chairs in the living room. I would study the layout, then navigate through it with eyes closed, counting the number of brushes and shin-whacks. I tried different preparatory strategies:

1) visually memorizing the maze,
2) calculating numbers of steps and the angles of turns, and
3) just getting a feel for the whole.

Tallying the number of touches and bruises with each approach, I found that, over time, my performance got better following every strategy, but the improvement was slow and unpredictable. More significantly, I got my first lesson in a truth I am still exploring: success came most readily when, rather than trying to gauge every step, I relaxed, letting my sense of the whole and my intuition guide my movement. The same recipe has brought my best results in the theater, business, the arts, and relationships.

In my boyish fascination, I focused on the story of a woman who had been born blind but as an adult underwent a new surgical procedure that miraculously granted her sight. Her experience obsessed me. I played imaginary games in which I was this woman, repeatedly improvising the moment of first vision. I would squint and then open my eyes shakily and look around my room, slowly, with reverential awe, as if for the first time, at my stuff: the red desk lamp, the worn rubber basketball, the geometric mobile. (My enactments were a bit histrionic: trembly eyelids, luminosity around the objects, slow panning camera sweeps.) This game imbued the everyday objects of my world—even the bookshelf with the wood veneer I had picked off—with an aura of significance. I now think the reason I loved this play-acting sequence was that it allowed me to rehearse my natural yearning for extraordinary experiences. At the heart of this game was the wonder of turning leaden stuff into personal gold.

Recently, I came across some medical reports about cases similar to the story that launched my childhood imagining, but without the melodrama of my inventions. Almost without exception, I learned, adults who have received sight through surgery have deeply upsetting and difficult experiences. The process of coming to see is long, hard work. One case told of a previously blind craftsman being taken to a museum where he encountered one of the tools he had worked with for years without seeing it. He stood before it, agitated in a way he couldn't articulate. Finally, encouraged to touch it, he exclaimed that the moment he felt it, he could see it. Some people in this situation find the difficulties of coming to see insurmountable and choose to live in homes with the lights turned off. In a study of many such medical cases, author M. von Senden quotes the eye surgeon Dr. Moreau:

> After the surgical intervention, the eyes have certainly obtained the power to see, but the employment of this power, which as a whole constitutes the act of seeing, still has to be acquired from the very beginning. The operation itself has no more value than that of preparing the eyes to see; education is the most important factor…. To give back sight to a congenitally blind person is more the work of an educator than a surgeon.[19]

The work of art is a kind of deep seeing. We all have the preliminary requirements, and we know how to use a subtle range of natural powers to accomplish this sight below the surface of things. We develop our skills over a long period of time, and the learning requires guidance, motivation, and practice. (Of course, blind people, as well as those with other limitations, have ample skills of art—many are wonderful practitioners. And truthfully, we all have blind spots among our repertoire of artistic skills.)

However, just as in the surgeon's prescription, our available skills of art represent only a starting point; we all require an education to tap our perceiving power, to become lively readers, responders, and makers of worlds. Indeed, the surgeon reminds us that the education part of the deep-sight equation is at least as important as the skills. The work of art is the optimum schooling for the use of our basic skills, and the artist in us teaches well if allowed. The curriculum for coming to perceive with fullest sight is years of hard work, made consistently engaging through a practice in the work of art. Yes, we can get along without this kind of deepest seeing, we can manage a life on the literal plane of living; those surgically sighted people lived adequately in their darkened homes—but we have the capacity to do so much more.

As you have read this book, you may have felt disquieted at some of its important but ineffable points. For example, what does yearning mean, *exactly*? (If I knew a simpler answer, I would have shared it.) You "know" the skills I am talking about; you "understand" what I describe—but there seems to be something more underneath. There is. The once-blind craftsman described above shook in disquiet when he saw the somehow-familiar tool of his craft on display. Like him, you may be looking at familiar tools with enhanced sight in these pages. His agitation disappeared, his newly extended powers of sight engaged, the moment he moved the work of deeper seeing from his head to his hands. I wish the same for you. We must intentionally lay your hands on these somehow-familiar skills of art to engage your deepest seeing. That is the goal of Part Four.

We met the work of art in Part One; we explored its skills in Part Two; we examined the three main modes of expression in Part Three. You are

The work of art is a kind of deep seeing.

Our available skills of art represent only a starting point; we all require an education to tap our perceiving power.

now well-versed in *the* attitude. However, because attitude without engagement is like potential without occasion—nothing—we will now dig into some practical issues to get you started in your daily artwork.

We will deal with beginning, a challenge that never ends. We will explore the exemplary, natural model of the amateur. We will attend to job-life as well, to make sure the work of art thrives there. Then we will study two overlooked support ideas that can make a critical difference in growing into the work of art. Finally, I will confess my secret faith that the work of art can make a difference greater than the reach of any single pair of hands.

Chapter Twelve:

In the Beginnings

Almost every cultural mythology around the world begins with a creation story. This is no coincidence: making worlds is one of the central acts of being human. Similarly, world-making is the master key to the work of art.

You Need a Regular World-Making Practice

Would that it were as easy to launch such a practice as the cozy preamble with which Julia Lang used to begin her children's stories on BBC radio: "Are you sitting comfortably? Then I'll begin." But beginning is not simple; indeed, the biggest blocks lie right in front of the starting gate. Resistances, anxieties, and excuses arise to stop us before the process can develop a momentum of it own. (Get used to this persistent difficulty; long-time practitioners, even masters, may handle the pressures of beginning with more facility, but they still *always* encounter things in the way of beginning.) Let's get familiar with some of the clever traps and detours you will encounter.

There are personal anxieties: I don't know how to do it. I'm not good enough to pull this off. Why am I doing this? There is worry about the work ahead: What the hell am I making here? Who am I kidding? And my personal favorite: Where will I find the time?

We each have our particular cast of pernicious characters that try to get parts in the drama of beginning. They come from central casting,

Beginning is not simple; indeed, the biggest blocks lie right in front of the starting gate.

quite literally they arise from personal history and from archetypal human history, from the center. No matter how puny or odd they may appear, they are powerful, effective, and determined to deter your creative process. I imagine them as the high-energy cast of an improv comedy troupe showing up in your work area to put on a show; the goal of the performance is not to entertain, but to distract.

Anytime you launch a new kind of creative project, you meet some of the members of your personal cast. Their voices sound like a parent, a particularly bad teacher, a competitor, a bully who once insulted you. For their lines, they will speak a hundred demeaning things you have thought about yourself. The troupe is always seeking new members and sharp new one-liners to try out on you. The casting director might be described as that little demon-critic who sits on your shoulder—the one who whispers those discouraging, belittling comments in your ear.

Here's another metaphor for the trouble at the start. The mind regards an exciting beginning as if it were an invasion. The radar detects a creative urge and sets off an alarm to arm against a potential attack on the status quo. The more significant your intuition about a new idea, the larger the blip on the radar screen, the larger and more varied the defensive reaction.

Any committed artist has tales of difficulties at beginnings—she has been through the air raid drill many times. She has calmed those defensive troops or cleverly slid around their positions; she knows their strategies. The defending troops are pretty good, but not inventive or flexible in devising new approaches. The weakness to exploit is that they don't devise new shut-down strategies readily if we have found a way around them. The experienced artist learns to begin quietly, so simply that the defenders will think it is just an inconsequential sparrow flying across the radar screen, too insignificant a threat to evoke a defensive alarm.

Some Startup Suggestions

No big deal. The less fuss you make, the better. Stay under the radar. Expectations and grand announcements may be exciting and feel good,

The mind regards an exciting beginning as if it were an invasion.

but they increase the difficulty of beginning. They alarm the resistance radar; they are more histrionic than supportive. Doing just a little something, and then doing just a little more—attentively and well—will serve you far better in the long run than any radical change.

Don't buy anything. You have everything you need to begin right now. You don't need to take a class or buy a speedy computer. If you want to write, begin writing today with pen and paper. If you want to undertake your family genealogy, don't buy a kit or special software, begin with a notepad and a call to a Aunt Mary. Learn small first, before you pressure the learning with new equipment. If you buy the "necessary tool" too soon, you may spend creatively useful time with your new "toys" and could suffocate the artistic yearning underneath.

Small steps, small successes. Set your sights with humility—that is, close to the ground, in modest stages. Worlds are made of many small yeses. Like the wise non-runner who decides to prepare for a marathon, your first days should be spent not in ten-mile sprints, but in fast-walking or in slow short jogs. The small focus and attendant satisfaction enable you to build the necessary muscles for long-term accomplishments.

If you stumble early, lower the hurdle. It is easy to give up in the early going. If you find yourself overwhelmed, take it as a signal of the need for adjustment, not as a disaster. Like the over-enthusiastic high jumper, you set the expectations too high—so lower the bar. Find a less-demanding task that goes part of the way you intend. Let's say the world you yearn to create is a painting of your favorite tree, and you can't get it to look good. Pull back and sketch a single leaf for a while, until it satisfies you, and then you're ready to move on. Remember that success is not the excellence of any single painting or project; success means sustaining the practice over time.

Include reflection. World-making is not a single kind of action; it inherently includes more than hands-on construction. The part that is most often overlooked is reflection. You will help yourself a lot if you take the time to attend to your process from the beginning. Take notes, keep a record about how the work is going; notice the minuscule

World-making is not a single kind of action; it inherently includes more than hands-on construction.

achievements and hiccups of satisfaction. Don't throw away the early work; keep it to look back on later. A habit of ten daily minutes of reflection on the front end will buy you ten hours of engagement down the road.

Play the triangle. The three kinds of world-work support one another, but in the early stages, the rustier stages, they can use a little nudge. To get their mutually supportive rhythm going, be very attentive to any impulses to explore something related to your project; follow every lead. Be very attentive to occasions when your thoughts return to your project while you are away from the task. Investigate related worlds made by others, especially masters. If you want to play the piano, listen to CDs of great players, listen for the piano part in radio tunes, notice how often you use musical metaphors, etc.

Put support people in place. In a continuing education course, a teacher would be there to guide you, and other students would be hard at work by your side, sharing your trials. If you are on your own, set some support in place. Pick the right people to be your confidantes (preferably not those too close, because proximity exerts pressure). The ideal supporter is an interested, encouraging friend, with a good sense of humor.

Get the habit. Habit will become your best ally in diminishing the difficulties of beginning, and there are beginnings to contend with every day. Rather than grabbing time when you can, try to make regular habits of as many things as possible: the time and place of your work, the atmosphere, perhaps even what you wear. A small steady habit will prove more effective than larger, irregular chunks of action.

Play. It is easy to get too heavy or serious in the early going; don't forget to have fun.

Common Bloopers of Beginning

I have seen many enthusiasts select challenges that stack the trouble cards against them. Here are a few to keep an eye out for:

A "should" project. This a project that you feel you should do, rather than one that your heart says you must do. The dictates of that "should" can come from cultural or family expectations (a Booth "should" act in the theater); personal history (you "should" get back to the piano playing you once enjoyed); necessity (you have to do something with that blank wall, so you might as well make it a mural); common sense (finish that old project that you left half-done). Shoulds don't last. On occasion, they lead to self-sustaining practices, but the chances are slim.

Inappropriate scope. Be careful not to select a project that is too large or too small, or that sets the stakes too high or too low. If you decide to write a novel, you have set your sights on a challenge that is extremely difficult even to those who have practiced the form for years. Your chances of "success" dwindle. Conversely, the scope of your project can be too small so that you feel you are pouring time and energy into an activity with negligible meaning—a thimble engraved with the titles from all the *Star Trek* episodes, for example. Remember the recipe for flow: a satisfying engagement in which skills are balanced with the difficulty of the challenge.

Unreasonably high expectations. This may be the most common trap people set for themselves. In the enthusiasm of the moment, some decide, "I will write poetry for two hours every morning," or, "I will design my dream house for an hour every night before bed until it's done." Within the first week, that two-hour poetry plan will smack into a crisis at home or work, a day will be skipped, and there will be a "failure" where there needs to be success. Start with *ten minutes* of poetry a day, and do it wholeheartedly. This nurtures the yearning that is the essential ingredient of a long-term habit. Other inappropriate expectations include grandiose views of your results. Of course your first nine hundred paintings are not destined for the Museum of Modern Art. Don't depend on enthusiastic responses from others to keep you sustained.

Goal dependence. Don't forget the redefinition of success; it is measured in quality of ongoing personal experience. The perfection of some aspect of your job need not be applauded by the boss or get you a raise to be "successful." It might have that result and it might not.

Extrinsic goals and rewards rely on value systems that are important and real, but, because of their dominance in life, they tend to smother everything else. You need to redress the imbalance with careful attention to your *intrinsic* success and satisfaction. If you find that you are working on a project for its outward signs of payoff, your yearning will be hard to sustain.

People goofs. There are all kinds of troubles you can create for yourself related to interacting with other people, like: sharing your ideas with someone who makes comments that hurt; giving away your secrets before they are fully formed (not because they get stolen, but because they get crooked). Be thoughtful about the people you include in your support network; carefully instruct those you do include about what you need from them. Don't be afraid to say, "I just need you to listen and tell me how interesting it sounds," or, "Don't talk about any details, just give me your general impressions." The people you love the most can sometimes damage your work the most. My wife and I have earned our way (by the painful route) to very careful rules about responding to one another's from-the-heart projects; we will sometimes go weeks without telling the other anything, until the time is right.

Let's say you have eased past the bugaboos of beginning; you are into a groove in your world-making habit. You are handling the ups and downs; you have your eyes on the main goal as well as the daily details; you are flowing like Old Man River; you are not talking to too many people about the work, and those you do confide in contribute good thoughts and energy. Hey, this is great; what was all that blather about difficulty?

Stay careful. Your resistance never quits. At any point along the way, your doubts or distractions can launch a sneaky surprise strike to stop you. This happens particularly at the seams. Seams are junctures: the start of a day; after you have been pulled away for a bit of time; the moment a major new idea appears that expands or redirects the scope of the task; when you are sharing your work with someone, getting praised or criticized; when you recognize that you are accomplishing something significant; when you are at the end of one piece before you bounce on.

To Forestall Trouble at the Seams

Don't end at the end of a day. Before you close up shop for a day, take the first step into the next day's work. Set a "bookmark" in place so you can pick right up and begin without scrabbling to rediscover where you were. If you are making a quilt, begin the next square; if you are making a poem, write down the seed of the next image; if you are making a garden, drive a stake at the spot where you will dig first the next day; if you are writing a book about making things, write the topic sentence of the next morning's section before you go out to mow the lawn.

Train for marathons, not sprints. Marathon training concurrently holds short- and long-term perspectives. A marathon runner keeps track of total miles a month, as well as how her legs feel each day. Both perspectives are essential. Each day's effort must be seen as complete and whole and valuable, even though it is also only a small part of a larger endeavor.

Continually attend to the process. The undercurrents are the ones that carry you, not the surface waves. It is the process that needs to become the habit, not the stream of products—that's merely manufacturing.

Set up a convenient, dedicated work-of-art space. Just as much as a potter needs a wheel that doesn't double as a night table, a writer needs a desk just for writing, one unlittered with bills or phone messages. Every practice requires its dedicated place. The more readily and smoothly you can slip in and out of creative work, the more often you will do it, the more easily it slips into your lifestyle as a habit. The fewer the distractions (physical, mental, and logistical) in your workplace, the easier it is to dig in.

Be prepared for trade-offs. To make room for a new habit in your life, something else may have to go. Change is exchange. (That is even etymologically true.) Make deals with yourself: cut your television watching back to just two favorite shows a week; experiment with new arrangements and schedules. But be gentle; pull back for a bit, provisionally, before you rashly lop off any significant part of daily life—old routines were established for good reasons that cannot be merely wished away or shrugged off.

Be *willing to seem a little eccentric.* You might develop daily life priorities slightly apart from American norms. There is a stigma attached to eccentricity, and a few people might shake their heads or make comments. But creativity takes our thinking outside the status quo, and creative people color their lives outside the conventional lines of behavior. They playfully, artfully resist the control of cultural norms, refusing to surrender their uniqueness.

A little idiosyncrasy is part of the positive modeling you give to the world. People will feed off your excitement; eccentricity that is full of joy becomes admirable. There is no such thing as "centricity" anyhow; the highly functioning human is idiosyncratic. A "centric" individual would have to be severely limited. The eccentric soul spends a lot of time out of stasis—that is, in ecstasy.

By the way, a recent research study of eccentrics proved that they are happier and healthier than the average citizen, and they are no more likely to be mentally ill. The researchers found five characteristics to be the top indicators of eccentricity, in descending order: nonconformism, creativity, strong curiosity, an idealistic desire to make the world better, and a happy obsession with a hobby.[20] Sounds like the work-of-art practitioner to me.

Develop a "wiser advisor." This may be an actual person, a caring, experienced guide who can keep you steady through ups and downs. But such a graceful and understanding mentor can be hard to find. It is likely that you'll have to rely on yourself for some degree of wise counsel.

I have an advisor in me who answers Eric's questions. I know this sounds goofy, but it works: I sometimes write letters and notes of guidance from him to me when I am troubled or stuck. Those "Dear Eric" letters really help when I am pulling out clumps of hair. My inner guide gives great advice, and, amazingly, he always knows exactly what is going on. Generally, he urges patience and reminds me of the "marathon" picture. He points out things that are going well, and he gets me to laugh at my blunders.

Setting new projects. Just as you develop a habit of setting down the next day's beginning before you close up shop, try to do the same

A little idiosyncrasy is part of the positive modeling you give to the world.

between projects. Seeds for new work sprout along the way; inspirations and ideas for new projects pop up at any time. Grab them in some way, all of them, and set them in a particular place. (You will forget them otherwise, and many are terrific ideas.) Then, as you complete one project, revisit this storehouse of possibilities. Follow those that pull you.

Sometimes when you finish a big piece of work, you don't want to slip right into another project. You may need a break, but make use of this time. You have taken notes on possible projects you might want to dig into, so your subconscious can begin its gestation work. Let ideas roil around inside you as you take your break. Notice your dreams and daydreams; attend to notions and noodling—keep a record.

Notice your dreams and daydreams; attend to notions and noodling.

I do this. Every time I feel that sweet flicker of interest in a new idea, I make a file for it in my desktop filing system. Whenever I have a related notion, I jot it on a scrap of paper and drop it in. Then, later, when I am casting about for the next project, I check those files, read through the notes, and see which have become irresistible. I am always amazed at how much good preliminary work is held in that collection of scraps.

Developing Over Time

Over the long haul, we all change significantly. We take up new pursuits, switch fields altogether. That's fine. The Census Bureau tells us that the average American worker now has more than three entirely different careers (not jobs, *careers*) in a working life. In our personal lives, we are even more changeable. There is nothing amiss in working intensely in one field and then switching to another.

There is nothing amiss in working intensely in one field and then switching to another.

I am reminded of children listening to fairy tales. A child will ask to hear the same one, say *Cinderella*, read over and over, sometimes twice a day for weeks—'til we are ready to crush glass slippers in our bare hands. Then suddenly she will ask for *Jack and the Beanstalk*, never to request *Cinderella* again. Smart kid. She is working on something with those repeated listenings to *Cinderella*. (Bruno Bettelheim and Marie-Louise Von Franz have written marvelous books that detail just how strategically, how effectively, children cobble together their inner worlds with those explicitly directed story explorations.) When that world is complete, the yearning satisfied by all that *Cinderella* has to offer, she moves right along to the next order of business in her development.

Similarly, you may drop one kind of world-making as you yearn to begin in a new field. You set down the handle of the loom you had worked on for a decade and put your fingers on the guitar. One does not marry any one medium of expression "'til death do you part." The relationship is "'til authenticity do you part," 'til a ravishingly attractive new yearning sweeps you away. Passionate, serial monogamy.

Chapter Thirteen:

Getting it to Work

There is a good model to emulate as you bring a dedicated practice of world-making into a life fulfilled through the work of art: the passionate amateur. Artists, non-artists, art-lovers, art-haters—all of us—have much to learn from the quiet wisdom of the amateur.

The Genius of the Amateur

Amateur is a dirty word in America. It conjures images that have a little something wrong: earnest-yet-dreadful productions of *Julius Caesar*, classes of elderly ladies creating still life paintings no one wants to hang. The word has a quaint timbre, with echoes of some charming bygone era, the sound of an instrument no longer played, a bagpipe rendition of "Rocky Mountain High."

The word "amateur" wears an apology. I often meet people who find out about my acting career and begin to share their own passion about acting, only to cut themselves off with: "But I'm only an amateur." In common usage, "amateur" implies professional or commercial mediocrity: the amateur golfer is an amateur precisely because he couldn't make it as a pro. The assumption is that if you have enough ability, you become a professional. An amateur is seen as a dabbler, a dilettante, a greenhorn; "amateur" equals "not a success."

It may, then, seem bizarre to say that I have tried to write this book in an amateur style but I have—not badly, not "amateurish," but with

The word "amateur" wears an apology.

Amateur (am´ə tûr´) n.
one who does something
for the love of it

*Just as the opposite of love
is not hate, but apathy, the
opposite of amateur is not
professional, but boring.*

the passion of an amateur. I want the style to be personal; I want you to feel the joy I took in making it just right. I wrote this book because I couldn't not write it.

The etymology of the word "amateur" suggests a lover, quite literally—one who does something for the love of it. But the love at the heart of the amateur does not require reciprocation. It is not sophisticated, or romantic, or self-conscious; it is grounded and irrepressible. It is the natural force that drives us toward the realization of our entelechy. Just as the opposite of love is not hate, but apathy, the opposite of amateur is not professional, but perfunctory, grudging, boring, required.

For a long time, I was uncomfortable with the connotative baggage that comes with the word amateur. (I often told the story of an amateur "extra" in a professional production of *Romeo and Juliet*. She was so absorbed in the tomb scene that when Romeo killed Paris just before he poisoned himself and he sadly said, "Lie thou there, by a dead man interred," this amateur whispered to the "extra" next to her, "Why do you think he's burying Paris in turd?") I had no impulse to stand up and brag that I was an amateur—hey, I was a hotshot entrepreneur, or a Broadway actor, a *professional something*; I didn't want to be lumped in with old Aunt Sadie who makes Christmas baskets all year to fill with her dreaded fruitcake. But now I feel honored to be linked to millions of inspiring amateurs throughout the country who quietly spend lifetimes discovering and making things of meaning; people who understand Kahlil Gibran's line in *The Prophet*: "Work is love made visible;" people who make work they love, and make love in their work a fundamental part of their lives; people who transform the ordinariness of the everyday into valuable grist for growth's mill.

The self-sustaining zeal of amateurism can drive more than individual lives. In his 1995 book *Seven Experiments That Could Change the World*, Rupert Sheldrake made a bold challenge to the scientific status quo. He proposed the return to a time when science extended beyond a professional society to include a lively arena for amateur contribution. He invited amateur scientists (plain folks who were intrigued by his proposed challenges) to perform basic experiments (he explains precisely how) and submit their findings to scientific centers as evidence toward understanding inexplicable biological phenomena. Sheldrake now has a database of over two thousand cases that amateurs have reported.[21]

I have had occasion to invite artists (more than sixty over the years) to act as amateur education researchers. They have been given only the most basic instruction in methodology and some guidance, but mostly left to their own common sense and enthusiasm to create projects and procedures. Their results have been invaluable, inspiring to many—most of all to themselves and those who joined in their projects.

The Amateur Lifestyle

The amateur has, of course, a consistent practice of making things that reward and inspire her yearning. This sequence of projects provides lots of flow, frequent and various kinds of satisfaction, and a reliable bounce into further curiosity.

The hands-on investigations in her own work lead her into explorations of related worlds others have made; masterworks offer many useful answers to her serious questions. Few people devour an art book the way an amateur painter does; few people thrill more at the theater, and reflect long afterward, than those who act in a local theater troupe for the love of it.

The committed world-making and world-exploring just described demonstrate exemplary practices in the work of art. However, it is the third habit, *the* attitude with which an amateur reads the world, that transforms the quality of her life. This allows her to attend under the surface, to make connections among the different parts of living, to spark further curiosity and creating.

The typical picture of an amateur's daily life features a regular time commitment to the hobby or practice, no matter what her other life commitments may be. There may be some ebbs and flows in the amount of time she spends in the thick of it, but the practice occupies a big part of her daily life and thought.

This typical picture is not the only amateur lifestyle. Many infuse their amateur practice into their professional lives so that it becomes less distinguishable. As an example, I think of the fresh-fish-for-sale window display designer of Citarella's on New York's Upper West Side. He makes a new fillet kaleidoscope, shellfish icon from the news, or some seafood work of art every day—this is someone who adores his work. To identify this kind of amateur-professional, look for the flow on the job, the evidence of yearning, the connected world-exploring, and the eagerness to carry insights into the full scope of life by reading the world for what it can offer. The home-amateur and the job-amateur are two good models, and a mixture may be even better.

Many almost-amateurs touch on a part of these optimum pictures. These amateurs may keep their world-making isolated in their lives, may keep it for vacations or every once in a while; they may restrict the natural playing-out of their curiosity, having "no time" for things like that; or they may resist the application of their insights to other parts of daily life. If you are such an individual, I hope this book makes the value of your amateur part palpable. I hope these pages encourage you to relax some of those boundaries and allow that amateur impulse to grow. Start with just a little expansion and notice the experiential rewards.

The Heart of the Amateur

The amateur is not only a literal person with a visible practice; it is an intangible aspect of us all. Being an amateur means more than having a good hobby; it means pursuing actions of the heart for the satisfaction of the process.

For clarification, let's contrast this amateur impulse with the professional impulse; it is often difficult to distinguish between the two. The area has been gray for thousands of years: Was the village herbalist a medieval amateur or pro? Was the carver of sacred masks an amateur? Were the Wright brothers professional inventors?

Even today the distinction between amateur and professional is not as clear as we may think. There are obvious distinctions we might draw:

Being an amateur means more than having a good hobby; it means pursuing actions of the heart for the satisfaction of the process.

the amateur works for love, the professional works for a living; the amateur plays in a personal arena, the pro plays in a public game. On the other hand, many professionals work primarily for love rather than for money, and many amateurs care desperately how their work is received. Many amateurs play in a very public arena (e.g. community theater), and many professionals follow subtle paths of passionate personal interest (e.g. scientists) or stay in very small arenas (e.g. psychotherapists).

Which is the appropriate label for the hopelessly bad actor who keeps performing non-paying parts in hopes of launching a big-money career? How about the highly successful concert pianist who hated traveling so much she now plays only for friends at her home? Which is an amateur?

If you are a dedicated amateur accordion player who gets so good that people start booking you into paying jobs, at what point do you become a professional?

Imagine you run a business, say a small basket shop, and get so interested in all the possibilities of baskets that you keep making and commissioning more innovations. You create baskets with antique cloth and feathers as part of the weave, baskets made of edible seaweed and dried guppies—even though no one would ever buy one. At what point do you stop being a business professional and start being a passionate amateur?

Ideally, amateurism and professionalism exist in a healthy balance in all the work we undertake. The full practice of the work of art brings them together. In the poem "Two Tramps in Mud Time," Robert Frost writes:

> But yield who will to their separation,
> My object in living is to unite
> My avocation and my vocation
> As my two eyes make one in sight.
> Only where love and need are one,
> And the work is play for mortal stakes,
> Is the deed ever really done
> For Heaven and the future's sakes.

Ideally, amateurism and professionalism exist in a healthy balance in all the work we undertake.

The Invisible Job Skills

Let's assume this book has accomplished its main goals to some degree: you recognize parts of your life in which you engage in the work of art, and you want to do more. That "more" must include an amateur practice at your job, as well as at home.

No matter what your job, no matter what your field, no matter your age or education, your abilities, responsibilities, or salary, you *must* have an amateur engagement in your work. Work absorbs the largest chunk of waking life—too much productive energy and opportunity to shrug off as a loss to the work of art.

If your job makes only logical sense and provides a view only through the single-eye of need, it cannot fulfill its pivotal role in a high-quality life. In other words, if you can articulate why you do your job only in terms of cash flow, job perks, "other, worse options," "not-so-bads," and "the future," you have suffocated the amateur to death in your work. And it isn't that "they" have done it to you or that the situation has done it—*you* have done it. Yes, the vast majority of workplaces are horribly faulty in supporting the personal fulfillment of their workers, but every active amateur I know has nonetheless found fulfillment at work, no matter what.

Let's face it—Americans are hard workers. And it shows. Research indicates that, compared to other cultures, Americans' hard work is one of the two main impressions visitors from other countries have of us. (The other is how young we appear for our years.) Our Puritan heritage has left the legacy of a deep respect for industriousness; this Plymouth bedrock belief has sustained across centuries, through many fads and vogues, and still serves us well in many ways. Hard work remains high on list of "American values," touted as the best medicine for many problems.

Few workers work harder than artists or amateurs; yet they are delighted and inspired by their work, rather than depleted and "owed." A recent study asked famous artists to identify the single most important key to their success. They were asked about talent, luck, education,

No matter what your job, you must have an amateur engagement in your work.

Artists and amateurs are delighted and inspired by their work, rather than depleted and "owed."

inspiration, insights, planning, etc. The researchers found near-unanimous agreement on one attribute, far above any others: diligence. Such diligence can derive only from self-motivated inquiry, the personal engine with get-up-and-go. Artists yearn a living. This is an essential ingredient to great success in any work, and to making a good life.

The work of art doesn't feel like work-work—those day-long tasks people perform, apart from their interests, in order to survive. It is an entirely different quality of experience, one that feels more like play no matter how labor-intensive it gets. Ask the panting, sweaty dancer on a rehearsal break about the difficulty of her work, and she will smile with pleasure as she towels her armpits and feet. The work of art, in any of its manifestations, embodies the magnificence of work—not work in the stoical, Spartan sense—but in the sense of flow.

Extrinsic motivation, doing work for outside reasons, no matter how good those reasons are—like making a living, gaining acceptance, getting a reward—does not support personal satisfaction in the work for long. It may "get you through" a project or keep you pushing on, but it desiccates the individual, kills the investment in the work, and ignores the entelechy. Working for rewards or to "get it done" entrenches the desire to not work, its opposite. Education research demonstrates that rewards and other forms of extrinsic motivation actually deplete the very interest and curiosity they seek to support. Systems that motivate through rewards deplete the inner trust in competence. Short term results; long-term cost. Promising a child a ten dollar bill for getting an A may drive her to get that A, but it will diminish her chance of becoming an A student in life.

Internal motivation is not merely a nice job perk for upper-echelon bosses; it is our hope, our only way to find success. Without a lively balance between internal and external reasons for doing our work, our yearning goes to sleep, gives up, or turns toward harmful expressions.

This book is for individuals. These pages do not offer corporate policies to nurture the amateur on the job. I do not argue for the work of art as "the answer" to employee problems or as a prescription for corporate change. I do not propose that part of the factory floor be

Systems that motivate through rewards deplete the inner trust in competence.

The effectiveness of the
work of art lies in its
particularity; it resists one-
size-fits-all programming.

Work (wûrk) v.
to engage in activities
with wholehearted
participation

Until we live in a wiser
world, few businesses will
invite and encourage this
amateur part of you—you
have to do it yourself.

dedicated to mats for choreography breaks. I avoid such suggestions, because the effectiveness of the work of art lies in its particularity; it resists one-size-fits-all programming. I do know, however, that meaningful work makes better workers and that the work of art provides something close to a single, comprehensive model for success within a maelstrom of change.

I invite readers who are business leaders to participate in the work of art for themselves, personally. It will change your life in the ways this book describes. And when a leader changes, the organization changes. The axiom that an organization is an expression of the person at the top rings true in my experience. I would learn more about the way an organization runs in an hour working side by side with the president making bowls in a pottery studio than by studying the annual report.

I do argue that work requires a regular dose of serious play to be healthy; personal and corporate success require rich personal experiences for the workers within their jobs; the workplace requires the amateur. Tell your colleagues this one tomorrow: the word "work" derives from an Indo-European root that spawned many words about engaging in activities, including "orgy" and "energy." Wholehearted participation is the etymological key to joyful involvement—as true in a job as an orgy.

Until we live in a wiser world, few businesses will invite and encourage this amateur part of you—you have to do it yourself. As you do, stay under the radar. Make no pronouncements, and ask for no special dispensations. But do allow yourself to dig deeper into the assignments that attract you. Give yourself over to flow wherever you can, make it a top priority. Grab challenges and problems, and make satisfying solutions. Bring *the* attitude to work and discover what is there. None of this disconnects you from work; on the contrary, it connects you more intimately.

And if it seems awkward, no one need know. You need not send out an office memo declaring that from now on Janet will be passionate about the mutually fulfilling relationship with those new young suppliers from Wyoming. You need not broadcast a loudspeaker announcement though the repair shop that Chuck is now investing himself in a comparison of which shock absorbers last the longest.

At a glance, the professional with an active, inner amateur at play may not appear much different from the disciplined, grind-it-out pro. Both exert themselves; both have drive and focus; both get results. The difference between the two appears over time. The former sticks around, works well with others, is a steady, positive presence, is the one you want on problem-solving teams, is happier, and misses fewer days of work. The latter leads to trouble of some kind, or stops developing, or leaves.

Finding where Your Amateur Appears at Work

Let's assume you want to find or expand a place in your job where you engage as an amateur. If you cannot readily point to such a place, how do you find it? Here are a series of provocative questions. Answer any or all to stir your awareness of places in your work where you can appropriately bring amateur interest.

* What part of your work do you find yourself telling people about in an excited way?
* What was the last occasion when you enthusiastically told a friend about a success you had at work?
* What is something you do at work that makes the world a slightly better place? (Once you find it, drop the "slightly.")
* Is there something unique that you bring to your workplace? If that talent could grow into fuller expression, where might it go?
* If you met a famous artist (pick one you admire) and were to try to impress him/her about your work, and were to slightly exaggerate what you do, what would you choose to exaggerate about; what might you say?

* Tell a whopping lie about what you do at work. (And then ask yourself: what important truth is buried underneath that particular lie?)
* Imagine you are sitting by a fire with native people from a remote, pre-industrial village in New Guinea, who miraculously speak English. They ask you to tell them what it is you do all day and why it is important. What would you say?

The Rounded Life

If you cannot find personal expression in a particular job, you will not make a career there, you will not make a life. You may survive for a period of time; you may keep the bucks coming in; but don't fool yourself into thinking you are going anywhere meaningful.

You may think this lofty approach is fine for certain situations, but what about the burger flipper at McDonald's—can such a person be fulfilled in his career? He may be going somewhere or may not be; he may be fully engaging in the potential of his work, or not. It all depends on his *the* attitude of responsibility, engagement, constructive-selfishness, and making-meaning. Remember, attitude means a chosen position in a landscape. *The* attitude enables him to engage in his position under the golden arches. If the position fits his sense of long-term process, if there are meaningful parts to the work, he will be involved there and may well manage that restaurant before long.

The meaning need not be cosmic. In that McDonald's, he may find no more engagement than in doing things with maximum efficiency; he may find flow in making great Big Macs; he may love finding personal connections with as many customers as possible; he may dedicate himself to helping new workers learn the ropes; he may try to figure out from the inside why McDonald's has become such a worldwide success. Every one of these tasks is worthy of his amateur passion. I'm sure you have met workers in fast-food joints who have a glimmer of the genuine joy of flow, who sparkle just a bit as they help you. Keep an eye out for them, they are inspiring to see.

Remember that the amateur part of professional work need only be a *part*. I do not picture an America covered with offices and workplaces of grinning, blissed-out amateurs. Only part of your work day need contain your yearning, just as my friends found only a part of their days needed flow in it to make the whole day "great."

Without an Amateur Place at Work

We need to do more than find a foothold for amateur engagement at work; we need to "keep walking the walk"—*sustain* the involvement—or we lose the advantages. This happens to artists. I have known many who begin careers full of the passion of the amateur. Their professional lives are perfect outgrowths of their personal lives, everything connects, feeding, and growing. But over time, the brutality of the art business warps their flow. They lose the love and become bitter or addicted to something. They come to live in anger, and even their productive hours become frustrating and depleting.

I have seen the same thing happen to promising people in business—successful people who get hollowed out inside or burnt out. Their need to succeed gets literalized into the corporate currencies. People give over their wonder, their yearning, and their curiosity, trading them for reasonable things, like doing what the boss wants and the company seems to demand. Entrepreneurs who seemingly enjoy the ideal arrangement for personal choice and self-expression can end up as slaves to the thing they create.

The key to avoiding their pitfalls is balance. The recipe is the same for all workers—amateur success within your professional life. The balance is sustained in little habits: the flexible way you can think about your work; the lively corners of the job you adore and exploit; the pride you take in small accomplishments; the connections you make to other parts of your work-of-art practice.

Serving Others

It may seem that all this focus on ourselves—our satisfaction, our fulfillment at work—is the kind of indulgent "me me me" thinking of

Only part of your work day need contain your yearning.

The mature skills of constructive selfishness enable us to get what we need, to grow from it, and be poised to give back.

a spoiled child. I see it precisely the other way. The cry of "me me me" comes from the immature person of any age who has not learned how to move toward what he yearns for and so is stuck in an endless loop of need and demand. The mature skills of constructive selfishness, on the other hand, enable us to get what we need, to grow from it, and thus be poised to give back.

The work of art, even when its practice is solitary, does not make us insular. On the contrary, the amateur connects more fully than others and rarely feels lonely. I see far more loneliness in those who are frequently with people, but not connecting with them in meaningful ways, than in the amateur who spends most of her day working alone.

The work of art is quite the opposite of selfishness; it is service. An amateur's constructive selfishness is generous concern for all of us. The work of art takes full responsibility for making something that counts and gives it to others. An individual hitting on all her work-of-art cylinders drives us all forward. This is the rugged individualism, the entrepreneurial zeal that leads and inspires. It is the best work we can do for ourselves and for those we love, which makes it the best work we can do for the world.

Let me introduce two slightly old-fashioned notions that can make a big difference to an amateur.

1) The first, apprenticeship, is one to relish if you can find it (but you can succeed just fine without it if it never appears).
2) The second, documentation, is an absolute necessity.

Apprenticeship

Apprenticeship is one particular way to learn an amateur practice — other good ways include classes, books, "how to" videos, and figuring it out on your own. Use any, use all. Apprenticeship is not possible for every amateur, but it is so potent a practice that I encourage it wherever I can.

Apprenticeship evolved thousands of years ago as a natural way for a beginner to acquire necessary skills, and it continues as one of the most effective paths to mastery. (Indeed, the root word of "apprentice" means "to learn.") The history of apprenticeship is tainted by abuses of child laborers or browbeaten workers slaving under cruel tyrants. However, the inherent relationship of apprenticeship is quite the opposite of abuse; it is profoundly attuned to the ways people learn at their best.

In the basic model of apprenticeship, a master with a particular expertise (usually in making something, most often in the arts or crafts) takes on a learner for a specified term, agreeing to share his expertise in exchange for the cheap help the apprentice provides. The assumptions of an effective apprenticeship are that the apprentice yearns to learn what the master knows; the master is willing to guide the apprentice toward his fullest competence and then let him go; the apprentice will follow the master's guidance, with the master building meaningful challenges for the apprentice's growth; they both make a commitment for more than a short period of time; and the apprentice can ask many questions, even dumb ones.

Here's why apprenticeship works:

The balance between head and hand understanding. As opposed to most other learning situations, in the dialogue of apprenticeship, words usually take a secondary position; the doing together is the means of conveying the information.

The poet Robert Bly speaks of this as an important missing element in the raising of young men today—they rarely stand and work beside their fathers in the field of the father's expertise. Bly's claim applies to mothers too and to children of both genders; a child learns as much from working beside a parent's hands as he does from being held in a parent's arms. This truth is perfectly embodied in the way apprenticeship works.

Context. Everything an apprentice learns is discovered in context. Nothing is abstract or incomprehensible or isolated; parts are presented within organized, meaningful wholes. Every small task the apprentice undertakes has real-world significance. The apprentice flower arranger

Apprentice (ə pren´tis)
v. to learn

Every small task the apprentice undertakes has real-world significance.

who trims low-stem leaves can see and feel the importance of her task when she views the beauty of the master's final arrangement.

Also, a real-world context teaches the apprentice to listen more widely and to read the signs of process. The master notices and comments, and tiny contextual cues become lively topics. The apprentice learns that, nothing ever happens in isolation, there is a web of interesting and subtle connections among things—mastery includes awareness of such connections and the ability to improvise in and around them. All those insights are, of course, critical skills of the work of art.

Master modeling. Rarely is a master so perfect a model that the apprentice seeks to become just like her. Even so, the apprentice sees and feels what it is like to be the master of something effective in the real world. The apprentice practices being a highly functioning human: one who has skill, patience, access to flow, real love for the work, and spillover into the rest of life.

Taking the time. The rhythm of apprenticeship is a learner's rhythm, not a system's rhythm. A learner's rhythm is an unpredictable fast-and-slow—a tango, a cha-cha, and then a dead stop—what we described earlier as Maker's Variable Time. It includes spontaneous rests and accelerandos, lots of trills, retards, and repeats. Apprenticeship allows for gestation and repetition—vital steps in understanding.

More rigid learning systems press on no matter what, walking roughshod over parts of the learner's process. They leave patches of incomplete learning, weak supports in the foundation of understanding. Apprenticeship allows the slow, idiosyncratic, constructed learning that makes a solid foundation.

Questioning. Inquiry is as basic a tool of apprenticeship as it is in the work of art. The apprentice asks specific questions, and the master answers in context, again and again. Sometimes, too, the master challenges the student with a question. Also, the apprentice's mind is constantly asking, "How do I…?" and, "Why is that better?" This is the organic inner monologue of the work of art. In school, a student's job is to get right answers; in apprenticeship, a learner's job is to find, ask, answer, and outgrow the right questions.

Apprenticeship allows for gestation and repetition—vital steps in understanding.

Applying Apprenticeship

I do not propose broadscale apprenticeship programs to make this effective learning available to all—in our culture that would be impractical. I propose that you find and build upon informal apprentice-like situations in your amateur practice. As an amateur, seek to work humbly beside someone who knows things you want to know. Be willing to help in exchange for this person's willingness to work with you and answer your questions. Even an approximate apprenticeship can provide some of the benefits suggested above.

Conversely, if you are a master at something, take on an apprentice. Don't go out and recruit one; that rarely works. Apprenticeships succeed only when the learner is hungry to learn what you know. However, stay open to receiving an apprentice if one should appear. If you catch a whiff of passionate interest, be open to becoming a resource—*you* will benefit too.

I have been both an apprentice and a master. My most significant apprenticeship was with a farmer. I took two summers during college to learn about farm work by shoveling the manure, stacking the hay, and milking the cows at Wilson's farm. Subsequently, I have guided apprentice-like relationships in business, in the theater, and in teaching. I have been a part of many "approximate apprenticeships" too, in which a new employee, a young actor, or an occasional student and I informally became master-apprentice partners in real-world situations. The unspoken, enormous truth of all my experience is love. Wilson and I never shared an extraneous word; my mentees and I never poured out feelings about how it was going. We simply dedicated ourselves to the work and found ourselves filled with love and gratitude.

What's Up, Documentation?

I heard a story several years ago from a proponent of Waldorf schooling, an educational approach that emphasizes attention to the learning process. She told me of her octogenarian father, whose memory was developing sizable holes. As a boy, he had gone to a grade school that included a portfolio of each student's learning process as a

As an amateur, seek to work humbly beside someone who knows things you want to know.

part of the schooling. My friend's elementary-school-aged son asked her father (his grandfather) about what he learned in school as a child. Much to her surprise, the old man led them up to the attic, dug into a dusty trunk, and pulled out his elementary school learning portfolio. He sat down with his grandson and went through it, vividly recalling every lesson, what was exciting about it, and where it had led. My friend was stunned by the depth and complexity of her father's recall and by the joy that accompanied it, since so much of his life had been forgotten.

My friend's story is no fluke; documentation of a learning process is a uniquely powerful practice. I have heard strong testimonials from many teachers who use portfolios to assess student learning. I am amazed by their students, even very young ones, who can explicitly articulate their learning journeys with precise reference to the documents that represent turning points in their understanding. In the early stages of my work with documentation and portfolios, the results seemed too good to be true. But the learning boost continues to be so extraordinary and sustaining that I have come to rely on the habit of documentation for my own work of art. It effectively clarifies many vagaries of the creative process and affirms the subtle accomplishments along the way. It is the most important adjunct to an amateur's practice that I know.

Documentation doesn't sound enticing. It sounds like paperwork, like a dreary housekeeping chore. That feeling derives from the way we use "documents" in life; we associate them with legal and financial recording. I propose a different purpose with different tools, and, I hope, a different resulting feeling.

The words doctor, doctrine, and document all derive from the same Latin word "docere," meaning "to teach." In Latin, a doctor was a teacher. In English, too, the word doctor meant teacher—a doctor of philosophy was not a guy who prescribed that you take two chapters of Plato and call him in the morning. (The association of doctor and medicine became common only around the time of Shakespeare.) The Latin "documentum" meant "a lesson," a specific written part of a

Documentation
(dok´yə men tā´shən) *n.*
the setting down of the parts of a creative learning process

learning process. That last meaning is precisely what I intend when I use the term documentation as an amateur's necessity—the setting down of the parts of a creative learning process. The amateur's documents are produced naturally in the work; they are the parts of the learning-through-flow process that constitutes an amateur's career; they need to be collected and attended to.

Many artists do their documentation, and keep it, in an organized way: in a notebook or sketchbook, with an audio or video tape recorder, or in a portfolio. They would feel lost without the habit.

The documentation habit need not become a major time-consumer; just a little bit on a regular basis will do the trick. Your documentation "tool" could be, but need not be, a binder or a bunch of papers, a hatbox, an Indian basket, an old boot. What goes into this collection of documentation? It can include anything—notes to yourself, maps, poems, doodles that strikes you as significant to the process. This includes those bits and pieces that occur along the way. A good question? A good spin-off idea? Don't trust them to memory, jot them down and keep them. Any reflection on what you are doing—thoughts sparked while exploring the work of others, notes from a book, an idea you get from a friend, a weird notion you had on a morning walk—is worth writing down. You might include a day-by-day set of notes, as well as an occasional description of how you think the work is going. A portfolio is a good place to keep the results from any activities like those in this book that you might try as a part of a project. Even if you find you are thinking of a particular metaphor or image or song or memory, if you have a dream or a coincidence—get it down. Your subconscious is sending you a message that it is important, whatever it is. And, of course, your finished works (whether painted, written, videotaped), or copies of them, belong in your collection.

Whatever practice you use for documenting your process—from an expensive trademarked system to a ratty old wire-bound notebook—there are certain benefits your documentation will provide:

You don't forget the good stuff. An amateur's work is jam-packed with small discoveries, fleeting insights, questions, and ideas that might be

The documentation habit need not become a major time-consumer; just a little bit on a regular basis will do the trick.

useful later. Unless you are in the habit of documentation, you will lose many of your best goodies. That is not to suggest that everything you document gets used later, it's just that without the habit of documenting, you drastically reduce the chance that you will retain and recall your best stuff.

I cannot count the number of times a small odd note in a process journal, a note I had completely forgotten, jumped out to serve me later. Sometimes I recall a vague feel of an idea I had at some point. When I snoop back into the process notes, I harvest the specifics of that notion and usually find a surprise bonus or two. I shudder at the thought of how much more difficult it would have been to create this book if I did not have the resource of my years of process documentation to refer to and draw from.

You notice small things of significance. Take the time, often only moments, to set down the specifics that made a difference in a project: a new idea, a surprise connection, a small step accomplished, a rephrased question, a change of direction, a strong feeling. This habit keeps you attending to personal resonance in the modest, undramatic places where projects really thrive. Your success as an amateur depends on your capacity to enjoy the journeys, as well as the arrivals. This requires that you notice and celebrate the value held in the steps along the way.

You stay creatively connected. Psychologists sometimes divide experience into two kinds: primary process and secondary process. You have a raw complex experience (primary process), whatever it might be, and you notice it. Then you take the next step, finding words or other symbols that hold it, capture some of it, stabilize it, document it (secondary process).

Documenting your amateur process is comprised almost entirely of those secondary process tasks: finding the best words, images, symbols, metaphors that feel right to capture the fleeting raw experiences of your creative process. Your documenting is itself the work of art. The steady dose of secondary process activity provided by ongoing documentation enables you to feel more satisfaction along the way, to be more patient, to tolerate the inevitable frustrations. You notice and use those easily

Your success as an amateur depends on your capacity to enjoy the journeys, as well as the arrivals.

forgettable little bits of experience along the way; apply a bit of documentary attention to them, and they keep you connected to the yearning that got you going in the first place.

You boost your creative potential. A regular dose of secondary process supports what some psychologists call tertiary process, the creative work of making connections between two previously separate things.

You are making scrambled eggs, you think you hear the doorbell ring, and go to answer it—no one is there. You come back and see the plastic spatula has partly melted. You are annoyed at yourself for forgetting about it and ruining the eggs and the spatula—primary process. Your anger turns toward noticing how the drippy flipper looks, the shapes the melting has assumed, the different textures—secondary process. You flash on the surface you have been trying to create in your model train landscape of a washed-out earthen bank and realize this is the look you have been seeking—tertiary process. Analogously, documentation of your raw experience makes it more available for you to work with and enriches that possibility of making inventive, creative connections.

You stay balanced. The habit of honoring your process through documenting keeps you in balance.

Do you recall the myth of Icarus and his father, the master-inventor Daedalus? They were trapped by a tyrant in an escape-proof maze. Daedalus built two pairs of giant wings, made mostly of feathers and wax, with which he and his son could fly to freedom. As they took off, young Icarus, against all warnings, became carried away by the thrill of flight and rose too high. He got too close to the sun, which melted the wax, and he fell to his death in the sea. Daedalus maintained a middle-path, not too high nor too low, and flew to freedom.

The documentation of process prevents you from flying too high because its regular attention to the pebbles of process keeps you close to the ground. Documentation offers the wisdom of middle ways and early warnings of danger by allowing the inherent soaring of creative engagement to be joined with the grounding that keeps it from getting too detached. Amateurs need the wisdom of the quick and the Daedalus.

You support clear self-assessment. Hindsight is commonly credited with 20-20 vision. In my experience of the arts, that is rare. Most people, myself included, tend toward something like 20-200 hindsight of our creative processes. We revert to a skewed, romanticized, or largely invented view of how things came into being. This indulgence retards our ability to learn from our accomplishments and mistakes, to grow from project to project. Unrealistic or romanticized notions of process obscure the necessary facts of creative life. Unclear self-assessment encourages our belief in the ups and downs of the waves, rather than trusting the deeper truth of the currents.

The ongoing tracking of your process—taking the time to note the small choices, setting down the actual steps along the way—supports your grip on the truth. Your *real* process, your creative style, your problem-solving improvisations are wonderful enough as they actually are, without romantic exaggeration or cosmetic adjustment. The habits of a documenting process keep your focus on the exquisite reality of your work, not on other people's assessment or judgment of it.

Your assessment belongs before, after, and above all others'. Without the reliable discipline of documenting what happens, other people's assessment can knock you around, can damage, deter, and mislead your long-term development. If you are assessing the process all the time, no one can mess with your journey of learning through experience.

You strengthen all the work-of-art connections. Documenting processes makes the world-work go 'round; it nurtures the healthy interplay of the three angles of the work of art.

Setting down the process encourages the impulse to make connections between:

* different parts of world-work happening in your life (the way you looked at a Mondrian painting and what you notice from the Empire State Building's observation deck).
* different projects (an insight from your job assisting your hobby at home).

> *Your real process, your creative style, your problem-solving improvisations are wonderful enough as they actually are, without romantic exaggeration or cosmetic adjustment.*

* different parts of any large project (the clever way you solved a problem at an early stage becomes useful again later).
* other people involved in a project (a technique you discovered, an insight, may be invaluable to others).
* the work in the project and ways to communicate with those not involved (the discovery of how a project came into being may open just the right metaphor to explain its significance to others).
* different periods in your amateur career (the ebullient ways you instinctively solve problems at twenty may reappear or develop into the ways you work even smarter at forty).

Give yourself the gift of learning about your learning in this vivid way. I believe that learning how to learn is the ultimate goal of education. I find it takes students a little while to get used to that idea; to value *how* they learn as well as *what* they learn, and to get accustomed to sustaining that perspective. Once they have the taste though, they don't forget. The same holds true with amateurs. They are naturally drawn to the action and results, and it takes a while to begin to value the *how*.

We need not be the child who whines, "Are we there yet?" We can be the adult who knows that getting there is half the fun—and we can document the steps that awaken that half of the fun.

Beginning a Conclusion

Scratched on a piece of paper on my bulletin board is a phrase Carl Jung carved into the stone lintel of the house he built with his hands: "Vocatus atque non vocatus deus aderit." Called or uncalled, the god will be there. Similarly, I believe that welcomed or unwelcomed, trained or untrained, acknowledged or not, the work of art is there.

Learning how to learn is the ultimate goal of education.

After the final no there comes a yes
And on that yes the future world depends.
No was the night. Yes is this present sun.

Those lines begin the poem "The Well Dressed Man with a Beard" by Wallace Stevens. What does he mean by that "yes"? The remainder of his poem suggests that it has to do with the irrepressibly curious, creative mind. Maybe the yes is no more than the present-tense moment of your engagement with his poem. Maybe it's his moment of constructing the poetic lines. Maybe it is the dialogue between you and the poem or the improvisation of thought that bounces out of your response, shedding light elsewhere. Yeses all.

Wallace Stevens was a successful businessman, the vice-president of the Hartford Accident and Indemnity Insurance Company. Like any working person, he was concerned about his projects, benefits package, and retirement plan options. He was also a dedicated poet, one of the greatest of this century. He wrote poems from his passion, from his unquenchable thirst to do the work of art, and he kept these two parts of his life in a delicate balance. Good businessman, good artist, he knew that making things at work and in poems chases away the dark, makes the future positive. In his lines, yes is always in the present tense. Making the poem, perceiving the poem, reflecting upon and using the poem—all bring out the present sun—in this moment, and this moment, and the next. The verb of art appears before the noun.

Of course, not all corporate vice-presidents develop passionate amateur practices; many seem far removed from the work of art. I see people in all vocations flailing to get more satisfaction out of life, struggling to know what Wallace Stevens and many millions of amateurs know through their way of life. I see people yearn to make disparate parts of life connect, find meaning in the stuff of daily life, and clarify what "making it" really means. But they are stuck—trapped in literalness, hardened by result-orientedness, adrift without the compass of their personal response-ability, not aligned toward the quality of experience, trusting ideological and simplistic answers to complex questions, played out.

I see people underequipped to pull themselves up by their emotional and spiritual bootstraps—people buying things, doing things, saying things that are supposed to provide meaning, but don't.

I see so many fine, committed people digging so hard for bones that are buried elsewhere, dedicating themselves to efforts that don't lead to the sources of their dissatisfaction, to actions that cannot clarify the questions or ignite the answering they seek.

These are the people that I meet in my workshops. By the end of our intensive time together, they are usually inspired to some degree, *and* they find their real-life problems have not disappeared. The weeds didn't pull themselves out of the garden, and the boss is still a creep. However, they have attained new attitudes. How?

It is the beginning of a workshop. I might give the participants a difficult Wallace Stevens poem to read. They encounter a lot of problems, feel they can't succeed. They blame themselves, mostly, and the poem, too: "Too vague, not clear." Everyone feels pretty lousy—stuck. I guide them into some poetry-making work, solving word-and-thought problems akin to those in which Stevens was interested. They work hard to create successful solutions, which spark curiosity to go back and discover how Stevens solved that problem. Now, they crack the poem wide open with a release of joyful energy. They turn that energy and light wherever they choose: to the friend they meet for tea; to a Maya Angelou poem; to a sticky real-life problem that makes them feel lousy. They have refreshed the skills that enable them to experiment with different perspectives until they can see some things clearly in the muddy mixture of their boss-from-hell problem. They can try out new ways to perceive the job's stuck status quo, finding a part that is interesting to play with, to loosen it up. They can remake "the way it is" into one of the ways they imagine it could be. The work of art transforming the quality of life.

The skills of art enable us to change our base metaphors; we can change the weeds into something other than the oppressive relentless enemy they were as the workshop began. Perhaps the weeds turn into a sparring partner or a contemplative routine. (My friend Carolyn Reynolds has transformed her infuriating weed-war into a treatise called the Nine Laws of Weeds that cleverly teach universal truths; so she weeds her way toward wisdom.) Problems are not huge, dark difficulties, they are parts of constructed wholes, and artists know that parts can be re-imagined and moved into different, more-rewarding, organizations.

Of course, we all want our problems to go away or get better. However, like the lousy scene in the second act that is taking the life out of the play, we have to re-"wright" the faulty part, put our best skills to work on it, to bring the whole to life. There is no magic bullet, no drug or secret formula, that fixes the scene or the problem; we have to get in there and work on it. To make a difference with our problems, we require the best of what artists know, the best of what we know as artists.

I hope the skills are familiar by now. We must perceive reality well, with empathy, compassion, and a patient hunger to penetrate more deeply into its complexity. We need to not-know a lot, seek the valuable in the unfamiliar, and allow ourselves daily doses of wonder. We must yearn to make things that make sense to us, developing an interest in the processes themselves and the balance that comes with a long-term view. We need to be master learners, improvisers, and active-reflectors. We need to be amateurs to engage in the work of art throughout our lives. We need the serious play of flow to run through the life of every home.

The Hundredth Monkey

I have an abiding faith that the work of art transforms people's lives; I know it has mine. But my ambition for the work of art reaches further than individuals. I think it can have an influence on the lives of so many that it could change the course of a nation.

That may sound naive, but the skills of art are hard-wired into our species survival mechanisms. The practices of art are our longest-

To make a difference with our problems, we require the best of what artists know, the best of what we know as artists.

The skills of art are hard-wired into our species survival mechanisms.

surviving human tool for social cohesion and development. In the work of art, it becomes unmistakably clear that people have a tropism toward the good and the beautiful, toward the development of self and humankind, toward greater understanding, toward bettering themselves and making better worlds—as surely as plants grow toward the sun. The work of art is the optimum growing medium for this tropism. If enough individuals dig into it, no problem is impossible to solve.

I have hope thanks to the hundredth monkey. The notion of the hundredth monkey comes from a 1950s study of animal behavior. Subsequent accounts have called aspects of the scientific evidence into question, so I can't guarantee that the startling findings are impeccably, hard-fact true. That bit of doubt as a result of reasonable skepticism doesn't perturb me, however, because the story is as compelling on a metaphorical level as on a strictly literal one. It holds a deep truth, whether scientifically replicable or not.

A team of primate biologists launched the experiment on Koshima, an island off Japan. They were studying a species of monkey called Macaca Fuscata. To feed their subjects while they studied them, the researchers dumped batches of sweet potatoes on the beach. The monkeys liked the sweet potatoes, but they couldn't quite resolve one problem: the sweet potatoes were covered in sand that didn't brush off, making them unpleasant to eat.

After some time, one adolescent female monkey, whom the researchers had come to refer to as Imo, accidentally dropped a sweet potato into the sea water and made a wonderful discovery: not only did the salt water wash off the sand, it also made the sweet potato taste delicious. Imo became a devoted dunker, and she enthusiastically tried to share her discovery with other monkeys in the group. First, members of her family picked up the practice, one by one. Then a few more converts adopted the eccentric habit. The number of dunking devotees slowly, haphazardly grew as a result of individual contact. The researchers observed, documenting the sequence. They found that when about the hundredth monkey embraced the habit of dunking the

In the work of art, it becomes unmistakably clear that people have a tropism toward the good and the beautiful.

sweet potato in the sea, something inexplicable happened. Spontaneously, every monkey in the group began dunking. One morning, dunking was a fringe phenomenon; that evening it was the status quo. Somehow, a hidden critical mass of participants had been achieved, and suddenly, the whole group appropriated the beneficial new habit. Right habit, right timing, right number to cross a threshold comprising a critical mass.

But there's more. Researchers on other islands observed that their monkey groups spontaneously began Imo's dunking and washing routine. These were islands completely cut off from one another, not even in visual contact. Even monkeys on the mainland at Takasakiyama began dunking around the same time. None of these separated populations had been involved in dunking before; but when a critical mass of one local population adopted the beneficial new habit, the whole population adopted it, and the course of their history changed forever. Right habit, right timing, right number crossed the threshold that constitutes the critical mass—adjusting the future for all who are connected in many ways, including ways we don't understand.

Of course, there is no analytical explanation for this occurrence. No simian email, loudspeaker, or smoke signal system. Any attempt to explain this phenomenon as coincidence or a result of swamp gas is, in Mark Twain's term, "a bit of a stretcher."

Among the various proffered explanations, I find Rupert Sheldrake's theory of morphic resonance to be compelling. He points out, as a part of arguing his comprehensive theory, that phenomena akin to the hundredth monkey happen all the time, even in the controlled conditions of laboratories. When scientists invent a new crystal in a lab at M.I.T., it suddenly becomes easier and faster to make the same crystal in labs around the world. When rats master a particular maze in England, they begin to master it faster in California. There is no logical cause-and-effect relationship to explain these phenomena (no microscopic crystal-seedlings are carried on the bushy eyebrows of itinerant chemists), yet this baffling reality exists.

When a critical mass of one local population adopted the beneficial new habit, the whole population adopted it, and the course of their history changed forever.

Morphic resonance, the phenomena of crystals and hundredth monkeys, carry on in some way beyond any understandings we currently have; they can seem as perplexing as a Wallace Stevens poem. We may feel a tendency to blame or reject them because they don't reveal their subtle truth to our logical questioning. To get a grip on them requires that we find our way to a more complex understanding, an enriched logic, by engaging our best skills in work on parts of it that we love. We crack open the stuck places through the work of art. Read the world for evidence of the hundredth monkey at work.

The habit? The work of art, practiced by amateurs in every calling, on every block; alive on the job in the hands of individual workers, sometimes in spite of tremendous constraints; suffused into home life in the questions asked, the moments noticed and celebrated.

The time? As soon as individuals want the sweet potatoes described in these pages badly enough: to try something less conventional, to set aside the common misconceptions of those artistic-dunkers, to sink their hands into a new kind of engagement.

The critical mass? I wish it were a hundred amateurs; I wish I knew the number. But we add dunkers every day. The time and the habit are such that the practices will continue; the rewards produce so much good, they will grow. This very old habit of the work of art and its strong, humble expressions throughout our lives may provide a future of new satisfactions for you, and for many more. No was the night. Yes is this present sun.

We crack open the stuck places through the work of art.

Notes

1. Robert Shaw, Music Director Emeritus of the Atlanta Symphony Orchestra, originated this quip.

2. J. M. Barrie, *Tommy and Grizel* (New York: Scribner's Sons, 1917).

3. Jacob Needleman, "Questions of the Heart," Noetic Sciences Review 26(Summer 1993): 8.

4. Roger von Oech, *A Whack on the Side of the Head* (Stamford: U.S. Games Systems, 1983): 122.

5. David N. Perkins, *"The Possibility of Invention," The Nature of Creativity*, ed. Robert J. Sternberg (Cambridge: Cambridge University Press, 1988): 379.

6. Franz Kafka, *Shorter Works: The Collected Aphorisms*, Vol. 1, no. 109, ed. and trans. Malcolm Pasley (London: Secker & Warburg, 1973).

7. Arthur Danto, *The Transfiguration of the Commonplace* (Cambridge: Harvard University Press, 1981).

8. Jerome Bruner, *Acts of Meaning* (Cambridge: Harvard University Press, 1990): 96.

9. Donald Polkinghorne, *Narrative Knowing and The Human Sciences* (Albany: SUNY Press, 1988): 150.

10. Arthur Zajonc, *Catching the Light* (New York: Bantam Books, 1993): 341.

11. Mihaly Csikszentmihalyi, *Flow* (New York: Harper and Row, 1990).

12. Theodore Roszak, "A Few Things Beautifully Made: An Interview with Theodore Roszack," by Suzi Gablik, Common Boundary 13, no. 2 (March/April 1995): 46.

13. James Hillman, *Kinds of Power* (New York: Doubleday, 1995): 52.

14. Adrienne Rich, *What Is Found There* (New York: W.W. Norton & Co., 1993): xiv.

15. William Blake, in "Auguries of Innocence."

16. Rich, 12.

17. Barry Sanders, *A is for Ox* (New York: Pantheon Books, 1994): 31.

18. Lynda Sexson, *Ordinarily Sacred* (Charlottesville: University Press of Virginia, 1992): 90.

19. M. von Senden, *Space and Sight: The Perception of Space and Sight in the Congenitally Blind Before and After Operation*, trans. Peter Heath (Glencoe, Ill.: The Free Press, 1960): 160.

20. David Weeks and Jamie James, *Eccentrics: A Study of Sanity and Strangeness* (New York: Villard, 1996).

21. Rupert Sheldrake, *Seven Experiments That Could Change the World* (New York: G.P. Putnam's Sons, 1995).

Bibliography

Arieti, Silvano. *Creativity: The Magic Synthesis*. New York: Basic Books, 1976.

Aristotle. *Nicomachean Ethics*. Translated by Martin Oswald. Indianapolis: Bobs Merrill, 1962.

Barrie, J.M. *Tommy and Grizel*. New York: Scribner's Sons, 1917.

Bateson, Mary Catherine. *Our Own Metaphor*. New York: Alfred A. Knopf, 1972.

Beardsley, Monroe. *Aesthetics from Classical Greece to the Present*. New York: Macmillan, 1966.

Bergson, Henri. *Creative Evolution*. London: Macmillan, 1911.

Brockman, John, ed. *Creativity*. New York: Touchstone/Simon & Schuster, 1993.

Bruner, Jerome. *Acts of Meaning*. Cambridge: Harvard University Press, 1990.

Campbell, Joseph. *The Hero with a Thousand Faces*. Bollingen Series, vol. XII. Princeton: Princeton University Press, 1972.

———. *Myths to Live By*. New York: Viking, 1972.

Coles, Robert. The Call of Stories. Boston: Houghton Mifflin, 1989.

———. *The Spiritual Life of Children*. Boston: Houghton Mifflin, 1990.

Csikszentmihalyi, Mihaly. *Flow*. New York: Harper and Row, 1990.

Danto, Arthur. *The Philosophical Disenfranchisement of Art*. New York: Columbia University Press, 1986.

————. *The Transfiguration of the Commonplace*. Cambridge: Harvard University Press, 1981.

Dewey, John. *The Philosophy of John Dewey*. Edited by John J. McDermott. Chicago: University of Chicago Press, 1973.

Fox, Matthew. *The Reinvention of Work*. San Francisco: Harper San Francisco, 1994.

Fritz, Robert. *Creating*. New York: Fawcett Columbine/Ballantine, 1991.

Greene, Maxine. *The Dialectic of Freedom*. New York: Teachers College Press, 1988.

————. *Landscapes of Learning*. New York: Teachers College Press, 1978.

Gablik, Suzi. *Conversations Before the End of Time*. New York: Thames and Hudson, 1995.

————. *The Reenchantment of Art*. New York: Thames and Hudson, 1991.

Gardner, Howard. *Art, Mind and Brain*. New York: Basic Books, 1982.

————. *Frames of Mind*. New York: Basic Books, 1985.

————. *The Unschooled Mind*. New York: Basic Books, 1991.

Ghiselin, Brewster, ed. *The Creative Process*. Berkeley: University of California Press, 1952.

Hillman, James. *Kinds of Power*. New York: Doubleday/Currency, 1995.

Johnson, Robert. *Inner Work*. San Francisco: Harper & Row, 1986.

Kafka, Franz. *Shorter Works: The Collected Aphorisms*, vol.1, no. 109. Edited and translated by Malcolm Pasley. London: Secker & Warburg, 1973.

Kubey, Robert and Mihaly Csikszentmihalyi. *Television and the Quality of Life*. Hillsdale, NJ: Lawrence Erlbaum, 1990.

Lakoff, George and Mark Johnson. *Metaphors We Live By*. Chicago: University of Chicago Press, 1980.

Langer, Suzanne. *Feeling and Form*. New York: Charles Scribner's Sons, 1953.

Maslow, Abraham. *Toward a Psychology of Being*. New York: D. Van Nostrand, 1968.

May, Rollo. *The Courage to Create*. New York: W.W. Norton & Co., 1975.

———. *The Cry for Myth*. New York: Dell, 1991.

Nachmanovitch, Stephen. *Free Play*. Los Angeles: Jeremy Tarcher, 1990.

Ozick, Cynthia. *Metaphor & Memory*. New York: Alfred A. Knopf, 1989.

Perkins, David. *Smart Schools*. New York: The Free Press, 1992.

Polkinghorne, Donald. *Narrative Knowing and The Human Sciences*. Albany: SUNY Press, 1988.

Remer, Jane. *Beyond Enrichment*. New York: American Council for the Arts, 1996.

Rich, Adrienne. *What Is Found There*. New York: W.W. Norton & Co., 1993.

Rothstein, Edward. *Emblems of Mind*. New York: Random House/Times Books, 1995.

Sanders, Barry. *A is for Ox*. New York: Pantheon Books, 1994.

Schlain, Leonard. *Art & Physics*. New York: Morrow, 1991.

Schubart, Mark. *The Hunting of the Squiggle*. New York: Praeger, 1972.

Senge, Peter. *The Fifth Discipline*. New York: Doubleday/Currency, 1990.

Sexson, Lynda. *Ordinarily Sacred*. Charlottesville, VA: University Press of Virginia, 1992.

Sheldrake, Rupert. *Seven Experiments The Could Change the World*. New York: Riverhead Books/G.P. Putnam's Sons, 1995.

Shusterman, Richard. *Pragmatist Aesthetics*. Cambridge, Mass.: Blackwell Publishers, 1992.

Smith, Ralph, A. *The Sense of Art*. New York: Routledge, 1989.

Sternberg, Robert J., ed. *The Nature of Creativity*. Cambridge, England: Cambridge University Press, 1988.

von Oech, Roger. *A Whack on the Side of the Head*. Stamford, Conn.: U.S. Games Systems, 1983.

von Senden, M. *Space and Sight: The Perception of Space and Sight in the Congenitally Blind Before and After Operation*. Translated by Peter Heath. Glencoe, Ill.: The Free Press, 1960.

Warnock, Mary. *Imagination*. Berkeley: University of California Press, 1976.

Weeks, David and Jamie James. *Eccentrics: A Study of Sanity*. New York: Villard, 1996.

Wilber, Ken. *A Brief History of Everything*. Boston: Shambhala, 1996.

Zajonc, Arthur. *Catching the Light*. New York: Bantam Books, 1993.

Acknowledgments

This book is forged from experience. It proposes theories and points of view that would take volumes to "prove" with scholarly rigor. It includes true stories of some of the experiences that have lead to my conclusions; and it offers activities for readers to try that have worked for many people. It is my hope that this book provokes and inspires readers rather than proves anything.

The following list of people I acknowledge for contributions is long. It isn't long enough to include everyone who has added to my learning process over decades and through several professional fields. I worry that my imperfect memory has overlooked a colleague where I ought to have said thanks. I apologize in advance for any unintended oversights.

I would like to acknowledge and thank the following colleagues and friends who contributed to this work.

Thanks to those who gave their time and insights to work on early drafts: my wife Le Clanché du Rand, my sister Katherine Miller, and stalwart friends Michael Bergmann, Gilbert Girion, Robert Landy, Will Osborne, and Carolyn Reynolds. The deepest thanks go to my wife, Le Clanché, who not only hacked through a difficult draft, but who also remained supportive through the years in which I was holed up in the study or on the road. The occasional mentions of her in the book hardly suggest the enormity of the impact that twenty-four years of learning with her have had on the person who wrote this book.

I would like to thank the team at Sourcebooks, especially my editor, Michael Lowenthal, my friend, Dominique Raccah, and Karen Bouris.

Like most teachers, I must thank my students everywhere who have gamely engaged in unfamiliar activities and honestly reported their experiences; some will find their stories in these pages.

I would like to acknowledge my professional art and education colleagues who contributed in so many ways, not least in discussions and feedback that have finally jelled into the perspectives in this book. You will read about the teaching-artists in the "Bob" group at the Nashville Institute for the Arts (NIA): Ed Bilous, Madeline Cohen, John Knowles, Andrew Krichels, Cynthia Word. You will not read about many others who helped me at the NIA, where I have led so many workshops, and through which I have worked with so many fine teachers and students. I must thank Roberta Ciuffo, Bonnie Hyde, Holly Martin, Scott Massey, Margaret Officer, Jane Perry, Carol Ponder, Ben Reynolds, and Susan Sanders.

I also have many people to thank at Lincoln Center Institute, where I was first introduced to aesthetic education: special gratitude to Maxine Greene who has deeply inspired so many people, and to June Dunbar, Christine Goodheart, Scott Noppe-Brandon, Mark Schubart, David Shookhoff, and Cathryn Williams. Thanks also to other art and education colleagues whose discussions have helped along the way: Barbara Andrews, Amelia Barton, Alexander Bernstein, Peter Rojcewicz, Larry Scripp, and Lou Trucks.

I owe much to the many artists I have learned from over the years, especially Eugene Gregan (whose paintings fill my home and heart) and Beverley Gregan, Laura Young, and John Toth. I would also like to thank my employees from Alert Publishing, Inc., who may be surprised to discover some of the invisible projects I was working on in the years we did so well together in business.

And a final few thanks to friends who said the right things along the way and who care that I care: Carl Frankel, Isabel Grandin, Bob Higgins, and Cleveland Morris.

Index

bounce, 131–132, 159, 166, 178, 194, 204, 221, 242, 249, 268; etymology of, 131
Browning, Robert, 197
Bruner, Jerome, 94

C

Cage, John, 45
Campbell, Joseph, 72
Carver, Raymond, 220
Catching the Light (Zajonc), 120
categorization, 156
catharsis, 28
Cézanne, Paul, 4, 27, 197, 198, 202
change, 36, 179, 204, 243
Chartres Cathedral, 87
choice, 104–106, 185
choreography, 5
Christina's World (Wyeth), 198
Christmas, 162–65
Cinderella, 245
Citarella's, 250
Citizen Kane (movie), 104, 196
classical music, 10
clean noticing, 67–68
Coleridge, Samuel Taylor, 90
Common Boundary (magazine), 143
connections, 176, 178, 179, 186–189, 155, 204, 211, 219, 221, 250, 258, 260, 266–67
connoisseur, 181, 225
connoisseurship, 131, 136–38, 200; etymology of, 136–137
conscious noticing, 58
Constitution, U.S., 196, 197
constructive selfishness, 110, 111–12, 258
constructive waste, 111
context, 259–60
contrapposto, 4
Cosi Fan Tutti (opera), 196
courage: definition of, 50

Cousins, Norman, 126
Crack-up, The (Fitzgerald), 113
creating, 85
creativity, 64, 123, 156, 208, 244
credit, etymology of, 216
Csikszentmihalyi, Mihaly, 121
curiosity, 131, 137, 204, 249, 250

D

Daedalus, 265
Dangerfield, Rodney, 158
Danto, Arthur, 82
data. *See* relevant data
daydreaming. *See* dreams
Death of a Salesman (Miller), 81
Declaration of Independence, 174
De Mille, Agnes, 11
de Vattel, Emerich, 175
Dewey, John, 91
dialogue, 73–74
dialogue level, 188
Diary of Anne Frank, The (Frank), 45
diligence, 252
discovering, 134
distinctions, 100
documentation, 261–67; etymology of, 262
dreams, 59–60, 158
Dreyfus, Richard, 18
Duchamp, Marcel, 26

E

eccentricity, 244
edges, 63–64
Edison, Thomas, 159
Emancipation Proclamation, 180
empathy, 29, 130
entelechy, 41, 81, 209, 248, 253
entertainment level, 187–88

About the Author

Photo by Marlis Momber

Eric Booth is an accomplished educator, businessman, author, and actor. Currently a member of the faculty of The Juilliard School, he has held positions teaching at Stanford, New York University, and Lincoln Center Institute and as Founding Director of the Teacher Center at the Leonard Bernstein Center. He has appeared in many Broadway plays and is an award-winning Shakespearean actor. His entrepreneurial efforts led to distinction as a major figure in American culture trend analysis, on which he has written three books. He is a frequent speaker and workshop leader for business, school, and civic groups, teaching about the arts, creativity, and learning. Former New York city auxiliary police officer, stage-combat director, marathon runner, and published poet, Eric Booth lives in upstate New York with his wife, Le Clanché du Rand, an actress, playwright, and therapist.